A HISTORY
OF THE
SALZBURG FESTIVAL

A HISTORY
OF THE
SALZBURG FESTIVAL

Stephen Gallup

SALEM HOUSE PUBLISHERS
TOPSFIELD, MASSACHUSETTS

First published in Great Britain by
George Weidenfeld and Nicolson Limited
91 Clapham High Street London SW4 7TA

First published in the United States
by Salem House Publishers, 1988,
462 Boston Street, Topsfield, MA 01983.

Library of Congress Cataloging-in-Publication Data

Gallup, Stephen, 1939–
  A history of the Salzburg Festival.

  Bibliography: p.
  Includes index.
  1. Salzburger Festspiele.   I. Title.
ML246.8.S2F355 1988   780′.7′94363   87–16540
ISBN 0–88162–315–6

To my mother

Contents

Illustrations

Wilhelm Furtwängler (Roger Hauert)
Herbert von Karajan (Keystone Press Agency Ltd)
The new Festival Hall (Oskar Anrather, Salzburg)
Von Karajan rehearsing *Der Rosenkavalier* in 1983 (Roger Vaughan)

Acknowledgements

Many have helped along the road, and to all my sincere thanks:

In Salzburg: Dr Albert Moser, President, Salzburg Festival; Dr Hans Widrich, Director, Press Office, Salzburg Festival; Hans Jaklitsch, Archivist, Salzburg Festival; Renate Buchmann, Residenz Verlag; Dr Ernst Hanisch, Professor of Modern History, Salzburg University; Hilda Spiel, critic; Gisela Prossnitz, Max Reinhardt Institute.

In Vienna: Gottfried von Einem; Dr Hans Temnitschka, Bundesministerium für Unterricht und Kunst; Dr Oliver Rathkolb, Ludwig Boltzmann Institut für Geschichte; Edda Führich, Max Reinhardt Gesellschaft; Österreichisches Staatsarchiv, Music and Theatre Collections; Dr Otto Biba, Archiv der Gesellschaft der Musikfreunde; Dr Dernberger, Haus-und Hofarchiv; Dr L. Mikoletzky, Allgemeines Verwaltungsarchiv; Dr Otto Strasser, Archiv der Wiener Philharmoniker.

In Germany: Dr Werner, Dr Réal, Bundesarchiv, Bonn; Berlin Document Center, West Berlin.

In the United States: Marion Hanscom, Director, Max Reinhardt Archives, State University of New York, Binghamton, New York; Diane Burgwyn, author; Harvey Sachs, author; Professors Vincent Learnihan, John H. Kemble, Pomona College, Claremont, California; Professor Henry Cord Meyer, University of California, Irvine; Professor Michael Meyer, California State University, Northridge; Ms A. Schmidt, National Archives, Washington D.C.

In France: Jacques Lonchampt, Le Monde; Marie de Montlaur Gallup, Ministère des Affaires Etrangères, Paris; Bibliothèque Nationale,

Acknowledgements

Fonds Montpensier, Paris; Bibliothèque de l'Arsenal, Paris.

In England: Public Record Office, London.

Finally, my special thanks to Alistair Horne, whose fellowship aided in the preparation of this book, Raymond Carr, Warden, Theodore Zeldin and the Fellows of St Antony's College, Oxford, Venetia Pollock, Robert Baldock, and Juliet Gardiner and Elspeth Henderson of Weidenfeld, all of whom have helped shepherd the book through to completion. All interpretations and mistakes, however, are my own.

Introduction

This is the story of a somewhat curious institution, the Salzburg Festival. Today the Festival lasts for about five weeks a year, roughly between the end of July and the end of August. The quiet provincial city comes alive with the sound of music and theatre, the excitement of the crowds, the packed hotels, restaurants and cafés, the elegance of visitors from all over the world. Shortly after the first of September the crowds drift away, Salzburg returns to its somnolence, the Festival administration runs on a skeletal staff, and the city quietly tiptoes through autumn, winter and spring, all the while gradually preparing for another July awakening.

The Festival was founded in 1920; it is not the oldest, but it is the most prestigious of music festivals. Its only real rival is Bayreuth, but the differences between the two festivals are so profound that there can in truth be no competition between them. If one man founded Bayreuth, and made it a tribute to his art, Salzburg had many fathers, not the least of which were three of this century's most important artists, Max Reinhardt, Hugo von Hofmannsthal and Richard Strauss. These men founded the Festival to resurrect the spirit and ideals of a former age of theatre and the music of Salzburg's most famous son, Wolfgang Amadeus Mozart. Since 1920 and through its often tortuous history, Salzburg has welcomed practically every great conductor, singer and musician of our century. Salzburg theatre, which began in 1920 with Max Reinhardt's production of *Jedermann,* has featured every major German and Austrian actor and actress.

From its earliest years, Salzburg welcomed the rich and well-born, who spent large sums to witness, in the city's extraordinary setting, performances of opera, concerts and theatrical works which were second to none. In 1920 Salzburg was a very sleepy town with about

30,000 inhabitants; today its population is seven times that number. Yet the charm and beauty of the early days remain; people come to the Festival every year, prepared to overlook the crowds and feast on the same pleasures to the eye and the ear as they did in the previous year, and relive the same joys that their parents and grandparents experienced.

I first visited Salzburg in 1960, between studies in California and England. In the intervening years I have paid occasional visits to Salzburg, and in 1980 had the good fortune to spend a year at Schloss Leopoldskron, once the home of Max Reinhardt, which is now the headquarters of the American-based Salzburg Seminar.

Once one has savoured Salzburg, attended an exquisite performance of *Così fan tutte* or *Jedermann*, or a Fischer-Dieskau recital, wandered through the streets and parks or just lingered over a *Kaffee mit Schlag* at the Café Bazaar, all objectivity about the place quickly disappears. It is very difficult *not* to love Salzburg. It is equally difficult to become irritated if this or that performance is less than good. The ambiance of the 'city as a stage', as Reinhardt once put it, still pervades the Festival today.

I chose to write about the Festival not only as an institution, but as an 'idea' and an 'ideal' which was somehow put into practice at a particular place and time, and which evolved and mutated against the background of our cacophonous century. Salzburg is, after all, in Austria. The history of the First Austrian Republic, born in the collapse of the monarchy after the First World War, is not a happy one. The Festival's fortunes in many ways mirrored those of the Republic: depression and fear in the early Twenties, growing hope and prosperity at the end of the decade, the brutality of the effects of the Wall Street Crash in 1929, the fearful consequences of Hitler's coming to power in 1933 and the final solution to the Austrian problem, the *Anschluss* of 1938. In these days the Festival was continually challenged and had to fight for its very existence. Until 1938 it met, and conquered those challenges, thanks to men of the stature of Max Reinhardt, Bruno Walter, the Salzburg Provincial Governor Franz Rehrl and above all Arturo Toscanini.

After 1938 Hitler tried to mould the Festival to his tastes, but unconsciously mimicked the 'Jewish' Festival, the Festival of the founders whom he so thoroughly despised. After 1945 a new Salzburg emerged, with its sights set not only on the past but also on the future. The new and the modern, even the experimental, began to play a more important role in the Salzburg repertoire, and personalities such as

Introduction

Wilhelm Furtwängler, Gottfried von Einem and, finally, Herbert von Karajan, took the torch from the first generation of founders.

I have tried in this book to combine a number of aspects of the Festival's history which might seem incompatible. This is a history of the Festival as an institution against the background of the history of Salzburg, of Austria and of Europe. It is not a musical or theatrical history. I have only discussed individual performances when I think that their singularity — or notoriety — warranted mention. In truth, especially in the pre-war days, Salzburg performances were not always notable — they were the same performances, with the same set designs, and often the same casts, as one would find during the winter at the Vienna State Opera.

After the Second World War, with the development of performances staged in Salzburg *for* Salzburg, a certain amount of inventiveness came in, and some identified a particular 'Salzburg style'. Moreover, Salzburg now had formidable competition from a host of new festivals which had sprung up almost everywhere. It could not afford to be second-rate.

Most of all, the history of the Festival is a history of fascinating individuals, from Max Reinhardt to Clemens Krauss, from Arturo Toscanini to Wilhelm Furtwängler, from Bruno Walter to Franz Rehrl. All worked their particular magic in Salzburg; none emerged from the experience unscathed. For if there is one constant in this story, it is that great art exerts a heavy personal price, that cultural politics is a refined method of total war, that the artistic temperament does not produce concord, harmony, or humility. Perhaps Salzburg has done its work so well because of this continuing creative conflict; at least that is the charitable way of looking at it.

In any event, the story of the Festival has never been told in English, and German works on Salzburg have not included the considerable amount of archival information which is available. Since it is impossible not to love Salzburg, let this then be a labour of love, though, to be sure, not blind love.

1

The Birth of the Festival Idea

1756–1920

On 22 August 1920, at precisely five o'clock in the afternoon, the Domplatz in Salzburg was filled to overflowing with Austrians and Bavarians, some sitting on hard wooden benches, others standing, while still more people were jostling for space far away at the back of the square, almost out of earshot of the dramatic event which was about to take place on the makeshift stage in front of the Cathedral doors. This small town of only about 30,000 inhabitants had never been so crowded. All the excitement was for the première of *Jedermann*, an adaptation by the Austrian poet Hugo von Hofmannsthal of the medieval English morality play *The Summoning of Everyman*, directed by Max Reinhardt with incidental music composed by Einar Nilson and Bernhard Paumgartner.

The day was cloudy with a hint of rain to the west. In Salzburg rain is never far away, so an open air performance, even before the House of God, was a considerable risk. But as legend has it, and in this case the legend is true, the sun broke through the threatening storm-clouds in mid-performance, as if on cue. As shadows lengthened and dusk fell, Everyman met and accepted his fate, and the Salzburg Festival was born.

Salzburg in 1920 was the capital of the province of the same name, located in the western Alpine reaches of the 'new' Austria created by the Treaty of St Germain in 1919. If this lovely baroque town on the Salzach river, surrounded by those gentle hills which, in German, aspire to become mountains (Kapuzinerberg, Gaisberg, Mönchsberg), could boast of the beauty of its setting and its architecture, it could lay no claim to any important role in recent or current Austrian life. Salzburg's glories were behind her.

The province had been ruled by powerful prince archbishops until 1803, and had possessed an important university. Three of these

1

archbishops had quite literally changed the face of the city in the sixteenth and early seventeenth centuries. Marcus Sittikus, Wolf Dietrich and Paris Lodron were secular leaders every bit as much as ecclesiastical. They loved music and splendour, and transformed the medieval town into an extravagant baroque fairyland of palaces, fountains, courtyards and gardens, where music, both sacred and profane, flourished. Indeed the first production of an opera north of the Alps took place in Salzburg in 1618, when Cagetti's *Andromeda* was performed in the garden of Schloss Hellbrunn.

Wolfgang Amadeus Mozart was born into this setting in 1756. The young genius, pushed by his ambitious father, spent much of his early life away from Salzburg, dazzling the courts of Europe with his musical brilliance and refining his composer's craft. Until Mozart was fifteen, Salzburg's Prince Archbishop, Sigismund von Schrattenbach, gave him enthusiastic support. After the Archbishop died, in 1771, his successor, Hieronymus von Colloredo, showed little esteem for music in general or Mozart's talent in particular. Mozart became completely disillusioned with his home town. For him, Salzburg, in comparison to the great courts of Europe, was a wasteland. The city lacked adequate musicians and singers to perform his works; worse, the taste of the music public was simple, unrefined and traditional; there was little local appreciation of Mozart's sophistication and inventiveness. He wrote of his frustration:

I detest Salzburg. . . . I refuse to associate with a good many people there— and most of the others do not think me good enough. Besides, there is no stimulus for my talent. When I play or when any of my compositions are performed, it is just as if the audience were all tables and chairs. . . . [Salzburg] is no place for my talent.[1]

In 1781 Mozart went to glittering Vienna, and remained there for the last decade of his life. Most of his greatest works were composed in the Imperial City, but his successes there were fleeting at best. In 1791 he died in poverty and obscurity. Salzburg provincialism had stifled him, Viennese indifference destroyed him.

Salzburg, which had taken scant notice of its greatest son during his life, did little to redress the balance after his death. It was fifty years before he received a memorial service there; in 1842 a performance of the C minor Mass was given at the Cathedral, attended by the composer's two surviving sons, Franz Xavier and Carl Thomas.[2] Later a bronze statue of Mozart was erected in what is now the Mozartplatz.

Sadly, his wife Constanza did not witness the event, for she had died six months earlier.

In succeeding years, Salzburg did at long last make sporadic attempts to honour Mozart. In 1870 a group of notables founded the International Mozart Foundation, known as the Mozarteum, with the expressed purpose of reviving interest in his music. Under the aegis of the Mozarteum, Hans Richter was invited to bring the Vienna Philharmonic to Salzburg in 1877 to conduct three concerts of Mozart's music. Richter had conducted the inaugural performance of *Der Ring des Nibelungen* at Bayreuth the previous year, at Wagner's special request. Richter believed that Salzburg should celebrate Mozart as Bayreuth had honoured Richard Wagner.[3] Unfortunately the Mozart concerts were not financially successful, nor were the local citizens very enthusiastic; they much disliked change of any kind.

Despite the lack of enthusiasm at the time, Richter's concept of forging a link between Salzburg and Mozart in the same way that Bayreuth had begun to be associated with Wagner was important, for it was to be the basis on which a festival at Salzburg was finally achieved.

Wagner, who may or may not have visited Salzburg (the evidence is conflicting) but who was known to have been an admirer of Mozart, was the most powerful force for change in the nineteenth-century world of music and opera, its thought and performance. Before Wagner came on the scene, vast numbers of operas were performed every year in Berlin and Vienna, London and Munich with little rehearsal and scant imagination. New productions were rare, the same flat painted sets were brought out again and again, no one moved on stage: the human voice was all. People flocked in to escape the tensions of their daily lives, to hear the soprano of the day; they gave little attention to anything else, and performances were shoddy. Wagner wanted to liberate opera from these constraints, from composers, librettists and stage designers who had conspired to create an art form totally lacking in any dramatic meaning, a showcase for the human voice, a mindless spectacle: he wanted to integrate the music, the drama and the voice into total works of art. At Bayreuth, Wagner hoped to put his theories into practice, to initiate a festival in a small Bavarian town far from the noise of the city, where people of all social classes could worship at the altar of one man's creative offering. There would be unlimited rehearsal time for a small number of operas which would be seen in an atmosphere of calm, providing a musical and dramatic experience of unparalleled quality.

Wagner's operatic texts reflected his interest in *völkisch* themes, the stories, myths and legends from the dawn of German history; they glorified values which he and many of his generation felt had been destroyed by the materialism, secularism and philistinism of the nineteenth century. Wagner idealized the 'pure' Ayrian *volk* in contrast to the rich, sophisticated and ennobled classes whom he purported to despise, but who nevertheless made up the vast majority of the operatic public of his time. He wanted all Germans, not only the rich, to make the pilgrimage to Bayreuth to rediscover their past. Bayreuth would be a 'people's festival'. It would also be a living tribute to his ideology.

Our own age would dispute many of Wagner's conceptions, his naïve notions of what constitutes drama in opera, his inability in reality to integrate the drama with the music and, it must be said, his absurd racial rhetoric. But Wagner's ideas emerged from a climate of thought which pervaded Central Europe in the nineteenth century, a climate characterized by the search for systems, the rejection of the materialistic excesses of capitalism, and the desire to rediscover values from the past. That these conceptions fused in a dominating personality who happened to be a great composer and who applied them to the world of art, meant that they travelled far beyond the confines of the quiet Bavarian town of Bayreuth.

Salzburg, only a few hundred kilometres to the south-west, made its earliest serious attempt to implement Wagner's ideas in 1887. Professor Karl Demel, a local architect, founded in that year an Action Committee whose purpose was to build a 'temple of art' on the Mönchsberg, a steep hill overlooking Salzburg to the west. The hall would hold 1500 people, and would be used to put on 'perfect' performances of the great Mozart operas. Demel pointed out that most Mozart performances to be seen in the major European opera houses were ragged with uneven singing and acting. Salzburg would remedy this by taking the 'best from the best' of these houses and then strive to create a superb rendering of these operas, impeccable in every respect. Mozart would be at the centre of this festival, though Demel also wished works from the German classical operas of Gluck, Beethoven and Weber to be included. Like Richter, Demel thought that as Bayreuth was the guardian of the creative patrimony of Wagner, so Salzburg should become the centre for Mozart and for the other composers of the classical tradition. There was however to be no competition between the two towns; each would pursue its lofty but complementary goals in its own way.

Demel knew that, as Vienna was the dynamic generative force in the cultural world of the Austro-Hungarian Empire, it would be essential to

4

ensure that the Viennese elite and the press were receptive to the idea. Salzburg could not create its festival alone. Demel's Action Committee went so far as to ask two prominent theatre architects, Ferdinand Fellner and Hermann Helmer, to draw up plans for the Mönchsberg Festival Hall. Neither Vienna nor Salzburg expressed interest in the project, and the Action Committee was dissolved in 1891.[4] But these inchoate ideas surfaced in later plans for the Festival, and were not entirely wasted. The principle that Salzburg should echo Bayreuth, that Mozart should be the central but not the exclusive composer, that the operas would achieve a level of excellence unknown in conventional opera houses, that Vienna should play a dominant role—all these major elements went into the making of the Festival realized three decades later.

Meanwhile funds were laboriously being collected for the building of a new Mozarteum. Lilli Lehmann, a renowned Berlin soprano, was a prominent member of the fund-raising committee. Strong-willed and imposing, Lehmann, who moved to Salzburg at the turn of the century, was known by some as the 'Cosima of Salzburg'. Full of enthusiasm and drive, she organized Salzburg's most elaborate Mozart festival to date in 1906, when she encouraged Gustav Mahler to bring the Vienna Philharmonic and conduct and direct *Le nozze di Figaro*. Mahler believed that the drama and the interplay of the ensemble was the key to success; he was the first major conductor to organize the entire production himself, and as director of the Vienna Hofoper, while working closely with scene designer Alfred Roller, he had revitalized the Viennese operatic scene. Lilli Lehmann defied convention herself at the 1906 festival, and staged *Don Giovanni* in the original Italian, which was most unusual at the time in German-speaking countries. Richard Strauss conducted his favourite Mozart opera, *Così fan tutte*, to complete the programme.[5] Strauss's fame, like Mahler's, was based in those days as much, if not more, on his conducting as on his skills as a composer.

While this imaginative venture was taking place, another kind of Salzburg festival was central to the concerns of Max Reinhardt and his close friend, Hermann Bahr. Already in 1903 the two men had discussed the possibility of using Salzburg as one of the four centres for new theatrical productions to be launched with Europe's greatest actresses, Sarah Bernhardt and Eleonora Duse, as the primary attraction.[6] Bahr was an imposing Viennese, a father figure to the younger generation of poets and playwrights such as Hugo von

Hofmannsthal and Franz Werfel. A consummate man of letters, a playwright, essayist and critic, Bahr made his salon famous. Reinhardt had left Baden in 1891 to make his stage debut in Salzburg, where he spent the next fifteen months, and so began his life-long love affair with the city. He then moved to Berlin where he worked under Otto Brahm, the foremost theatre director of the day. After ten years' apprenticeship Reinhardt felt confident enough to strike out on his own, and bought the Deutsches Theater in Berlin; his productions there would promote his name throughout the world. Reinhardt invited Bahr to Berlin in 1903, and the two became close friends and collaborators. Bahr was profoundly impressed by the younger man's genius, and used his own position as Austria's best-known critic to champion Reinhardt's productions.

The discussions between the two in 1903 about the four-city theatrical network came to nothing; financial backing was not forthcoming. Two years later, Bahr made a new suggestion to Reinhardt, that they found a festival in Salzburg where both theatre and opera would be performed: Reinhardt would supervise the theatrical side, Bahr and his soprano wife, the operatic. Again, lack of financial support doomed the project. Yet Bahr's place in Salzburg Festival prehistory is secure, because he stimulated Reinhardt to consider the possibilities of the place. Fifteen years later Reinhardt, at the height of his powers, with his reputation made, his ideas nurtured and deepened by experience, did indeed move to Salzburg.

Ironically, it was two enthusiastic amateurs, Friedrich Gehmacher and Heinrich Damisch, who in the next years would join forces to provide a vital stimulus to the Festival idea.

Friedrich Gehmacher was born in Upper Austria in 1866, and completed his law studies in Berlin. Later he moved to Salzburg and became the government director for unemployment insurance in the same area. But his real love was music, and in 1900 he became a member of the Mozart Society in Salzburg, a major fund-raiser, alongside Lilli Lehmann, for the building of the new Mozarteum. Heinrich Damisch, born in Vienna in 1872, had begun his career as a professional soldier, but poor eyesight had forced him to resign his commission. He then turned to the theatre and to music, and established himself as a critic, founding the Viennese Academic Mozart Society in 1913. That same year Gehmacher, whose friendship with Damisch dated back to the early years of the century, wrote an eloquent report to the Mozarteum. He urged the directors to raise money to build a new hall which would

6

create a permanent site for a Salzburg festival. Salzburg, he argued, should become an 'Austrian Bayreuth'. Echoing the Action Committee's views of 1890, Gehmacher wrote that Salzburg was the ideal place where artists and 'theorists' could join forces to present Mozart's operas to their best advantage. The advantages to Salzburg would be great, not only artistically but financially: 'I think it is superfluous to point out what enormous economic effect the Salzburg festival would have. . . . It would bring to Salzburg a rich and elegant public.'[7] Gehmacher had underlined a point that others had neglected: a Salzburg festival could serve both Mammon and Mozart. Despite Gehmacher's clear vision, his colleagues at the Mozarteum were unenthusiastic and used the outbreak of war in 1914 as a pretext for postponing decisions.

Undeterred, Gehmacher and Damisch continued to make plans. While walking across some fields near the Maria Plain pilgrimage church to the north of Salzburg in 1916, they decided that this was by far the best site for the large new musical auditorium, for it was in full view of the old city, the fortress and the majestic Alps. Both agreed that it was an ideal spot. The ground would be cheap, the peasants could be bought out, and the magical beauty of the surroundings would entice benefactors to support the project. Franz Schalk, conductor of the Vienna Philharmonic, expressed interest, but Lilli Lehmann was less keen. She had heard rumours that Reinhardt himself was planning a festival, and she feared that if he became involved, such an understanding would become a mere business venture. This to her would be an 'irreversible disaster'. The other notables at the Mozarteum were equally negative about the project.

Throughout the autumn of 1916 Gehmacher and Damisch tried to find a way out of the impasse. Neither believed that the opposition of the Mozarteum was wholly straightforward; it concealed personal rivalries, frustrated ambitions, the old Salzburg jealousy of Vienna — and class rivalry. Damisch felt that the Mozarteum leaders were opposed to the Festival idea because some of its most prominent Salzburg supporters were only 'Biertischgrossen' (fat beer drinkers). Lilli Lehmann wanted only 'nobles, famous singers, bankers, privy councillors' to be associated with any proposed festival. Finally Gehmacher and Damisch had had enough. They decided to forego the support of the Mozarteum and to create a new Salzburg Festival Society centred in Vienna. To them time seemed of the essence, the war would soon be over and then new people with new ideas might come forward and wish to create something entirely different.[8]

The Salzburg Festival Hall Society bye-laws were officially recognized in August of 1917. A sister organization was set up in Salzburg a few months later; the organization's leadership and most of its financial resources were in Vienna. Its president was Count Alexander von Thurn und Taxis, President of the Society of Friends of Music in Vienna, and its few hundred members came mostly from the musical establishment of the city. But it was an unpropitious moment to found such a society. Gehmacher learned that the price of land near Maria Plain had inflated, and there was now no hope that the Society could afford it. The Society existed, that was a positive factor; but it had limited funds — and nowhere to spend them. And the autumn of 1917 was the saddest and darkest of the war.

Into this position of stalemate stepped Max Reinhardt. His marriage was breaking up, he was no longer attached so strongly to Berlin, and he had lost his taste for city life, which he felt was an unsuitable background for theatrical works which should 'touch the heart'. [9] Personal and artistic reasons therefore combined to encourage him to renew his interest in Salzburg. Moreover he was full of enthusiasm to bring new plays to new people, to cut through the constraints of the conventional theatre and break fresh ground; a man of tremendous energy, his wide-ranging mind never ceased to conceive original and exciting projects.

In the spring of 1917 he wrote to the directors of the Imperial Theatre administration in Vienna to suggest that the government should build a theatre at Hellbrunn Palace in Salzburg 'away from the hurly burly of the city'. He would be delighted to direct plays here where people could come during their summer holidays to escape the stresses of their daily lives and to enjoy all the rich natural and artistic beauty that the town offered. He even suggested that a smaller hall be built next to the major festival theatre which could be used for German *Singspiele*. He never mentioned the name of Mozart.[10]

The following year Reinhardt bought Schloss Leopoldskron for his own use from a German businessman. Though today the castle is surrounded by modern clutter, at the time he bought it, Reinhardt could sit on his balcony and gaze over a huge artificial lake to the German Alps to the southwest (which hid the then insignificant village of Berchtesgaden). Built in 1736 by Prince Archbishop Firmian, the castle was in a sorry state by 1918, and Reinhardt during the next twenty years spent all the money he did have, and even more that he did not, beautifying Leopoldskron and turning it into a private fantasyland which was to become the most fashionable 'artistic' salon of the inter-war period.

Heinrich Damisch was sceptical about Reinhardt's motives, but Friedrich Gehmacher though that Reinhardt should be encouraged to go ahead with his theatrical plans, in the hope that he could eventually be persuaded to become interested in music and opera. Given his great prestige, Reinhardt's presence in Salzburg could only be of value. Gehmacher therefore convinced the Salzburg Festival Society that it should cultivate rather than oppose the new lord of Leopoldskron, as the townspeople now called him.

In July 1918, while Reinhardt was on holiday in Badgastein, he received a visit from the writer Ferdinand Künzelmann, who had been sent by the Society to probe Reinhardt's interest in the idea of a festival. The two men had a series of long conversations during which Künzelmann was able to fire Reinhardt's imagination. Shortly after-ward Reinhardt sent an elaborate and constructive letter to the Society, in which he suggested a framework for a festival that would incorporate music, opera, theatre and much more.

He wrote that, despite Austria's magnificent cultural tradition, many of her greatest artists were abroad; he wished them to return. Salzburg, with its central position in Europe, its natural beauty and architecture, its history and memories, its 'virginity', would bring together the 'countless men who would be redeemed from this horrible time through Art'. The festival must have a humanitarian character: 'No one of us should today think about Art without wishing to fulfil his duty towards the poor victims of our time.'

Reinhardt proposed to create theatre which would reflect Salzburg's own history. Of course he wished to produce the classics as he had done in Berlin, but the programme would also include mystery dramas, religious representations, nativity and morality plays, all of which stemmed from poetic and literary traditions which were centuries old. He pointed out that the term *Fest* or *Festspiele* referred to more than a mere series of operas or plays produced in one brief season. Histori-cally, a *Fest* had meant a coming together of people, of rich and poor estate, usually under the leadership of the Church, to experience in words, music and drama a sense of community which related to their deepest spiritual needs. The modern theatre had become entertainment and amusement for urban people of affluence; he intended to return to the medieval and Renaissance traditions of Bavaria and Austria, traditions which he felt had never been truly lost.

Reinhardt rejected the notion of a 'star theatre' attracting the upper class from the cities. He wanted to produce drama which would appeal to the heart of the local country people, which would use the best Austrian actors available; he would also arrange for performances of operas and concerts by Mozart to take place, for Mozart's works, in conjunction with the plays, would give the festival its 'spiritual unity'.

Reinhardt wanted neither the theatre of entertainment nor that of spectacle but theatre in the medieval and Greek sense, where barriers between audience and actor were broken down, where class and caste played no role, where drama was a means of invoking a quasi-religious experience. He was willing to commit himself totally to this new type of festival and would work with the Festival Society towards that end. [11] Gehmacher had won.

Oddly enough, however, the real spiritual mentor of the Salzburg Festival was not to be Reinhardt but his good friend and sometime collaborator Hugo von Hofmannsthal, for it was he who would emerge as the most influential publicist for the Festival idea. Reinhardt's international fame gave his proposals credibility, but it was von Hofmannsthal who brought together all the neo-romantic ideas which had been in the air since the end of the nineteenth century and unified them into an integrated concept which enabled the Salzburg Festival to come into being.

Born in 1874, Hugo von Hofmannsthal was an elegant and sensitive intellectual from a patrician Viennese family. By 1918 he had gained a sturdy reputation as a playwright, poet, essayist and opera librettist. His background and demeanour contrasted sharply with those of his two closest collaborators, with whom he had been creatively entwined since the early years of the century: Max Reinhardt, the self-made man, the fantasist, the introvert in extrovert's clothing, and Richard Strauss, the jovial though sometimes crass Bavarian whose operas had taken Europe by storm. Strauss had composed *Salome* after having attended Reinhardt's production of Oscar Wilde's play. Von Hofmannsthal wrote the brilliant libretto for Strauss's *Der Rosenkavalier* which Reinhardt staged in 1911, and that same year von Hofmannsthal reworked *Jedermann* to enable Reinhardt to stage it in Berlin's Schumann Circus in front of three thousand people, a spectacle which received universal acclaim. The following year the three collaborated yet again on the first version of *Ariadne auf Naxos*.

Once von Hofmannsthal became seriously involved in the Salzburg Festival idea, his dedication became total; he spent the last ten years of his life in the service of Salzburg, producing some of his most eloquent prose in support of his notion that Salzburg had a 'moral mission'. This mission was to act as a regenerative force, to renew old traditions, to employ art to bring peace to a troubled Europe. Salzburg's geographical and spiritual position at the crossroads of Europe should be a symbol for reconciliation of a generation torn and divided by war. [12]

Von Hofmannsthal suffered, as did so many others of his generation, from a dislike of his own times. He hated modern fashions, he loathed the new psychology. He could not abide realism; for him modern life obscured rather than elucidated truth. He preferred to escape into the past, into the world of the seventeenth and eighteenth centuries, but in particular into the classical world of Goethe's Weimar; this was his spiritual homeland, and now he would make Salzburg into the new Weimar.

Von Hofmannsthal was fully aware that the 'new' Austria faced a crushing problem of identity. By the end of 1918 the old Austro-Hungarian Empire had collapsed. It had become the new sick man of Europe, surrounded by hostile new nations, Hungary, Czechoslovakia and Yugoslavia. What remained of Austria was a sliver of land, overwhelmingly German, reaching from Styria to the German–Czech border, from Burgenland to Vorarlberg. Though von Hofmannsthal was not himself a political thinker, he was sensitive to the potentially catastrophic effect that Austria's diminished position might have. He argued, and history has proved him right, that Austria's cultural heritage, as transmitted through the institutions which had made that culture dynamic, the Church and the old concept of the Holy Roman Empire, had created an identity — and a purpose — that could never be destroyed. As Weimar was the centre of German classicism, the Vienna of Maria Theresa in the eighteenth century was the synthesis of the 'Austrian idea'. Despite the physical collapse of the Empire, Austria could still retain her 'imperial' status, not through force or physical occupation, but through the continuation of her age-old spiritual traditions. And Salzburg would be the centre of the propagation of that idea. [13]

For von Hofmannsthal, that spiritual tradition had deep roots.

The [Salzburg] Festival is the true idea of art in the minds of the Austro-Bavarian people . . . the Festival Hall on the very border between Austria and Bavaria is the symbolic expression of deeply rooted tendencies, which are half a thousand years old. . . . The powerful underlying basis of these tendencies is medieval. Gluck was their forerunner, Mozart their peak and centre. According to them, dramatic and musical life are one; exalted drama and opera. . .were already united and inseparable in the baroque theatre of the seventeenth century. Here Weimar approaches Salzburg; the real dramatic element in Goethe, as the Salzburg Festivals will show . . . [is] a unified structure of all the forms of theatrical expression which spring from the South German soil.[14]

Between 1918 and 1922, von Hofmannsthal wrote a series of tracts in support of the Festival. He shared Reinhardt's view that class divisions did not exist in great art which had been created in the historical period before capitalism and hunger for money had divided the people, isolating them from each other and from their cultural roots. He established, in more detail than before, the programme for the Festival. It would centre, of course, on the classical age. In addition to Mozart, operas by Gluck, Beethoven and Weber should be performed, and mystery and nativity plays would alternate with the works of Calderon, Shakespeare, Schiller and Goethe.[15]

Von Hofmannsthal knew that he could also count on help and encouragement for his ideas from his old collaborator Richard Strauss, who had been a member of the Festival Society since 1917, largely because of his friendship with Franz Schalk. Indeed Strauss had been asked to join the organization's Artistic Council (*Kunstrat*) before von Hofmannsthal had. Born in 1864, Strauss had spent most of his life in the small Bavarian village of Garmisch, barely a hundred kilometres from Salzburg. As Germany's best-known living composer Strauss now vowed to bring others into the movement, to help raise funds and to put his not inconsiderable conducting skills at the service of the Festival. He was one of the great Mozart interpreters of his day, and his love for Mozart shows in the spirit and plot of his own works, in *Der Rosenkavalier* and *Die Frau ohne Schatten*. He was an eminently practical man, unlike his librettist, and focused his efforts before 1920 on finding solutions to the Society's major weakness, its lack of funds.

Strauss and Schalk in their turn encouraged stage designer Alfred Roller to become involved. Roller's long collaboration with Mahler at the Hofoper had brought him to despise the reliance on 'star' singers. Many great voices did not in themselves make for an integrated and dramatically compelling operatic experience. Like Reinhardt, who had created his own ensemble in Berlin, Roller and Mahler had brought the Vienna Opera to its apotheosis by developing a closely-knit ensemble. Roller wanted Salzburg to create a 'Mozart style' which would set a standard for the world.

Encouraged by all this enthusiasm, Damisch's Festival Society began in 1918 to publish a monthly report filled with supportive quotations from celebrities in the fields of both music and drama, and telling its members about the various charity concerts which were being held to raise money for the projected concert hall to be built in Salzburg. Such men as Bruno Walter, then General Music Director in Munich, Felix von Weingartner, another prominent conductor, and playwrights Anton Wildgand and Gerhart Hauptmann supported the movement, as well as the writer Thomas Mann. Hauptmann spoke for many:

> A Mozart Festival in Salzburg, that is the most natural and happiest thought that I can imagine—the eternal springs with pure poetry in this wondrous town with its magnificent setting. Who, before his death, would not wish to make a pilgrimage there to celebrate peace with his fellow man, and escape this sad and ravaged world?[16]

In 1918 and 1919, when the Society was growing not only in Vienna and Salzburg, but in other German and Austrian cities, Central Europe was in the midst of war, revolution and severe economic dislocation. There were shortages of food, the currency was in chaos, transport was difficult. People had more urgent matters on their minds than the 'Austro-Bavarian tradition' or a 'Mozart style'. Yet the author Stefan Zweig, who himself moved to Salzburg in 1919, described a contrasting mood, when he wrote on the Vienna Opera in the days immediately following the war.

> I shall never forget what an opera performance meant in those direst days. . . . There was never any certainty that the Opera would last into the next week, what with the sinking value of money and the doubts about coal deliveries; the desperation seemed doubly great in this abode of luxury and imperial abundance. The Philharmonic players were like grey shadows in their shabby dress suits, undernourished and exhausted by many privations, and the audience, too, seemed to be ghosts in a theatre which had become ghostly. . . . Then the conductor raised his baton . . . and it was as glorious as ever. . . . Never have I experienced so powerful a surge of life as at that period when our very existence and survival were at stake.

To Zweig, 'the collapse of money made us feel that nothing was enduring except the eternal within ourselves.'[17]

Zweig himself was to play only a peripheral role in the Festival, but for the next fifteen years he held court in his house on the Kapuziner-berg and entertained most of the artistic elite visiting Salzburg. His description of Opera performances in Vienna, where both audience and performers wore overcoats to combat the cold, strikingly portrays the reality of von Hofmannsthal's vision: in Austria art was life.

Meanwhile the Festival Society had commissioned two avant-garde architects, Hans Poelzig and Josef Hoffmann, to submit plans for a Festival Hall to be built in the grounds of Schloss Hellbrunn.[18] Reinhardt, however, was too impatient to wait for something to be built. To him, plans, promises and building designs did not make for a festival; performances did. He therefore planned to produce a modern rendering (by Max Mell) of the traditional nativity play given annually in the church at Hallein, a village to the south of Salzburg, during Christmas 1919. The young conductor Bernhard Paumgartner, recently appointed director of the Mozarteum, would organize the music, and the proceeds would be used to help poor Salzburg children.

Reinhardt, although himself a Jew, received permission from Ignatius Rieder, Archbishop of Salzburg, to perform the nativity play in a church, but no performance ever took place. Impossible travel conditions, and lack of coal to warm hotels, forced him to cancel the play just weeks before the first performance.

Reinhardt, however, remained optimistic. In January 1920, he proposed staging *Jedermann* in the summer, when heating would not be a problem. In April he decided to stage the play in the *Felsenreitschule*, or Outdoor Riding School, which made up part of the complex of the old Archbishop's riding stables; in July he changed his mind and proposed using the Cathedral square, a decision of extraordinary import for the future.

The reasons for Reinhardt's decision remain obscure. Bernhard Paumgartner's memoirs provide one version, Erwin Kerber gives us another. Paumgartner describes his first meeting with Reinhardt in a shabby Salzburg hotel where they sat in a gloomy entrance hall and drank 'horrible' cups of coffee; the next morning the two of them walked to the Cathedral square together and it was then that the idea was born.[19] The other interpretation credits Erwin Kerber, the business secretary of the Society, as having suggested the idea to Reinhardt while the two drank coffee with Hermann Bahr.[20] In any case the decision was made. The next vital step was to secure permission from the Archbishop. Fortunately, unlike many of the people of Salzburg, the prelate did not object to the Cathedral's being used as a 'set'. In response to Reinhardt's request, Rieder wrote 'it will bring joy to my heart if this deeply moving play is a success.' Reinhardt had assured the Archbishop that 'this medieval play has a great future. . . .'[21]

The story of *Jedermann* is simple: a conceited rich man, who lacks any respect for human suffering, is at the peak of his power when he is visited by Death, who warns him that his end is near. The rich man strives to reverse this decision; he begs for time, invoking the gods of Mammon for protection, but without success. At this point he is enlightened by Faith; he falls to his knees, says the Lord's Prayer and is taken off to his heavenly reward.

Hugo von Hofmannsthal had extensively reworked the text of this old English morality play for Reinhardt's Berlin production of 1911, enabling the rich man to be saved by a combination of Faith and Good Works, both of which were personified in the new version. Von Hofmannsthal, as Eugene Weber explained, 'incorporated into the drama a religious concept (salvation through faith) usually considered purely Protestant. Thus he has included two normally divergent points of view carefully presenting them in such harmonious and delicate interplay that Protestants and Catholics alike can see confirmation of their own belief here.' But the playwright did more than create a theologically pleasing compromise. He gave the morality play, whose principles were abstract and allegorical, a compelling life of its own. He added a banquet scene, a comic devil and a long conversation between Mammon and Everyman. In other words he took an ancient theological argument and made it contemporary and realistic.[22]

Yet *Jedermann* owed its impact, its ability to touch the hearts of its audience, not so much to von Hofmannsthal as to Reinhardt's brilliant direction. He created a new concept which was to be indelibly associated with the Salzburg Festival for all time: the concept of the city as theatre. Salzburg in its baroque eloquence was to be his public stage, just as Leopoldskron was his private one. When Death called Everyman during the banquet, his voice was heard coming from the imposing medieval fortress, the Hohensalzburg, which towered over the city. Various actors emerged from the audience to take part in the play, thus breaking down the barriers of conventional theatre; the sounds of organ and chorus emanated from the Cathedral; doves were released and church bells tolled when Everyman was saved. All these special effects worked powerfully on spectators. Even the timing of the play, which began in the late afternoon and ended at 7.30 in the last rays of dusk, was no accident. For Reinhardt the allegory was clear: day into night, life into death.

The actors whom Reinhardt chose for that first performance were those with whom he had worked for years. He had discovered Alexander Moissi, an Italian from Trieste, seen his natural talent and made him into a star before casting him as Everyman. For the next eleven years no one could conceive of the play without Moissi in the title role. Werner Krauss played Death. No one associated with the production received any payment, although Krauss did request a pair of *Lederhosen*; his wish was granted.

Reinhardt and von Hofmannsthal together had created in the Cathedral square a powerful religious experience which moved Archbishop Rieder, and many others, to tears. As Reinhardt wrote two years later:

> Everyman came to life. . . . Priests said that the play was stronger than any sermon . . . that the accomplishment of the *régisseur* and his dramatic collaborator had consisted of making this old folk-play really alive, filled with the spirit of today, and once more a community possession for the people. In fact, the giant post-war social revolutions, the new wealth arising everywhere, the dangerous materialism of today, all gave a great contemporary significance and deeply penetrating moral effect to this old play about the death of a rich man.[23]

Many of the locals had been unable to attend performances because of the influx of Bavarians and Viennese, so on 29 August a special performance of *Jedermann* was given exclusively for the people of Salzburg, for Reinhardt wanted to emphasize that it was indeed their Festival. There were no other plans that year, no operatic performances, no orchestral or chamber concerts. *Jedermann was* the Salzburg Festival of 1920. The idea of a Festival Hall was still only a sketch on a drawing board, and the Society's funds were no greater in September than they had been in August. But Reinhardt's bold initiative had at long last broken the deadlock. Through *Jedermann* the Salzburg Festival had come into being.

2
Difficult Beginnings
1921–5

The singular success of *Jedermann* did not in itself secure the future well-being of the Festival. In some ways it raised false expectations and encouraged leading members of the Society to set their sights too high and to assume that somehow huge amounts of money would now be forthcoming; in reality, the next few years proved to be a period of intense economic struggle.

The international public began to attend the Festival in ever-increasing numbers, but it was not exactly the public which Max Reinhardt and Hugo von Hofmannsthal had imagined in their earlier more idealistic moments. Many of the rich and aristocratic streamed into Salzburg for social reasons; the common man could not possibly afford the high ticket prices. Great art cost money, and most of that money had to come from the box-office.

This did not please the citizens of Salzburg, who saw some of their taxes going to subsidize a venture from which they were effectively excluded. As a result, local support for the Festival was half-hearted at best. The locals may have felt proud that Max Reinhardt entertained the cultural élite of Europe in his salon at Leopoldskron, but they resented not being invited to join in. Shopkeepers may have profited from the growing sales of fancy peasant costumes and *dirndl* skirts to well-heeled New York society matrons, but they were not enthusiastic about having so many foreigners in their midst; in the very predictable world of a small Austrian provincial town, foreigners brought unpredictability, flashy, expensive cars and questionable *mores*; Salzburgers were shocked when they read, later in the decade, that American flappers had actually danced the Charleston in the stodgy old Hotel Europa. In addition, there was a small, though virulent, anti-Semitic movement in the province which poured continuous scorn on Reinhardt, von Hofmannsthal and their international friends, and by implication questioned the *raison d'être* of the Festival.

Thus the line between politics and art was never clear. The success of the Festival was very much dependent on the dynamics of local and national politics. The nation was confused and troubled. In the space of four years the proud multi-national Austro-Hungarian Empire had been reduced to the status of a minor power with a weak currency, high unemployment and little consensus between the two major political parties, the Socialists and the clerico-conservative Christian Social Party (CSP), regarding her new role in the world. Austria's most pressing problem was, at least to many observers, her lack of identity, and this issue was inexorably linked to her relations with the new German Republic.

Many Austrians looked for their salvation to some kind of union with Germany. For the Socialists, the question was simple: the party would profit if Austria merged with a Germany controlled by the German Socialist Party. Many members of the CSP longed for Austria's attachment to a large and powerful German state, a cause which conservatives had promoted as far back as 1848. Intellectuals tended to view the Austrian cultural tradition as an exclusively Germanic one made manifest through the language.

Despite this climate of opinion, the federal government was in no mood to upset the victorious Allies; it would be a suicidal act. When therefore the Salzburg provincial authorities announced an 'unofficial' plebiscite for 29 May 1921, the federal government immediately declared it illegal, but to no avail. With the support of the leaders of the two major parties, as well as the newly-formed German Nationalist Party (the forerunner of the Nazi Party), the province voted over-whelmingly for union (*Anschluss*) with Germany. The vote was an act of desperation taken during a period of acute economic crisis. Local politicians of all stripes had incited the passions of their followers, and therefore had refused to accept the ultimatum from Vienna. But the plebiscite achieved nothing, save to add a footnote to history.[1]

Though on the surface this illegal plebiscite may make it appear that the Salzburg populace was prone to extreme measures, in reality the province was run by moderate men who eschewed radical measures from the right or from the left. From 1919 until 1934 the CSP controlled the province and exerted its leadership through the person of the Provincial Governor and through its comfortable majority in the Assembly (*Landtag*), which had considerably more power than the Salzburg City Council. Election to that Assembly was by proportional representation, and the Socialists regularly controlled one quarter of the seats. The budget for the province required unanimous consent. Herein lay, at least structurally, a reason for the relative stability between the majority and minority. Salzburg could function only if there was a will to compromise rather than to confront. But reasons for the development of what Salzburg historian Ernst Hanisch has called 'consensus' politics ran deeper. The leaders of both political parties were men of moderation. They left flaming rhetoric to their fellow party members in Vienna. Both Franz Rehrl, the CSP Provincial Governor, and Robert Preussler, the Socialist Deputy Governor, were pragmatists to the core. Furthermore, their personal relations were cordial. And the leaders of both parties realized that in a province which knew no extremes of wealth and correspondingly less class consciousness, local interests would be better served by working together. Salzburg could not afford the luxury of meaningless political strife.[2]

A third, more unstable, element in the Salzburg political picture was the small German Nationalist Party. Many of its members held important positions in the city administration, but in the Twenties the party's political power was limited because of factional infighting. Its platform echoed that of the National Socialists north of the border: *Anchluss*, anti-Marxism, anti-clericalism and anti-Semitism. This party became the most vocal opponent of the Festival, whereas the Socialists and the CSP eventually came to favour it.

If there was one issue that all local political parties could agree upon, it was the province's relationship with Vienna. Vienna, whose two million inhabitants made up almost a third of the country's population, was the enemy. The capital city was run by radical Socialists. 'Bolsheviks' were a threatening minority, as was the city's large Jewish population. Most of the powerful politicians, bankers and industrialists worked there, and they had no interest in Salzburg' fate. As a result, the relationship between party leaders in Vienna and Salzburg—and this was true of both major parties—was at best 'correct'. In private, local party notables decried the excesses of their national leaders and kept the Salzburg sections of the party private armies, the Socialist *Schutzbund* and the CSP *Heimwehr*, as politically toothless as possible.[3] Certainly these tensions between Salzburg and Vienna did little to encourage central government support for the Festival. In 1919 the government gave the paltry sum of 2000 Kronen to the Society, as well as a few words of encouragement—nothing more.

Richard Strauss believed that he could use his reputation and contacts to raise the necessary funds from private sources, and in late 1920 he sailed for America. On board ship he met a wealthy American who offered to build a huge Festival Hall in Salzburg if only Strauss would persuade the Austrian government to give him a mine exploration monopoly in Austria. In New York a wealthy socialite promised to raise 100,000 dollars for the building of a concert hall. But nothing came of these projects. Later, while travelling in South America, Strauss wrote to von Hofmannsthal about his difficulties in publicizing the Festival: 'What is Salzburg to a Brazilian, or even worse, to a German living in Brazil?' [4]

It was a chimera to think that Strauss—or anyone else—could convince individuals to contribute the huge sums that were necessary to build a concert hall. Funding on such a scale required government involvement. But the only way to convince the government of the desirability of such a venture would be to prove that a festival in Salzburg would be advantageous to the nation as a whole.

Instead of thinking of ways and means of doing this, the Festival Society director wrote to the Minister of Finance less than two months before the 1921 Festival was due to open, requesting a government guarantee of 4,000,000 Kronen against expected losses.[5] The Society feared that there might be a deficit because inflation was rampant and it had provided a large number of cheap tickets for the citizens of Salzburg, which might upset visitors who had to pay correspondingly higher prices for the remaining seats. Already, due to the government's conspicuous silence, the Society had been forced to cut back on its ambitious programme for 1921.

The Minister of Finance was not moved, and replied curtly that if the Festival authorities wished to have a guarantee against losses, they should find some rich capitalist to give it. The Treasury was in no condition to bail them out.[6]

The Society had acted much too late and, with no federal guarantee, was forced to cancel the proposed performances of *Così fan tutte*, *Don Giovanni*, and Molière's *Le Bourgeois Gentilhomme* with Strauss's incidental music. Instead the Festival was reduced to performances of *Jedermann* and a series of orchestral and chamber concerts conducted by Bernhard Paumgartner with members of the Mozarteum Orchestra and a few extra musicians imported from the Vienna Philharmonic.

If the 1921 Festival was only slightly larger than that of previous years, it had at least established continuity. Press reaction was enthusiastic. The *Neue Freie Presse*, Vienna's most prestigious daily newspaper, wrote that 'the call of *Jedermann* rang from Salzburg to the whole world'. In the American *Theatre Arts Magazine*, Herman Scheffauer wrote that the Festival would

> serve man and life. . . . Something of the radiance and joy of poetry, art, music, drama, the dance, undefiled by profiteering, by war, by nationalism is to dwell here, a kind of League of Arts of the world in a world sick to its gorge with the sermons of internationalism, the insolence and cretinisms of self-styled Leagues of Nations.[7]

Others were not so pleased. Strauss, who had a strong dislike for Paumgartner and the Mozarteum, wrote to Schalk telling him that the Festival programme had been a 'dilettante' one, that neither he nor his co-conductor at the Vienna Opera had been consulted. Strauss said that he would give up his 'protectorship' of the Festival, which, in Paumgartner's hands, was only an 'artistic swindle'. He feared that the deficit that the Mozarteum was incurring would be transferred to the Festival Society. [8]

The composer gave vent to his wrath in a letter to von Hofmannsthal in late August. Why had Reinhardt gone ahead with *Jedermann*? Since the Festival Society had been unable to raise funds for 1921, it should have cancelled the whole undertaking. Better no Festival than an inferior one. Did the Festival Society expect to see Paumgartner on the podium one year and he and Schalk the next? Strauss's *amour propre* was injured, and he threatened to resign. [9]

Strauss's outburst is indicative of the atmosphere which pervaded the Society during this difficult period. As personal feuding between artistic prima donnas increased, it could only harm future prospects. The old Salzburg–Vienna rivalry now took the form of poisoned articles in the Vienna press accusing the people of Salzburg of provincialism, and complaints by the latter that, with one exception, the Society was being run by 'outsiders' who wished to impose their will on Salzburg. The Artistic Council seemed incapable of ensuring continuity. The President of the Society, Count Alexander von Thurn und Taxis, did not exert sufficiently strong leadership, and neither Damisch nor Gehmacher had the necessary political connections to control events. Thus personal and institutional squabbling threatened to undermine the Festival.

However, Max Reinhardt was undeterred by these problems. He asked the Archbishop for permission to perform in 1922 Hugo von Hofmannsthal's revised version of a seventeenth-century allegorical

Spanish play by Calderón de la Barca, called *The Great World Theatre*, in Fischer von Erlach's Kollegien Church. This request met with considerable resistance from Nationalist Party groups in both Salzburg and Vienna. Only when Reinhardt threatened to stage the play elsewhere did he receive permission to go ahead.

Fortunately the Austrian government was feeling more generous in 1922 and allocated 250,000 Kronen for that year's Festival, which enabled the Society to publicize the event and send prospectuses throughout Europe and to the United States.[10] Although the Vienna State Opera was on tour in South America, thirty-seven musicians had remained behind, and these were promptly engaged. Among them was a young new second violinist, Otto Strasser, who came to Salzburg in the summer of 1922 and was dazzled by the town's 'dreamlike' quality.[11] He played in four Mozart operas at the local Landestheater, *Così fan tutte* and *Don Giovanni* under Strauss, *Figaro* and *Die Entführung aus dem Serail* (*The Abduction from the Seraglio*) under Schalk. The small size of the orchestra caused no great difficulty—the tiny theatre could not have accommodated any more players.

The casts, strengthened with guest singers from Dresden and Munich, read like an operatic *Who's Who* of the time. They included Richard Tauber, Richard Mayr (Strauss's favourite bass, and Salzburg's favourite son), Alfred Jerger, Selma Kurz, Elisabeth Schumann, Rosa Pauly, Lotte Schöne and Elisabeth Rethberg. The Vienna Philharmonic also gave two early morning concerts consisting solely of music by Mozart.

This was the only summer Festival during Reinhardt's tenure when *Jedermann* did not appear in the schedule; his energies were focused entirely on *The Great World Theatre*, which was performed fourteen times. In this play, the Master of the World gives out different parts: one soul is to be a king, another a merchant, a third a beggar and so on. The beggar initially revolts against his lot, but finally acquiesces. Allegorical figures play militarism, commerce, luxury, labour, religion, wisdom and beauty. After a chilling dance of death all the characters except the merchant (here von Hofmannsthal shows his loathing for capitalism) are admitted into paradise. Setting, production and acting are crucial for a play of this kind, and here Reinhardt excelled himself, although one English critic could not understand why such an historical curiosity was being staged at all. Another suggested that, although the play was piffle from both the intellectual and poetic standpoints, he had enjoyed the baroque exuberance of the setting in the old Benedictine church, the bold rigorous rhetoric of the actors and the sustained melodrama of the performance. Moissi played the central figure of the Beggar and was roundly acclaimed. The Salzburg and Viennese press were universally laudatory with one notable exception, Karl Kraus of the satirical Viennese review *Die Fackel*.

Kraus spent thirty-seven years, from 1899 to his death in 1936, castigating his enemies and praising his prodigies in the columns of his one-man newspaper. Although not particularly remembered today outside German-speaking countries, he was the most deadly critic and satirist of his time. Neither his opponents nor his supporters could deny his extraordinary lucidity and command of the German language.

Kraus could not abide Reinhardt or the Jewish establishment in Vienna. That the critic was himself a converted Jew suggests something of the complexity of the man. In any event, he found *The Great World Theatre* a blasphemy; he felt that Reinhardt, Moissi and von Hofmannsthal, all Jews, had turned the House of God into an attraction for tourists. The Archbishop, he noted with irony, was honouring God by allowing 'high ticket prices'. Kraus was so incensed, by some accounts, that this incident prompted his departure from the Catholic Church.[12]

Kraus's review was intemperate and exaggerated but that was his style: to provoke. In Salzburg itself, criticism of the Festival was more prosaic. The *Chronik*, a strong supporter, complained that, despite free general rehearsals, tickets were still too expensive for citizens: a financial subsidy would have to be found. A journalist for the *Neue Zürcher Zeitung* mentioned that he had seen many local inhabitants who did possess tickets selling them to hotel porters at a profit.[13]

At the end of August two thousand Socialists demonstrated in front of the provincial government offices, demanding that tourists be asked to leave as soon as possible. The prices in the shops had gone up, the people of Salzburg were given no discounts and the tourists were depriving the locals of their daily bread. There was some truth in all of this, for a Swiss journalist had been amazed at the huge increase in prices displayed in the shops on the eve of the Festival. The Socialist Deputy Provincial Governor spoke to the angry crowd and promised that the tourists would be asked to leave by 3 September, and a proclamation to this effect was published the next day.[14]

Kraus's diatribe, the ill humour of the Salzburg crowd and the complaints about the use of the church seemed misguided; many pointed out that Reinhardt's creativity, hard work and genius had worked miracles. The Viennese *Allgemeine Zeitung* complained that no one in the Festival Society had even bothered to give Reinhardt formal thanks for his contribution.[15] As before, Reinhardt had refused all payment, and had pledged the profits of the play to the restoration of the church; von Hofmannsthal had accepted only half of his salary. The Festival Society had, by comparison, given only a minuscule amount.

The *Neue Freie Presse* saw the Festival in a broader perspective. It had shown that Austria's desire to strive toward certain ideals had not been destroyed by the war. 'We will cling to our great tradition and document it.' [16] The foreign press echoed these sentiments. The London *Literary Digest* wrote:

> Only a traditional and passionate love of music—a language which all nations speak—can explain the keenness with which a bankrupt, derelict country enters into the production of a festival of such importance. . . . It is indeed, though perhaps unconsciously, Austria's cry to the world. 'Can you,' she asks of the rest of the world, 'allow so zealous an art, so earnest a zeal for culture, to perish?'

The *Eclair* in Paris thought that through the Festival, the 'young republic' would restore itself to its 'allocated place in history' despite the sufferings caused by the Peace Treaty.[17]

Indeed, there was room for optimism. The Festival, as expected, had run at a deficit; but Salzburg, and Austria, had received international acclaim. Concurrent with the Festival performances, the newly-founded International Society for Contemporary Music had put on a number of chamber music concerts, highlighting the works of Strauss, Busoni, Webern, Milhaud, Poulenc and Schoenberg. To one of the founders of this Society, the Viennese writer and critic Paul Stefan, the combination of traditional and new music was fortuitous: Salzburg was celebrating at one and the same time its ancient traditions in the mystery plays, its greatest composer, Mozart, and the fruit of the newest generation of musical genius in Arnold Schoenberg. Unfortunately Stefan's hopes for a conjunction of new and old music in Salzburg were short-lived; the Contemporary Music Society moved to London, and never held concerts in Salzburg again. [18]

The high point of the 1922 Festival was the ceremonial laying of the cornerstone for the new Festival Hall at Hellbrunn, which took place on 19 August. The Austrian President, Michael Hainisch, spoke warmly of Salzburg's mission in the presence of Archbishop Rieder, Reinhardt, von Hofmannsthal and most of the artists who were performing at the

Festival; but behind the pomp and ceremony, doubts lingered. On his way back to Leopoldskron, accompanied by von Hofmannsthal and Helene Thimig, Reinhardt remarked: 'It will never happen.' Reinhardt had throughout his life built on existing foundations; he never laid his own. He was to be proved right. Poelzig's fantastic designs would never be realized.[19]

The relative success of the 1922 Festival could not mask the continuing conflicts within the Society itself. That autumn the President, Count Alexander von Thurn und Taxis, resigned. The Society asked Richard Strauss to replace him. At first the composer hesitated, for he thought the natural candidate should be Reinhardt. Von Hofmannsthal's reaction to Strauss's hesitancy was immediate. Strauss should take the job, for he alone could give the Festival real artistic direction.

> These philistines *[Spiessbürger]* will never make Reinhardt President. They hate him several times over, as a Jew, as a *Schlossherr*, as an artist and as an individual whom they cannot understand.[20]

Von Hofmannsthal described his own frustration and irritation with the people of Salzburg. 'I gave them my share of the profits, thirty million Kronen, and instead of thanks . . . they said I should have given them all of it.' If Strauss did not take the job, another cultural 'big wig' would step in, and all would be lost. Strauss accepted the position. [21]

His tenure lasted two years; it was not a happy period, and it inhibited the Festival directors from appointing another performing artist/composer for the Presidency for nearly forty years. Hyper-inflation prevented the building of the Festival Hall, and tensions between the Viennese and Salzburg factions intensified, thus paralysing the organization. Strauss, in the eye of the storm, withdrew into himself. He was much more comfortable composing in his cottage in Garmisch or conducting prominent orchestras. Bureaucratic conflict bored him.

In October Strauss suddenly announced that the 1923 Festival would take place without him; all the momentum which had been gained in 1922 was lost. He would only take up active participation in 1924, when he promised to conduct *Ariadne auf Naxos* and the Suite from *Le Bourgeois Gentilhomme*. [22]

In March 1923 the *Neues Wiener Journal* reported from Vienna that, because of local pressure in Salzburg, the Archbishop had rescinded his permission for the Kollegien Church to be used for *The Great World Theatre* and the provincial *Landtag* had refused to allocate funds to rebuild the indoor Winter Riding School for theatre performances, although the Salzburg City Hall supported the subsidy.[23] Damisch, whose eyesight was failing, now resigned. The Viennese section of the Society was in tatters. Reinhardt threatened to stage no play if the Winter Riding School was not rebuilt, and when funds were not forthcoming, he abandoned his Salzburg plans and decided to concentrate his energies on preparing Carl Vollmoller's pantomime play *Das Mirakel* (*The Miracle*) for Broadway.

Many people shared responsibility for the failure of the 1923 Festival. Schalk and Strauss had announced at the last moment that they would take the Vienna Opera company on a lucrative tour of South America, and so had cut Salzburg off from one of the sources of its lifeblood. At the eleventh hour the Festival directors held discussions with the Berlin Philharmonic—the Vienna Philharmonic's great rival—but these fell through because of the poor facilities in the Salzburg concert halls.[24] Those members of the Vienna Philharmonic not on tour then offered to play some concerts in Salzburg, but the Festival leadership could not meet their price. The refusal of the government to grant a healthy subsidy to the improverished Society was the final straw. Altogether 1923 was a grim year.

Reinhardt, however, was not a man to hold grudges, and he saved the Festival from total collapse in his own unique way. He decided to put on Molière's *Le Malade imaginaire*, first in a general rehearsal at Leopoldskron, then for a few performances at the Landestheater. Reinhardt had engaged the great comedian, Max Pallenberg, to amuse and beguile the well-dressed guests as they arrived at the door of Leopoldskron for the general rehearsal on 20 August 1923; his son Gottfried has described the scene in charming detail:

> The guests were arriving. For a brief moment feelings of high anticipation gave way to a twinge of awkwardness. . . . Had the invitation been for a masked ball? But reassurance came quickly . . . was [Reinhardt] not *l'homme de théâtre par excellence*? So why should one not be greeted by a garrulous buffoon surrounded by his servants, all decked out in seventeeth-century costumes? . . . The shameless fellow seemed riddled with disease and spared no detail in describing symptoms, aches, malfunctions, examinations, therapies—the clinical lot. . . . He introduced himself as Monsieur Argan. Some beat him to it and addressed him as Herr Pallenberg. . . . Soon a sea of laughter filled the vast entrance hall and the ornate staircase as, the party now assembled, he and his retinue joined the rear guard ascending and entering the grand ballroom where the remainder

26

of the cast of Molière's *Malade imaginaire* mingled with the *tout Salzburg*—which in the Twenties was *le tout monde* for drinks and a sumptuous banquet and the subsequent surprise performance in its very midst.[25]

The *Malade imaginaire* kept the Festival idea alive in 1923, but in 1924 the malady was the Festival itself, and the sickness was not imaginary. The cornerstone in Hellbrunn was buried in undergrowth, the Viennese and Salzburg factions of the Society were at war, and Strauss had ceased to be President in all but name. He had written to Kerber in the autumn of 1923 that he would be unavailable for the 1924 Festival after all. 'I must work in the summer.' His only contribution was to suggest a few operas for the following season.[26]

Press passions replaced the sweet sounds of Mozart in 1924. Political infighting in Salzburg was added to the perennial Vienna–Salzburg tensions. The local Socialist paper, *Die Wacht*, launched an attack on the bourgeois leadership of the Festival Society, which it accused of trying to build a Festival Hall without having any idea where the money was to come from. 'Salzburg string-pullers' were only indulging in power politics; they would not even raise enough money to buy a lavatory for the new Hall. All their talk about local interests ceased when it came to spending money. Their only goal was to win power from their colleagues in Vienna. The Festival itself was secondary.[27]

The *Wacht* ridiculed this state of affairs. Socialists had as much stake in the Festival as anyone else, for it was of vital importance to the city, both economically and artistically. But it could not survive without backing from Vienna. Salzburg itself had neither the financial nor the artistic weight to put on its own Festival.

There was also another Salzburg newspaper, *Der Eiserne Besen* (the Rod of Iron) representing the German National Socialist viewpoint until it was banned in 1933, which was no friend to the Festival, for its pet hates were 'Max Goldman-Reinhardt', von Hofmannsthal and 'Bruno Walter-Schlesinger'. It was the conduit for Salzburg's anti-Semitism and loathed the two major parties with equal fervour. Although few responsible people in Salzburg took the *Besen* seriously, it was sometimes able to exert considerable pressure and had been largely responsible for the campaign to prevent Reinhardt from producing the *The Great World Theatre* in 1923. The line it now took was that the Festival might be an economic boon for Salzburg shopkeepers, but it had used a church as a theatre where 'foreign races and enemies of religion have presented their un-German art.' The *Besen* wanted all the 'Jewish elements' which ran the Festival expunged; then a real German

Festival could come into being. The paper campaigned against Reinhardt in 1924 in order to prevent the director from staging his New York triumph *Das Mirakel* in the Kollegien Church. Chagrined when the Archbishop did give his permission, it was able to crow when the star, the fashionable English beauty Lady Diana Manners, became ill and performances were cancelled.[28]

The Society had begun lethargic negotiations with the Vienna Philharmonic, but had had to call them off because they were unable to meet the orchestra's salary demands.[29] Strauss became increasingly remote. Without Reinhardt, plans for the 1924 Festival went up in smoke. Whatever disagreements the Society had had with him in the past, they were now fully aware how totally dependent that were on him for his ideas and his drawing power; he, at least, was willing to try to keep the spirit of the Festival alive.

Strauss finally decided to resign, allegedly because he had heard rumours from the people of Salzburg that the Vienna section had secretly dug up the cornerstone of Hellbrunn.[30] This turned out not to be true, but Strauss's resignation was inevitable; he had become a mere figurehead, and had lost interest in the project. Simultaneously other members of the Vienna section resigned, as did Gehmacher in Salzburg.

Once the dust had settled, and after several weeks of confusing manoeuvres, the whole structure of the Salzburg Festival administration was seen to have changed. The Vienna section was no more; a new Society, based solely in Salzburg had been formed, with Robert Hildmann, Deputy Mayor of the city, as President.[31] At long last Salzburg was prepared to take the responsibility for the Festival upon itself. The Provincial Governor, Franz Rehrl, had decided to preserve the Festival at all costs.

From late 1924 until 1938, when he was jailed by the Nazis, Rehrl was the driving force behind the Festival. Indeed he is still considered a hero in Salzburg. Without him it is doubtful whether the project could have survived. Rehrl never claimed to be a cultural leader; he left that to others. He was, however, an astute politician and an organizer who exerted all his energy to promote the interests of the province he led. He saw clearly that tourism was the key to salvation: 'Culture equals business.'

Rehrl, like his classmate and friend, Erwin Kerber, was Salzburg born and bred. Always dressed in a loden jacket, sloppy grey trousers and a green hat with a feather, his squat, rather dumpy figure made him appear at first glance to be a country bumpkin. He was not. He was

28

immensely clever and remarkably single-minded, with an exceptional ability to charm his enemies. His friendship with Reinhardt was based on genuine affection, and his relationship with important national leaders like Ignanz Seipl and Kurt von Schuschnigg, as well as the trust he inspired among the local Socialist leaders, enabled him to lobby extensively and successfully for the Festival. He was to be particularly ingenious in persuading the national government in Vienna to provide revenue and publicity, and then convincing them that Salzburg's success was also their success.[32]

Rehrl's opening gambit was a carefully phrased letter to the Minister of Education outlining the reorganization plan and notifying the Minister that he, Archbishop Rieder, Chancellor Rudolf Ramek and the Mayor of Salzburg, Josef Preis, now constituted a 'protectorate' for the Festival. He asked that the State President lend his name to that list. Rehrl pointed out that Salzburg would now run its own Festival; it would no longer depend on private individuals in Vienna and Salzburg to master the complexities of raising funds, engaging artists—and building a Festival Hall.[33]

Alfred Roller and a local architect, Eduard Hütter, had produced designs for the rebuilding of the eighty-year-old Winter Riding School, and this project would start immediately. Rehrl did not ask explicitly for federal funding, but he did point out that, from both a cultural and an economic standpoint, the Festival benefited not only the city and the province, but the entire nation. He hoped that the chief of the Ministry's Cultural Section would become a member of the newly-established 'Kuratorium', the body which had been created to oversee the programme and the finances of the Festival.

Within a week the new Society was immersed in planning the 1925 Festival. Hildmann asked Reinhardt if he might stage *The Great World Theatre*, *Jedermann* and *Das Mirakel*. *Figaro*, *Don Pasquale* (under Bruno Walter) and *Don Giovanni* were the probable operas, and the Festival hoped to engage Schalk, Strauss and Wilhelm Furtwängler. Of course if Reinhardt wanted to stage other plays, he was perfectly free to do so, since 'your productions are the central point of the Festival'.[34]

The next step was to engage the Vienna Philharmonic; this involved a series of negotiations conducted by Kerber. Unlike the previous two years, the Society was determined to succeed despite the financial gap between its proposals and the Philharmonic's demands. When the orchestra manager baulked at Kerber's salary scale, he wrote to the Minister of Education claiming that the Society could not increase its offer. Much as he had hoped to have the Philharmonic's participation, Kerber made it clear that he might be forced to hire an (unnamed) German orchestra which had accepted the Society's conditions. Kerber's threat was decisive. One week later the Philharmonic signed the contract.[35]

In May, after borrowing funds from several major German and Austrian banks with Rehrl's help, the Society began work on the Riding School, and within two months it was ready to be used as a theatre. The programme was published in mid-May, and, according to the Society, created 'great excitement abroad'.

Meanwhile the Austrian government promised to provide immediate visas for all tourists who held tickets for the Festival, and to institute late trains between Salzburg and Vienna. Reinhardt had used his influence to provide information to American and European tourist agencies who were preparing 'package deals', and he encouraged his flamboyant American friend, the producer Morris Guest, to publicize the Festival and 'put it on the world map'.[36] When Guest later arrived in Salzburg, he was immediately made a member of the Kuratorium and wined and dined by the Austrian 'establishment'. He deserved this warm welcome, for more than six hundred Americans were to make the long trek to Salzburg that summer.

During the last two and a half weeks of August 1925, 38,000 people could choose between Reinhardt's three spectacles, Max Mell's *Apostelspiel* (added at the last moment because of the unforeseen increase in attendance), one Donizetti and two Mozart operas, two ballets, three orchestral concerts (featuring Walter, Karl Muck, Schalk, and the young Hungarian pianist Rudolph Serkin) and two chamber music recitals by the Rosé Quartet.

As a whole, the actual performances probably received less critical approbation than ever before, or since, for such a splendid selection of alternatives had overstretched the site, and a great deal of improvisation had taken place under conditions which were not ideal. The Landestheater was much too small to allow first-rate performances of operas to be given. What had been acceptable in 1922 was no longer so in 1925. The reconstructed stables had been designed with Max Reinhardt's spectacles in mind, so that the stage had been built to resemble the apse of a baroque church. Facilities for the actors were nonexistent, seats were uncomfortable and accoustics poor; one critic likened the hall to a garage.[37] *The Great World Theatre* was much less effective in the Festival Hall than it had been in the church. Paul Stefan,

Reinhardt's friend and a loyal supporter of Salzburg, expressed an intense dislike for *Das Mirakel*. He thought it overproduced, a mere pretext for 'endless litanies and hymns, an accumulation of ceremonies, wild battles and drawn-out orgies'. Still, the critic supposed that 'we must allow what gives pleasure'; Salzburg could not say no if America said yes.[38]

In general, in 1925 as today, the further away one gets from Salzburg, the more positive are the reviews. Americans in particular were fascinated by Salzburg's beauty in the Twenties, by the towering charismatic figure of Reinhardt, and by the Festival's clientele. The *New York Times* correspondent was dazzled by it all.

> The little mountain town is filled to overflowing with visiting celebrities, including former royal princes, American beauties, international film stars, actresses, singers and world-famous orchestral conductors.[39]

As usual, the people of Salzburg criticized the high ticket prices, the presence of so many rich foreigners who were contributing no money to the Festival Society, and the high living of the actors and singers.[40] Meanwhile they were pocketing the considerable sums that the visitors were bringing in. Gusti Adler, who was Reinhardt's *factotum* during his Salzburg years, wrote later about the city's 'Janus face'. The moment the Festival was over, the people of Salzburg, profits in hand, would revert to their usual state of somnolence. They could live for a year on the profits of the Festival, and they would make good use of the year to criticize it.[41]

1925 was a watershed for the Festival, but its very success would lead to subtle changes in format and concept in the following years. Though Reinhardt had told the *New York Times* of his desire to preserve Salzburg's old theatrical traditions, he would never again stage a mystery play (with the exception of the hallowed *Jedermann*) in Salzburg. The democratic and *'völkisch'* sentiments of Reinhardt and von Hofmannsthal, the idea of the Festival as a venue for both rich and poor, were belied by the well-heeled international élite which descended on Salzburg that summer, and every summer thereafter. How could the democratic ideal be reconciled with the natural desire to make the Festival self-supporting and a source of enrichment for the local population? No event of this kind, before or since, was ever founded upon such a base of profound and disinterested idealism. After 1925 those ideals were challenged.

Despite all the criticism, as the *Neue Freie Presse* said, the Festival had demonstrated the cultural and political values of Austria.

We are used to a life which brings us unhappiness. . .finally something positive had been created. Austria is working again at its real mission, which is to consecrate itself to the goals of harmony and unity. This Austrian Festival in a troubled time is something that we will treasure with joy.[42]

The journal had recognized what others, too involved in the day-to-day struggle, had failed to see. Something unique had happened that summer, something that gave pleasure, something that touched all Austrians. And it would endure.

3

The Search for Stability

1925–30

Barely had the 1925 Festival ended when the twin spectres of bankruptcy and scandal stalked Salzburg. Eduard Hütter had spent four times the expected estimate on rebuilding the Winter Riding School, the Festival itself had run a deficit, and neither the city nor its citizens wished to foot the bills.[1] Rumours abounded, and as they spread, the details grew. An English journalist published an article in *Music Courier*, which appeared in America, in which he stated that expenditures for the Festival Hall had exceeded forecasts forty-fold, and that the local citizens were incensed; the 1926 Festival would probably not take place.[2]

Franz Rehrl immediately realized the danger of such exaggeration; American support was crucial. He dashed off a letter to Austria's ambassador to London, Baron Franckenstein, asking him to seek out the anonymous British journalist who had written the offending article to force him to recant in public.[3] The Baron was unable to convince the *Music Courier* to name its correspondent, but the journal did write its own retraction and announced in the next issue that the 1926 Festival was now on secure financial grounds.[4] Rehrl had staked his credibility and a considerable part of the financial resources of the province on the success of the 1925 Festival, so he was determined not to panic at the first setback, but to consolidate what had been done and drive ahead to make the following year a success. Despite press polemics and predictions of doom he therefore set about negotiating new loans with banks, engaging leading artists, sending out publicity world-wide and expanding the Festival's programme.

For the first time it was decided to include an opera by a living composer: *Ariadne auf Naxos*, which Strauss himself would conduct. *Die Zauberflöte* and *Die Entführung aus dem Serail* would be complemented by Pergolesi's *La serva padrona* and Johann Strauss's *Die*

33

Fledermaus (this was the sole occasion in Festival history when an operetta was in the programme). There would also be several ballets, and two evenings of singing by the Vienna Men's Choir. Bruno Walter, Franz Schalk and a rising young conductor and close friend of Strauss, Clemens Krauss, would direct the operas.

Rehrl requested and received limited participation from the government in publicizing the Festival through its foreign embassies and consulates, for he was well aware that survival depended on tourists from countries with strong currencies, in particular from England and America.[5] In order to convince the *Landtag* of this he commissioned a report entitled 'An Economic Policy for Tourism' which convincingly backed his case and strongly argued that primary responsibility for the tourist industry be taken out of the control of private individuals and groups and put squarely in the hands of the city and the province.[6]

This led to a heated debate in the *Landtag* in April 1926. The Festival's fate was now in the hands of the politicians. The Socialists, while aware of the potential benefits to the province, used every occasion to accuse the 'bourgeois parties', essentially the CSP, of corrupt involvement in the building scandal. Rehrl responded that the Festival must be saved, whatever the cost, and proposed a series of measures, including a reorganization of the Festival Society, further improvements in the Festival Hall, reconstruction of the outdoor Riding School and a series of complex financial measures, including huge loans from Bavarian and Viennese banks, which would be guaranteed by the province. Rehrl's arguments won over the sceptical Socialists, though they called his reform a 'peculiar Easter Egg'.[7] They were willing, despite their distrust of the 'local groups' who in their view had precipitated the crisis in the first place, to guarantee the loans with the backing of provincial funds.

Deputy Mayor and Society President Hildmann, embarrassed by the scandal, resigned in May and was replaced by Baron Heinrich Puthon, a retired military officer who had recently come to live in Salzburg. Some said he was tone deaf, and in truth Puthon did not participate in artistic planning for the Festival; instead he devoted all his subtle and delicate diplomatic skills to dealing with artists, composers, politicians and local dignitaries alike. He was a rock of stability during the next thirty-four years of turmoil. Those who knew and worked with the Baron all described him as 'a perfect gentleman' ('*der war ein Herr*').[8]

The reorganization plans obliged the city and the province to back the necessary loans to carry out modifications to the Hall, which were now entrusted to an old friend of Rehrl's, Clemens Holzmeister. This Viennese architect was commissioned to make the Festival Hall capable of staging operas as well as plays. The Supervisory Board (*Aufsichtsrat*) was granted powers to veto expenditure and now included representatives from the city and provincial governments; von Hofmannsthal, Reinhardt, Strauss, Roller and Schalk continued to make up the Artistic Council.[9]

The 1926 Festival thus began on a note of optimism with a new administrative structure, solid financial backing, a promising programme and the presence of a growing international public. Bruno Walter conducted the music of his old mentor, Gustav Mahler, for the first time at Salzburg. Reinhardt had wanted to direct *Faust*, but the state of the Festival Hall (the new reconstruction had not yet been completed) forced him to choose a lesser play, Carlo Gozzi's *Turandot*.

Turandot almost caused Reinhardt's demise in Salzburg. This eighteenth-century play, which had recently been adapted as an opera by Puccini, included elements of tragedy, farce, pageantry and revue. One American critic found the play magnificent, and thought it should be brought to New York; he would have liked the opportunity to see it 'a dozen times', but for most critics, once was enough.[10] The *London Morning Post* described the production as 'rather extravagant', as Reinhardt had turned the play into a 'kind of English pantomime'.[11] Gusti Adler was more candid, when she wrote in retrospect that the play was a 'disaster'.[12] Reinhardt had hired five of Germany's best-known actors, including Max Pallenberg, to create a *commedia dell'arte* ending for the play but mutual jealousies and petty bickering ruined the scene. On a deeper level, Reinhardt fell into a trap which was to dog him during his Salzburg years. On the one hand he wished to please the non-German-speaking audience, to overproduce, to use fantastic (and expensive) costumes, to highlight the musical background, to exaggerate emotions. On the other hand, so as not to betray German speakers, he included scenes replete with doggerel and dialect jokes, which were completely lost on the foreign visitors. In the end no one was satisfied. What had worked with *Jedermann*, a simple story presented in an extraordinary setting, failed with a lesser but more complex play in an ordinary theatre.

When Reinhardt chose simplicity, however, he triumphed. His staging of Goldoni's *The Servant of Two Masters* on a small stage within the confines of the Riding School was a great success. This gentle comedy turned out to be much more convincing than the grandiose attempt to make Gozzi's rather bizarre tale of the Princess and the Calaf into a fantastic baroque comedy. And *Turandot* had cost a fortune, not only because of the expensive scenery and costumes, but also because of the huge salaries demanded by so many famous actors. Of course the *Eiserne Besen* blamed Reinhardt for the opera's failure; after all, the paper had blamed him for his successes. [13] But Paul Stefan, no enemy of Reinhardt and a consistent Festival supporter, had to be taken seriously. Stefan was 'numbed' by the overproduction in *Turandot*, and disappointed that the announced plans for *Zauberflöte* and *Faust* had been scuttled. If the Festival could not renew itself, it would lose its audience.

> It is not enough to depend on the beauty of the scenery, on the Vienna Opera, on Reinhardt's name . . . on the magic name of Mozart and Mozart's birthplace. [The Salzburg Festival needs] artistic leadership, an ideal which connects with our own time.

Improvisation had been carried too far. If older men such as Reinhardt and von Hofmannsthal could not fulfill their responsibilities to Salzburg, then the younger generation must take their place. [14]

The operas fared better. Von Hofmannsthal had used all his persuasive talents to convince the directors to add *Ariadne* to the programme. Strauss himself conducted two performances, and Krauss, the Director of the Leipzig Opera, the third. Lothar Wallerstein, a talented stage director, worked with Lotte Lehmann, Strauss's favourite Ariadne. Initially the Festival directors had wished to avoid the precedent of putting on a modern opera for fear that Salzburg might be forced to accept other, less congenial contemporary works. Von Hofmannsthal too saw the danger, and feared that the German composer Hans Pfitzner, whom he heartily disliked for the latter's National Socialist leanings, might try to have his operas staged in Salzburg. [15] But all had finally agreed that Strauss would be an 'exception'. Concern had also been expressed that *Ariadne* might not draw a large audience, and this turned out to be justified. It was also expensive to mount because of the considerable salaries demanded by Wallerstein, Krauss and the world famous singers, Lotte Lehmann and Selma Kurz.

In the end 1926 saw yet another deficit, despite celebrities, increased ticket costs and high quality performances which, with the exception of *Turandot*, received generally positive reviews from critics and the public alike. The press searched for scapegoats, and Rehrl was the chosen target. He was held responsible for the costly productions, the inadequate publicity, the lack of more famous stars, the meagre housing for tourists, the unfinished state of the Festival Hall and the poor scheduling.[16]

Though there was some truth in these criticisms, it must be said that after the building scandal, the resignations and the restructuring, it was an accomplishment to mount a Festival at all. And critics failed to take into consideration the somewhat parochial tastes of the Salzburg public, which flocked in great numbers to see Mozart, Johann Strauss and *Jedermann*, but abhorred anything else. Even Strauss could not sell out *Ariadne*, the ballet programmes were poorly attended, and Walter, Krauss and Schalk filled only half the seats for their orchestral concerts, which featured the works of Mahler, Bruckner. . .and Richard Strauss. Salzburg audiences, then and now, preferred the familiar to the unknown.

Vienna's prestigious journal *Musikbote* blamed not the audience but the Festival's administration, which had presented a programme showing no consistency, no 'fundamental idea'. Instead it was a potpourri of everything from mystery plays (*Jedermann*) to revues (*Turandot*), poor Mozart (Krauss) to routine ballet. Only the major Mozart operas, Paumgartner's serenades, Messner's church concerts and *Jedermann* were of festival quality. Echoing other journals, the *Musikbote* argued that the Festival in its present state was untenable. Only strong artistic leadership and a well-planned and unified programme could save it.[17]

Given these attacks which contrasted, it must be noted, with the often almost reverential reviews to be found in the foreign press (English, American and French), it is instructive to note the changed attitude among the people of Salzburg. The previous year they had criticized the high ticket prices and the influx of tourists, and voiced fears that performers might bring moral degradation in their baggage. Rehrl had changed the terms of the debate. He had convinced the people of Salzburg that they would eventually profit from the Festival, and had made them, because of the guaranteed loans, metaphorically silent partners in the whole affair. The Festival deficit was now Salzburg's deficit, and high ticket prices were perfectly acceptable, so long as one could find rich foreigners to fill the seats.

But the deficit meant that Rehrl had to undergo searching criticism in the *Landtag*. Two measures saved the 1927 Festival: a large loan from a

Bavarian bank, and the creation, by an act of the *Landtag*, of a 'Fund for the Promotion of Tourism in Salzburg Province' which would be based on the contributions from hotels and businesses; this fund would be used both to help run the Festival and to advertise various other local attractions.[18]

Rehrl took a number of other initiatives that winter. He proposed Dr Paul Kerby, a music critic for the *New York Times*, for the Artistic Council, in order that Kerby could be a travelling ambassador for the Festival, using his contacts in France, England and America to publicize Salzburg. In late January 1927 Kerby went to Vienna and was received by Chancellor Ignanz Seipl, who gave him encouragement and promised Austrian government support.[19] It was unusual for an Austrian Chancellor to meet an American music critic; Seipl's action suggested that the government might be willing to go beyond the rather tepid support that it had given in the past.

This was Rehrl's goal. To insure even closer government involvement he now proposed that the head of the state subsidized theatre administration, Wolfgang Schneiderhan, be made a member of the Artistic Council; in this way he hoped to involve Vienna's renowned Burgtheater in the forthcoming Festival. This initiative was not a success, since it was quickly leaked to the press, who made it appear to be a poorly disguised attempt to run Reinhardt out of Salzburg, and replace him with a state theatre director. Rehrl had overplayed his hand, and the initiative backfired. Schneiderhan wrote to Rehrl in December to say that, if it came to a choice between him and Reinhardt, then Reinhardt must stay. Rehrl had to agree.[20]

These intrigues were not lost on Reinhardt, nor were the attacks that appeared in the *Deutschösterreichische Tageszeitung* in February 1927. This pro-Nazi journal accused Reinhardt of using the money he was making in Salzburg to finance performances in Berlin and America. Even *Jedermann* was described as 'old rubbish' which had been 'warmed up' for the Festival. Reinhardt's profligate spending would no doubt cause another Festival deficit in 1927. 'It is perhaps time to bring Salzburg dilettantism to an end. The idea of an Austrian festival cannot remain with Salzburg.'[21]

Reinhardt returned to Europe in the spring of 1927, after completing a highly successful American tour with the Deutsches Theater. While on holiday in Sicily, he wrote a long letter to Rehrl in which he described his present fears and future hopes. He was not unaware of the rumours, denigrations and press polemics directed against him, he said, but none of this bothered him. He was used to being in the public eye, and was no stranger to criticism. He wanted no special privilege in Salzburg, and had no objections to the eventual participation of the Burgtheater. It was a 'laughable absurdity' that he sought to be the Festival's 'dictator'; he was much too busy to involve himself in the daily tasks of administration. But did the Festival directors really *want* him in Salzburg?

He believed that the Festival was just coming into its own, that its possibilities were endless. There were some in Salzburg who did not share this view, but he realized that Rehrl did, and despite the financial uncertainties, the problems of inadequate rehearsal time and scheduling, which had caused him so many difficulties in the past two years, he was ready to give Rehrl his closest cooperation. He reminded Rehrl of his years of dedication, the financial sacrifices he had made, the opportunities he had turned down so that he could sustain his beloved Festival. He accepted that all the vicious rumours, the backbiting, the production problems were merely natural 'growing pains'. He wanted only one thing: the unqualified support of the Festival directors and their willingness to allow him the means to stage his plays to their best advantage. With that backing, the success of Salzburg would be unlimited.[22]

There is not a false note in this long letter. It is the genuine cry of a man who had indeed been hurt not only by public criticism, but by the lack of any firm indication from Puthon or Kerber that the Festival directors stood behind him.

As months passed, Rehrl became more optimistic. Chancellor Seipl said that he would have liked to grant direct subsidies but that the constitution did not permit this; he promised that the Festival would be publicized through consulates and embassies.[23] True to his word, Seipl, through the agency of the Foreign Ministry, sent out letters to twenty-six capitals and ordered Austrian officials to approach local newspapers and important dignitaries in their respective countries in order to obtain publicity for the Festival programme, to display posters in strategic positions and to take every measure possible to encourage foreign visitors to come to Salzburg. The Austrian Consul in Matto Grosso, in the Brazilian outback, drily replied that no one ever travelled abroad from where he was posted. However, other initiatives were more fruitful: the Austrian Vice-Consul in New York encouraged American Express and Thomas Cook to create special Salzburg package tours.[24]

Ticket sales increased and the 1927 programme, first published in early spring, underwent no last-minute changes. Then, in early July, bloody riots broke out in front of the Palace of Justice in Vienna, and immediately everything was in jeopardy. Though Salzburg remained quiet, many feared that adverse publicity would cause visitors from abroad to cancel their reservations. Rehrl convened the local Chamber of Commerce on 9 July, and convinced them that the Festival should go ahead regardless; he claimed that, even if the expected crowds did not appear, the government would step in with last-minute financial aid.[25] In mid-July the city issued an official proclamation declaring that 'there exists no danger to foreign travellers from these disturbances in Salzburg.' A few weeks later, tourists streamed in, apparently paying no attention to what Gusti Adler saw as the first storm signs that would lead to Austria's demise.[26]

1927 saw the largest attendance in Salzburg's brief history. Reinhardt delighted many with his flamboyant production of *A Midsummer Night's Dream* and Schiller's *Kabale und Liebe*. Besides the usual Mozart — *Figaro* and *Don Giovanni* — Schalk conducted Beethoven's *Fidelio*, with Lotte Lehmann as Leonore, in the Festival Hall, the first opera to be performed in the now completed edifice. Paumgartner gave six Mozart concerts with the Vienna Philharmonic, and Messner expanded the church concerts to three. For the first time Paumgartner performed Mozart's C minor Mass in the splendid baroque Church of St Peter, where Mozart had first conducted the work in 1782.

Critics were less enthusiastic than the public. Reinhardt's Shakespeare was frankly geared to please an international audience. Dream-like fantasy and dance predominated over the serious parts of the plot. Critics from Boston to Vienna (though not the always-faithful French) found fault. To the *New York Herald* the ensemble playing 'became that of a music hall'. [27] The *Christian Science Monitor* was awed at the 'tremendous apparatus' that Reinhardt had created on the stage, but decried the 'merciless cuts' in the play, which left it almost un-recognizable. The critic Paul Bechert was frankly disappointed by the Mozart operas, with their 'familiar casts, shabby Salzburg scenery and complete absence of productive stage management'. Only *Fidelio* reached Festival standards.[28]

Theatre Arts Magazine suggested, somewhat ingeniously, that Shakespeare's *A Midsummer Night's Dream* should not be confused with Reinhardt's *Sommernachtstraum*. But, after pointing out what merit there was, the critic Ashley Dukes remarked that 'the action turns always to spectacular and theatrical over-statement, and little or nothing remains of the enchantment of suggestion that is the spirit of the Shakespearean piece.'

He added:

> The problem of Salzburg is no longer how to attract visitors to the *Festspiele*, but how to give them a roof over their heads. There is a greater problem before Reinhardt, for his stage cannot live by classics alone. Young Germany and France and England must be brought to the festival, which means that young art must be put upon the stage. With their assured audience, a great opportunity is opened to the artists at the head of affairs — such an opportunity, perhaps, as the theatre has not known for generations.[29]

It took two decades for Salzburg to address itself to this subject.

In Vienna, *Die Stunde* observed that Reinhardt's exaggeration might suggest a certain 'exhaustion' of his creative impulses. On the other hand, *Commoedia* in Paris could hardly find words to express its praise. The critic was so stunned by the beauty of Salzburg and its setting, that he freely admitted the impossibility of writing an objective review; to him *A Midsummer Night's Dream* was the apotheosis of Salzburg's baroque flavour.[30]

In truth Reinhardt was not 'exhausted', but his interests were shifting. He was openly fascinated by Hollywood; film stars and film moguls were added to the list of the elect who visited Leopoldskron and discussed film projects during Reinhardt's late night parties. For in 1927 Hollywood had come to Salzburg in a spectacular way. Cecil B. De Mille's *King of Kings* was given its European première there that August. Its world-wide success was symbolic of the sea change which was about to envelope twentieth-century mass entertainment, a change which would turn Reinhardt's theatre into an anachronism. For the cinema had endless capacity and unlimited resources to create an illusion far greater than Reinhardt could on the stage. His spectaculars — *Jedermann, Das Mirakel, A Midsummer Night's Dream, Turandot* — paled in comparison with the effects that a De Mille could produce.

Reinhardt quickly understood what was happening; he began to distance himself from his past and gradually to shift his focus to Hollywood. Ironically the work for which he is best known to the non-German-speaking world is his only film *A Midsummer Night's Dream*, which was based on the Salzburg version so maligned by the critics in 1927. Reinhardt, as it happened, was able to grasp the revolutionary possibilities of Hollywood, but was incapable of changing media; he just could not adapt to that world of glitter — and stringent budgets. That, however, lay in the future; his status in Salzburg in 1927 was still, at least in the eyes of one rather cynical critic, secure. Paul Bechert remarked that, if Salzburg had to choose between Mozart and Reinhardt, it should choose the latter. While Mozart was certainly the greater of the two, 'Reinhardt has the advantage of being present himself and of possessing without doubt greater business acumen than the modest music maker of the rococo age.'[31] As time was to prove, the critic was wrong on both counts.

If there was a small profit at the end of the 1927 Festival, and a large measure of rejoicing, some of this mood dissipated when production costs were analysed. *Fidelio* and *A Midsummer Night's Dream* (where Reinhardt had spent copiously on fantastic costumes for the entire cast) had led the Festival back into deficit. However, this news was only discovered well after the event, when plans for the 1928 Festival had already been made.

Again Rehrl was forced to plead with the government to go beyond its passive support and guarantee at least 100,000 Schillings for 1928. He wrote to the Minister of Education to tell him that, thanks to Max Reinhardt, the Festival was now a world-wide success, the personi-fication of the 'Austrian idea'. Its political importance was not to be discounted, for American, English and French visitors' perspectives on Austria in particular and '*Deutschtum*' in general had been altered by their new appreciation of Austria's cultural genius and her ability to overcome obstacles. He pointed out that not only Salzburg, but all of Austria had benefited from the large number of visitors who had some in 1927. Attending the Festival was starting to become a habit for the upper classes of Europe and America, who had previously summered in Biarritz or Trouville. Over three times as many French, American and English visitors had come in 1927 as in the previous year, and the Festival had welcomed guests from Japan, Africa, Australia and India. Rehrl estimated the value of international press criticism, which gave free publicity for Austria's natural beauties, at 200,000 Schillings. Why then, he asked, should not the government grant a sizeable subsidy for an event which advertised not only Austria's national cultural heritage, but also her general tourist attractions?[32]

Rehrl's plea met with only moderate enthusiasm from a central government advocating a policy of austerity. The Minister of Education granted only 3,000 Schillings to publicize the Festival abroad. Decisions concerning a more substantial subsidy were postponed. If a subsidy were to be given, however, the government would wish to have a representative permanently on the *Aufsichtsrat* who would have veto rights regarding the Festival programme; the Minister promised, however, that there would be no interference in the structure of the Festival Society's leadership.[33]

Over the next few months, there followed the dance of indecision known to all bureaucracies. The Finance Ministry was opposed to giving any subsidy to Salzburg, and thus came in conflict with the Ministry of Education. After much internal debate, the government finally decided on the small sum of 10,000 Schillings. This was little more than would be necessary to pay the salary of *one* conductor for a summer in Salzburg. Yet in return Rehrl was forced to promise that he would alter the Festival bye-laws to allow an Education Ministry representative to become an *ad hoc* member of the Artistic Council.[34]

These endless negotiations, which were concluded almost on the eve of the 1928 Festival, played havoc with programme planning. The general atmosphere of uncertainty was increased by leaks to the press. Reinhardt had originally suggested putting on a Nativity play, which had been successful at the Burgtheater, but it was clearly going to be expensive to mount, and the idea was eventually rejected. In March, General Secretary Kerber announced publicly what Rehrl had written privately: that the state was gaining a huge amount of foreign currency through the Festival: 300,000 of the 520,000 Schillings spent at the 1927 Festival had come from abroad. Kerber also pointed out that the Education Ministry's recalcitrance to grant a sizeable subsidy was based on the Minister's mistaken assumption that Salzburg was not interested in inviting the Burgtheater to participate. Such was not the case; Reinhardt had no objection. It was simply that the Festival Hall had already been booked for plays and operas during the coming year, and the resources of the Burgtheater could not be properly employed in the small Landestheater. Despite these obstacles, the Festival would take place. The city, province and tourist fund would act as guarantors.[35]

The Festival directors took two gambles in 1928 and lost them both. One was an expensive new production of *Die Zauberflöte*, the most problematic of Mozart's operas, given in the new Hall. Despite the imaginative scenery of Oskar Strnad, the entire Viennese repertory cast, with the exception of Richard Mayr, was roundly berated by the critics. One remarked that 'for a Festival performance, it was a meagre effort.' The *Eiserne Besen* was predictably horrified that a Jewish scene designer and a Jewish stage director (Wallerstein) had produced 'an advertisement for freemasonry'.[36]

The second gamble, decided upon at the last minute, was to bring a foreign opera company to Salzburg for the first time. The Leningrad Studio Opera Group, under the leadership of Emmanuel Kaplan, presented four operas, including *Bastien et Bastienne*, that charming product of the twelve-year-old of Mozart, Paumgartner's *Die Höhle von Salamanca*, and Russian operas by Rimsky-Korsakov and Gargomyschskij. Even the loyal French critics were horrified, and the public almost boycotted the proceedings. *Candide* wrote:

> We will pass over in silence the unpleasant interlude of the Leningrad Studio . . . [whose presence can be explained] only by a respectable concern for eclectisism in art. . . . Smiling Salzburg shook off the effects of these painful hours.

Another Parisian daily, *La Volonté*, wrote that 'these unfortunates cannot do anything . . . they are lacking the essential understanding of art: taste. It is cruel to see . . . *Bastien et Bastienne* treated like this.'[37]

The Leningrad Studio was not unknown in Europe; it had often performed in Germany. But the guest appearance of a foreign, indeed a 'Bolshevik' company, was an unwelcome shock for many Festival-goers. Yet the idea of bringing foreign ensembles to Salzburg — and thus making the Festival truly international — had been in the air for several years. Preliminary discussions about bringing the New York Metropolitan Opera and the *Comédie Française* to Salzburg had been mooted back in 1925. Early in 1928 La Scala, Milan, had asked the Festival Society if it might appear, but had been turned down.[38] Only Stefan criticized the narrow attitude of the locals who had not wanted the Leningrad Studio and who seemed intent on excluding non-Austrian ensembles, because he thought such an attitude short-sighted: foreign groups should be made welcome. Many of the purely 'Austrian' performances in Salzburg were themselves not very convincing advertisements for the excellence of Austrian art. Stefan might praise the Leningraders, but he again found fault with Reinhardt, this time for the staging of Schiller's *Die Räuber*. Reinhardt might think he was putting on a 'show' for American visitors, but he doubted that the stage director really understood his American audience. In the United States, they did not appreciate overstatement and overproduction in their plays.[39]

All in all, the 1928 Festival saw a slight drop in attendance and a considerable deficit, which was disappointing after the 'good' year of 1927. The result was the unleashing of the most passionate and vitriolic press polemic in Salzburg history. For the deficit was not abstract; it came out of the pockets of the people themselves, most of whom still could not possibly afford to attend the Festival.

The *Volksblatt* launched a broadside in November. Local taxpayers had been providing 100,000 Schillings a year for the Festival, each individual had therefore now incurred a debt of 350 Schillings; in modern terms approximately £150 or $200). The directors had had eleven months to prepare for the Festival each year, and still they managed to run a sizeable deficit. There was no effective planning; costumes and sets were used for one play only, then discarded. Singers and technical personnel from Vienna were housed in Salzburg at great expense, and their wages, it was claimed, were too high.

The Festival Hall, according to the *Volksblatt* editorial, was totally inadequate, and technically inferior to the average German provincial opera house. Salzburg had set out to create a 'Mozart style' which would be admired and copied around the world, but despite inflated salaries, the Festival could not afford the best singers, and it was artistically impossible to produce great Mozart with only eight days of rehearsal. Lilli Lehmann's pre-war production of *Don Giovanni* was mentioned as an example of what a real Festival performance should be.

Who was responsible for this catalogue of sins and omissions? The 'idealistic, theoretical and amateur' directors. What was needed? Practical men who knew how to run a festival. Otherwise, the foreign visitors who were the life blood of Salzburg would gradually realize that they were paying high prices for poor quality, and so would drift away.[40]

Blood-letting in Salzburg gave ample opportunity for the Viennese press to heap scorn on the narrow provincials who 'belittled themselves' by their constant complaining about the taxes they had to pay for their Festival, but who conveniently remained silent about the huge profits they made by raising their prices in the shops during that same Festival. Unseemly conflict served only to negate the idealistic underpinnings of such a great enterprise, which could only succeed if people were willing to make sacrifices. The Festival could not, and should not, be judged in purely materialistic terms.[41]

It was all very well for Vienna to be so high-minded, but there was some truth in Salzburg's complaint that Austria as a whole was profiting from the Festival, which improved its image abroad and brought in a useful infusion of foreign currency, yet the Austrian government gave only token support. This impasse could not continue. Something would have to be done to put the Festival on a sound financial footing.

Into the breach came a curious soldier of fortune called Camillo Castiglioni, the son of a rabbi from Trieste who had made millions in various enterprises ranging from car and aircraft factories, mines, banks and steel works to paper mills. Castiglioni lived in a sumptuous house in Vienna next to the Rothschilds, and prided himself on being a patron of the arts. He had befriended Reinhardt in the early Twenties, and had bought the Theater an der Josefstadt in Vienna for him. Scandal dogged much of his life, for he seems to have operated close to the edge of the law, but his wealth, his connections and his oft-repeated desire to help Salzburg made him appear in a heroic light to the beleaguered Festival organisers, though his being Jewish made him instantly unpopular among certain segments of the Austrian population.[42]

Castiglioni, Reinhardt and von Hofmannsthal decided to save the Festival by an infusion of private capital. Rehrl was not, in principle, opposed to this, though Kerber feared outsiders might gain control and Puthon felt that the State ought to be made to make a commitment. Highly complex semi-secret negotiations dragged on for months, but they foundered when it was learned that financial backing would come from a Dortmund bank and from Castiglioni's Viennese organisation, Wiener Schauspiel A.G., both of which would be represented on the Festival's *Aufsichtsrat* and would control the purse strings. Another element of the plan — to expand the powers of the Artistic Council and turn the Salzburg Festival Society into a mere propaganda organ for the Festival — was equally unacceptable.

Rehrl, Kerber and Puthon realized that the new plan would effectively deny the people of Salzburg all control over their Festival. Von Hofmannsthal, though a direct party to the negotiations, now began to have doubts about Castiglioni, for he feared that the rich man's unquenchable ambition might end by distorting the 'Salzburg ideal', an ideal which von Hofmannsthal himself had done so much to create. In Salzburg the rumour spread once more that Reinhardt, through the agency of the Artistic Council, was planning to become the city's 'dictator'.

Finally, on 15 December 1928, Rehrl wrote to von Hofmannsthal to say that he had broken off negotiations because he believed that the Viennese group wanted to set up a dictatorship in Salzburg. He had never been so disgusted before as he had been trying to negotiate with 'so called serious men'. [43]

Reinhardt himself was not present at any of the discussions, as he had gone to Hollywood in late 1928 to make a film with Lillian Gish, one of his numerous guests of the previous summer. The advent of the talkies, however, had caused the project to be cancelled. When he returned to Europe, in early 1929, Reinhardt informed the Festival authorities that he would produce only *Jedermann* for the forthcoming Festival. He dared not plan anything more, given the precarious financial situation in Salzburg; although he hinted that he might send over some productions from the Theater an der Josefstadt intact, but in the end this did not occur. [44] Reinhardt, after his lack of success in America, was doubtless demoralized. The failure of the Castiglioni scheme, in which he had been involved, and all the bad feelings it had aroused, could not have made him feel any friendlier towards Salzburg, which alternately embraced and rejected him.

Reinhardt's apparent lack of interest (the press suggested that he was 'tired of Salzburg)' the failure of the rescue scheme, the bad press of 1928, continuing financial instability, all now stimulated the Festival leadership to reflect and analyse. Reforms were necessary now; they could not wait. What emerged were three reports; two were anonymous, the third appeared under the aegis of Gehmacher, Paumgartner, Messner and various local businessmen and bankers. All were exceptional for their depth, the frankness of their analysis and the breadth of reform which they proposed.

Paumgartner and other Salzburg notables agreed, in essence, with the newspaper critics. Programme planning was a shambles, and works were often staged solely for the purpose of pleasing Americans. This unbalanced approach could have been defended if it had worked, but Festival programme brochures were sent out too late to encourage American visitors, and last minute changes were more the rule than the exception. Furthermore, the programmes were becoming ossified. There was justice in some of the critics' complaints that Salzburg was deaf to new music. If programmes had no variety and were just rehashes of old productions, then newspapers would not send critics and there would be no publicity. Performances themselves were often of less than first-class quality. Would it not be better to sign up the greatest international artists rather than transfer operas part and parcel from Vienna?

After describing the various problems of the Festival Hall itself, its noisy seats, its all too brief intermissions, its uncomfortable foyer, and the policy of allowing latecomers immediate entrance, the authors shifted their focus to an aspect of the Festival which was of critical importance, but often neglected. Salzburg was an 'artistic-social' event, which made it different from other festivals; this was too easily forgotten in the excitement of putting on operas, concerts and plays. The Festival authorities should make greater efforts to draw famous personalities to Salzburg, and, at the same time, should involve more of the locals in the social side of the Festival. This would serve two purposes: Salzburg would get more publicity and the local people would feel a greater personal sense of commitment.[45]

Because it was signed, and was the result of a committee's deliberations, this study outlined problems that were well known to everyone; it tended to pull its punches. The anonymous author of the report entitled 'The Programme of the Salzburg Festival' could allow himself to be more outspoken.

To him, Salzburg's financial problems were in part the result of lack of federal funding; middle-sized German towns received more help than Salzburg. They were also in part a result of having performances for only a few weeks each year, which meant incurring huge initial costs for every new production, and the need to negotiate new contracts annually with singers, stagehands, actors and the Vienna Philharmonic. Ticket prices, no matter how high, could never cover such costs. The only way Salzburg could pay for itself would be to cut its budget dramatically, but if it did so, the public would cease to come. Only performances of the highest quality could assure Salzburg of an audience, even if it also meant a deficit.

He then went on to explain that the real reason for the 1928 financial crisis had been the failure of the directors and the Artistic Council to present an attractive programme. The Artistic Council, with its famous names, lived a shadowy existence. Roller and Strauss had lost interest in Salzburg, Reinhardt was rarely there, and difficult to reach. Hofmannsthal and Schalk, together with Puthon and Kerber, put the programmes together. Much depended on their personal likes or dislikes; they took little note of the necessity of preserving a consistent artistic tradition, the 'idea' of Salzburg. New blood was needed from top to bottom. Reinhardt and his co-founders were all in the twilight of their careers, and were no longer in the forefront of artistic creativity. Reinhardt's failure in Hollywood proved his fallibility; the directors must now summon up the courage to turn down Reinhardt's expensive notions, as well as von Hofmannsthal's proposal to revive *The Great World Theatre*.

The anonymous author feared that the 1929 programme invited further disaster. A Viennese production of *Fidelio* was being produced that spring in both Sweden and France; this would correspondingly diminish the interest of Frenchmen and Swedes in coming to Salzburg, even if they did get Schalk to conduct. *Der Rosenkavalier*, though a popular opera, was frequently staged in Europe. Why not ask Strauss for a world première instead? Schalk's rendition of *Don Giovanni* was pedestrian; only Bruno Walter could give the opera life, and he was not available for 1929. Nor did the orchestral concerts look promising, given the Festival's inability to engage Furtwängler, Strauss, Mengelberg or Walter. Krauss was unlikely to prove an international attraction. Given this singular lack of famous names, and Reinhardt's refusal to put on a new production, the Festival was risking total failure. The Viennese would not come to see operas that they could hear throughout the year, foreigners would not visit Salzburg to hear repertory Viennese operas performed by little-known singers. Bayreuth was able to acquire the best artists in the world for its productions. Salzburg could not, or would not.

What then, was to be done? The report proposed a series of reforms which included:

(1) Close collaboration between the Directorium, the *Aufsichtsrat* and the Artistic Council, and the commissioning of outside experts on music and theatre to become occasional members of the Council so as to perfect programme choice.

(2) Publishing programmes for the coming year at the end of the Festival.

(3) Seeking out the best singers in the world, so as to generate real excitement.

(4) Avoidance of the practice of allowing conductors to choose their favourite works. A consistent artistic policy should be elaborated, and conductors must follow this line.

(5) Bringing in a wider selection of plays, both from Austrian and foreign sources.

(6) Inviting more foreign conductors and artists, in order to strengthen the Festival's international aspect.

(7) Performing world premières of new music.

(8) Encouraging the involvement and participation of the people of Salzburg in the Festival, including music and folk dance evenings so as to highlight the province's popular culture.

(9) Treating Festival visitors as honoured guests. Salzburg might not

have the luxury hotels to be found in Switzerland, but it could compensate for this lack if its citizens treated guests with friendliness and warmth, if they tried to create the kind of atmosphere which went with the intimacy of the city and its beautiful setting.

If these measures were taken, concluded the author, the Festival would have new vitality and embrace an exciting future.[44] It is interesting to note that only a few of these reforms were carried out in the next decade, whereas today practically all have been accomplished.

The last anonymous report, entitled 'The case of Max Reinhardt', reflects the extremely ambivalent attitude that the Festival authorities had towards Reinhardt: they could not live with him nor could they live without him. The collaboration was hardly more than a marriage of convenience.

This anonymous author missed no opportunity to denigrate his subject. Reinhardt was criticized for his refusal to present a new play in 1929 and for using his position in Salzburg as a springboard to publicize himself in America. The old charges were trotted out again: in Salzburg, Reinhardt was only trying to please American 'snobs'. Though the stage director's artistry was not in question, his business acumen made him avoid giving an intimate play in Salzburg, for this would have no future in the American market. Even Reinhardt's wealthy contacts were criticized, for they had never contributed one schilling to the life of Salzburg. Reinhardt himself was depicted as 'cold-blooded' and was said to have dismissed without a trace of remorse performers who did not measure up to his standards. He was also said to have complained about his treatment by the people of Salzburg. Though it was true that the National Socialist groups had attacked him, he had never seemed bothered in the past by such treatment.

But, despite possible alternatives, such as other directors and summer visits by the Burgtheater, the writer concluded that Reinhardt was 'the most powerful magnet for the future of the Salzburg Festival'. Only if the choice meant the Festival's 'total collapse' could Salzburg even contemplate breaking with him. Despite Reinhardt's alleged drawbacks, the Festival needed him. The report concluded that it might be a useful tactic to engage in sham negotiations with the Burgtheater, so as to 'reawaken' the director's interest. One is reminded of von Hofmannsthal's famous letter to Strauss about Salzburg's attitude to Reinhardt in 1923. Nothing had changed. Salzburg was using Reinhardt more than Reinhardt was using Salzburg.[47]

The prophecies of doom, both public and private, were proved wrong. The Festival of 1929 drew the largest crowds thus far, and in the end showed a small profit. There were various reasons for this. The Festival chose not to run risks, not to put on expensive operatic productions, and thus kept costs down. Secondly, despite another late beginning (the final programme was only published in March) the Austrian Foreign Office made considerable efforts to publicize the Festival.[48] By May the world press was giving ample space to Salzburg. Only Vienna printed negative (and inaccurate) news about Reinhardt's alleged decision to leave Salzburg.[49] Meanwhile the government had authorized a subsidy of 10,000 Schillings and promised more for the 'jubilee' year of 1930. Furthermore, the government announced that it would send a permanent representative to the *Aufsichtsrat*, a decision which must have given Rehrl great pleasure. Despite the small size of the subsidy, the State had now given *de jure* recognition to the Festival, and in effect promised its continuing and growing involvement in the enterprise.[50]

The critics, so difficult to please the year before, were now full of praise. Stefan hoped that, since the deficit problem had been solved, Salzburg could now afford to bring Reinhardt back to centre stage. It was a mistake to think that Americans were too unsophisticated to appreciate theatrical works, even if they were in German. The *Neue Freie Presse* quoted an American woman who claimed that the week that she had spent in Salzburg was 'the most beautiful of my life'.[51] The hotels, guest houses and pensions were filled to overflowing, and the weather was perfect.

One critic painted a picture of Salzburg's social side. He spent one evening with Stefan Zweig, a second at the Café Bazaar and another with the playwright Carl Zuckmayer in the nearby village of Henndorf. It was in these and similar locales, as much as on the stages of the Festival Hall or Landestheater, that the magic and the memories of Salzburg were forged. Zweig had become one of the best-selling authors in the German-speaking world, and his fame had spread throughout Europe. His *soirées* at the house on the Kapuzinerberg were as recherché as those of Reinhardt, although his salon was smaller, more intimate and more oriented towards musical artists and writers. He loved to show his guests his great collection of musical memorabilia, including his recent acquisition, Beethoven's writing desk.

Then as now, the Café Bazaar, overlooking the Salzach, was the 'in' place. Alexander Moissi held forth at the '*Stammtisch*' (regulars' table) with his unforgettable voice and effervescent good humour. Actors, actresses, musicians and hangers-on gathered there after every Festival performance. Unlike today, when Salzburg's artists flee the crowds to the relative obscurity of a house in the Salzkammergut or on the Gaisberg, in those days performers seemed at ease in the cafés and *Gaststuben* of the city.

Carl Zuckmayer, when he met the critic, was spending an evening at a small hotel in Henndorf owned by the brothers of the great bass, Richard Mayr. Zuckmayer was in good spirits, having just completed a play. He, Mayr and the reporter drank in the *Gemütlichkeit* from dusk to dawn, as Salzburg's special ambience cast its spell.[52] For in a real sense the charm of the place had much to do with the accessibility of both the famous who attended and the famous who performed. The entire city became a giant house party; people drifted from plays to concerts, stopped at cafés for drinks, glimpsed the stars in restaurants or on the narrow streets.

In contrast to the joys of the Festival, the summer of 1929 was a bleak time for Reinhardt, for within a week in July he lost both his brother Edmund and Hugo von Hofmannsthal. The former had been ill with a heart condition for some time. On 13 July von Hofmannsthal's son, Franz, committed suicide. Two days later, as his father was dressing to attend the funeral, he had a seizure. A few hours later he died. Reinhardt was utterly inconsolable, and spent only two weeks in Salzburg during the Festival, just long enough to make a touching speech in honour of von Hofmannsthal. He later wrote:

> In this summer full of death and sadness, I have left Salzburg. I could find no peace there, everything makes me sad. . . . It has become difficult for me, and will remain so; now it is so dark around me that I see no way out; I must wait and see how things go on.[53]

The Salzburg press took little note of Reinhardt's depression, and the *Chronik* even gloated that the public seemed to appreciate music more than theatre decorations. The fears that Reinhardt's inactivity would hurt the Festival were unfounded; it seemed that 'music alone attracts the rich, famous and cultivated public to Salzburg.'[54]

Reinhardt's one loyal friend in Salzburg, Rehrl, was determined to make up for the insults and insinuations that the great director had suffered at the hands of the local press and the Festival authorities; he therefore suggested to the President of the Republic that Reinhardt be granted an honorary Cross of the Republic in 1930, the Festival's tenth anniversary. The outlook was promising: the government had agreed to increase its subsidy to 35,000 Schillings; the Foreign Ministry negotiated with the Germans; and the festival cities of Munich, Bayreuth and Oberammergau agreed to work together with Salzburg to publicize their festivals throughout the Western world. As part of this campaign, which would take on a new importance in following years, Salzburg became friendly with the newly-founded *Société des Etudes Mozartiennes* in Paris, whose goal was to promote the music of the master and encourage French attendance at the Festival. [55]

Clemens Krauss was named Director of the Vienna State Opera in 1929, replacing Schalk, and for the next five years this elegant, sometimes dictatorial conductor, along with Bruno Walter, renewed Salzburg's musical life. Krauss, a close friend of Strauss and a talented interpreter of his music, was young and ambitious; he wished to reinvigorate the musical life of Vienna and Salzburg after the years of neglect under the ageing Schalk. A powerful and compelling figure, he longed to become the musical director of the Festival, although no such post existed. Krauss had no love for Walter, nor Walter for Krauss; it took the not inconsiderable skills of Puthon and Kerber to keep the two stars from conflict. Fortunately they were drawn to different composers; Krauss to Strauss and Walter to Weber and Gluck. There was enough Mozart to be shared. Krauss had a formidable task ahead of him, for the Director of the Vienna State Opera was in a highly visible and vulnerable position, his every move subject to press gossip and rumour. But Krauss's youth, talent, energy and elegance worked in his favour. To Otto Strasser, Krauss represented the new blood that Vienna — and Salzburg — had been seeking.[56]

Wall Street crashed in October 1929, but the effects were slow to reach Europe. The 1930 Festival was both grander (six operas instead of three, four Reinhardt productions) and longer (lasting throughout the month of August) than ever before. In addition to *Jedermann*, Reinhardt produced *Kabale und Liebe*, *The Servant of Two Masters*, and Somerset Maugham's *Victoria*. Besides the old productions of *Don Giovanni*, *Fidelio*, *Rosenkavalier* and *Don Pasquale*, Krauss conducted an entirely new production of *Figaro* and Walter brought his genius to Gluck's *Iphigenie in Aulis*. Hans Knappertsbusch, Krauss, Walter and Schalk shared the well-attended orchestral concerts, which included for the first time an all-French programme, including works from Rameau to Ravel. Krauss delighted his audiences with an evening of light music by Johann and Josef Strauss.

The crowds were huge. Sixty thousand tickets were sold (twice the population of the city), eighteen thousand more than in 1929, and the Festival made a sizeable profit for the first time in its history. The British Labour leader Ramsay MacDonald, the Conservative MP Winston Churchill, and Gaston Doumergue, the President of France, were among the visitors, which included the cream of international high society. Critical reviews were, on the whole, ecstatic. Despite the odd quibble, most reviewers believed that Salzburg had now truly come of age; they praised the imaginative programme and masterly concerts directed by men of different techniques, memorable podium person-alities and efficient administrative direction. Reinhardt's plays pleased even the non-German speakers.[57]

Present pleasures excited hopes for the future. Krauss, in an interview asserted that Salzburg should no longer be dependent on Viennese productions, but should now begin to create its own. He implied that the 'natural characteristics' of the city were not always well served by staging and scenery created for a different context, and vowed to expand the programme in the years to come. At the same press conference Schalk pointed out that Salzburg had become an inter-national event where music, not theatre, would dominate in the future. Alexander Moissi, also present, disagreed; Salzburg's theatrical life could thrive, but only if a large number of non-German works, especially those of Shakespeare, were presented. He voiced hope that the long postponed *Faust* would eventually be staged. [58]

The high point of the 1930 Festival was a formal ceremony, on 10 August, to honour Reinhardt. Rehrl spoke with great warmth of Reinhardt's contribution, and in his reply Reinhardt reminded his listeners of his youthful experiences in Salzburg, which had instilled in him a love of the place, an appreciation of its endless beauties, of its extraordinary musical and theatrical heritage. He would do all in his power to continue these traditions.[59]

Rehrl had also arranged to have a bust of Reinhardt displayed in the Festival Hall, and for the square opposite to be named Max Reinhardt Platz. Reinhardt was moved by such thoughtfulness, and commis-sioned a bust of Rehrl to be made. Reinhardt then wrote to Rehrl:

I have learned during my life . . . that it is as difficult to put into practice an artistic work as it is to create one . . . in the theatre, dream and reality, more than in any other art form, come into conflict . . . . I have also learned that in this life, gratitude is a rare commodity. . . .[60]

Reinhardt marvelled that Rehrl, the activist, the politician, the unshakeable supporter of the Festival, could exhibit such a deep sensitivity to his own feelings; the bust of Rehrl was to thank him for his extraordinary contribution.

Both a French and an American critic contrasted Bayreuth and Salzburg in 1930, and both preferred Mozart's birthplace. To Paul Bechert, writing in the *New York Times*, Bayreuth's productions were no improvement on those that one could view in any other opera house, and some of the singers lacked first-class ability. Salzburg's programme, on the other hand, was 'wider in scope as to both the choice of works performed and the artists for them'.[61]

More poetically, Henri Bidou of *Le Temps* pictured Bayreuth as a place where the 'faithful' journeyed to the 'sacred' opera house, where they were separated from the 'human universe by the mystical abyss and the ocean of sound'. In Salzburg no one 'sacrifices to a cruel god'. The masterpieces were on a human scale; spectators were moved, they might weep at the beauties they heard, but they were tears of joy. There was something upsetting, almost inhuman about Bayreuth; pleasure there bordered on the self-destructive.[62]

A small Viennese daily, the *Volkszeitung*, reminded its readers of what Hermann Bahr had said thirty years before, that Salzburg should become the capital of the 'good Europeans'; now this dream had been accomplished and in a more profound way than at Oberammergau or Bayreuth. Austria had such a tiny population that it was exceptionally fortunate to have such a great artist as Reinhardt; it should remember this.[63]

Altogether it had been a glorious August and the people of Salzburg could look back on the ups and downs of the last ten years with pride. Although the Festival had seemed to lurch from one crisis to another, all the conflicts, the financial chaos, the arguments and problems had finally resulted in real and lasting accomplishments. As Salzburg attempted to cope with the new realities forced upon it, as it modified the original ideals, it also experimented and created, although not all the experiments succeeded. The image of Salzburg was now well established in the minds of many; it had become the summer meeting ground for the titled and the wealthy. Hollywood film producers, stars, writers, kings and princes, generals and prime ministers all mingled in the festive air of the little town on the Salzach to listen to music, to gossip, to relax, to hear plays and to see one another. Reinhardt had been the magnet which originally brought them together, but soon the movement maintained its own momentum. Naturally this summer influx brought increasing prosperity to the city, but this in turn tended to remove some of the earlier air of improvisation. Perhaps this was inevitable.

The great ideas with which Reinhardt and von Hofmannsthal had initiated the Festival had gradually been superceded. Reinhardt was himself about to withdraw, slowly and imperceptibly, from the centre of the Salzburg scene, as Bruno Walter and Clemens Krauss began to dominate. The international language of music would take over from the mystery plays, the costly spectaculars and the medieval dramas.

The central element which had inspired Reinhardt had gradually disappeared; von Hofmannsthal too, before his death, had seen many of his ideas discarded. Salzburg's success in attracting the rich, famous, titled and powerful, who were willing to pay inflated prices, effectively nullified the idealistic notions about uniting businessman and peasant. Paradoxically it had been the renown of von Hofmannsthal and Reinhardt which had brought the élite to Salzburg in the first place.

But the unsung heroes of those early years were Bernhard Paumgartner and Joseph Messner, who between them had enabled the public to hear so many of the—until then—less well known works of Mozart. Before Paumgartner appeared on the scene, most people knew only the major operas and the widely renowned liturgical works, such as the C minor Mass and the Requiem. Few were acquainted with Mozart's piano concerti, his chamber music, concert arias, marches, divertimenti and serenades. But thanks to Paumgartner, the Salzburg visitor could experience some of this little-known canon, could stand in the Residenz courtyard and hear a divertimento just as his forebears in the eighteenth century might have done. Joseph Messner, the Cathedral's choirmaster, initiated the first concert of church music dedicated to Mozart in 1926. For the next forty years, with the exception of the Nazi era, Messner provided the public with an opportunity to hear all the major, and many of the minor, Mozart masses and occasional liturgical works.

In mid-August 1930, Arturo Toscanini, who had just finished his first Bayreuth summer, slipped quietly into Salzburg. The directors of the Festival asked him if he would conduct for them the following summer, perhaps to give a guest performance with La Scala Opera. The maestro said he would consider the idea. But that autumn he decided to return to Bayreuth for a further year, and leave Salzburg for another day.[64]

4

The Depression and Hitler's Challenge

1931–3

Those who attended the Salzburg Festival in the early Thirties, or whose parents or grandparents took part, never cease to talk about this period as a golden age. But the nostalgia seems to relate less to the heights of an individual's performance or the greatness of a play than to a mood, which can never be recaptured.

The Thirties produced a unique set of historical events in the Depression and Hitler's rise to power in Germany, which had immediate and far-reaching effects on the course of European culture. Jewish artists fled, or were forced out of Germany, and many gravitated to Salzburg where they practised their art in one of the last bastions of liberty in the German-speaking world.[1] Their performances were acts of commitment to freedom and, in a deeper sense, to the nation which guaranteed it. For Austria, despite her own local Nazi followers who looked to Hitler for salvation, was still an independent state.

Austrian authorities gradually realized that Salzburg's artistic freedom was a dynamic symbol of their nation's political independence. To the outside world, support of the Festival was a subtle guarantee of that independence. Equally, the Nazis viewed the Festival as an open challenge, and attempted to destroy it. Salzburg thus became, for those few weeks in July and August, a manifestation of the struggle between the Nazis and their enemies.

After 1931 the Depression began to damage the province of Salzburg. Unemployment, which had been negligible in the late Twenties, affected thirty per cent of the work force by 1933. Simultaneously, the good will and consensus that had characterized the relations between the two major parties, the CSP and the Socialists, began to disintegrate. This collapse was not precipitated by any intrinsic local instability, despite the high unemployment and growing Nazi influence; it was imposed from Vienna, the scene of serious and sometimes bloody

57

political strife, which now proceeded to remove many of the provinces' rights to make decisions.

The moderate Salzburg Socialist party began to lose members after 1930 because of its inability to cope with the economic crisis; local Socialist leaders did little to combat the slow erosion of their liberties imposed by Vienna, and lost credibility with the rank and file. The CSP, which in 1934 merged into the Fatherland Front, as Austria became a one-party state, now appeared to have total control; but this was illusory. Under Rehrl's leadership, the party was neither vindictive nor ideological. But they were goaded by Vienna to take extreme measures which now destroyed the delicate equilibrium that had existed for over a decade. They outlawed the Socialists and thus deprived themselves of an ally against the real threat, the Nazis.

The National Socialist Party, despite a brief period of political strength in the early Twenties, had declined in Salzburg. By 1930 it was only of marginal importance, but the impact of the Depression changed all that. By 1931 the Nazis could bring out a thousand people to their rallies, and such party leaders as Heinrich Himmler, Robert Ley (later Minister of Labour) and Wilhelm Frick (later Governor General of Poland) were able to mobilize crowds of three to five thousand in 1932. Local Nazi followers called Rehrl ' *Franz der Kleine*' and ' *Franz der Dicke* ' (Franz the Small and Franz the Fat). They created a *Gau* (district) in Salzburg that year, and by April of 1933, there were thirty-two Nazi organizations in the province. The Nazi Party was outlawed in June 1933, so that there are no membership figures available after that date; illegal members as well as sympathizers invaded all walks of Salzburg life, however, and it must never be forgotten that the city lay close to the German border, that the German town of Freilassing was only a few kilometres from the Domplatz, and that the Bavarian resort of Berchtesgaden was only fifteen kilometres away, a short tram ride.[2]

After the Nazis were banned, they set out to strike at Salzburg's life-blood: tourism. The high point of this campaign came in the summer of 1933 and included bombing telephone booths and dropping propaganda leaflets from Luftwaffe overflights.[3] The Salzburg authorities reacted to this terrorism by throwing 700 local Nazis into prison; many others escaped to Bavaria. The provincial government then promulgated a series of laws which attempted to fit the punishment to the crime: singing the Horst Wessel song, the anthem of the Nazi party, brought a fine of 50 Schillings; greeting people with the *Heil Hitler* salute landed the perpetrator in prison for anything from three days to three weeks; a party rally in a church brought a minimum six-week sentence. Enforcing such laws would have been difficult at the best of times, but with so many Nazi sympathizers in the city and provincial administrations, it was virtually impossible.[4]

Nazism and anti-Semitism went hand in hand, and although the number of Jews living in Salzburg was extremely small, foreign Jews who spent their holidays in the province were tempting targets. Much of the anti-tourist propaganda of the early Twenties had been barely disguised anti-Semitism, and this increased as the decade wore on.[5] In 1929, a visiting foreigner chanced upon a copy of the *Eiserne Besen* which caused him to write a letter to the *Salzburger Volksblatt*. This letter was published . . . without comment.

> I am a German American, a Jew . . . and have just arrived in Salzburg. I happened to read a copy of *Der Eiserne Besen*. I was struck speechless. How is it possible, in a city which publicizes international tourism, that such a paper, with such shameful language, which is really a cultural disgrace for Salzburg, can be tolerated? I immediately left this otherwise beautiful city, and I plan to propagandize against the Festival. . . .[6]

Salzburg authorities were fully aware that this sort of bad publicity could be catastrophic for the Festival, which drew a large Jewish clientele, mostly from the United States. But the press laws were such that they were powerless to censor the *Besen*.[7]

A curious, almost absurd, by-product of Salzburg anti-Semitism was the movement, created by an anti-Semitic group in the village of Seekirchen in 1922, to set up villages 'free of Jews' which would be forbidden to Jewish summer tourists. In the end, though the movement remained alive throughout the inter-war period, few of these villages managed to retain their 'purity'. Economic interest overcame racial prejudice. Since most of the villages involved were relatively distant from Salzburg itself, the policy does not seem to have affected Festival visitors. It is difficult to explain the deep-rooted nature of Austrian anti-Semitism, which by all accounts was more virulent and widespread than in Germany. The number of Jews living in Salzburg province was 350 in 1935. Ardent anti-Semites comprised many times that number.[8]

The soaring optimism which had attended the 1930 Festival was dashed by the world Depression which hit Germany with exceptional force and consequently made huge inroads into German tourism in Salzburg. In the next two years Salzburg ran large deficits, yet these Festivals were of very high quality, both in terms of the variety of programmes and the level of artistic excellence.

Since 1931 was the two hundred and fortieth anniversary of Mozart's death, heavy emphasis was put on his operas, five of which were to be performed. But Kerber did not want the Festival to turn into a one-man show, even for this special year; he planned six other operas as well, four of which would be presented by the visiting La Scala Opera. Clemens Krauss now made his first bid for artistic control by requesting that Bruno Walter be excluded. He clearly wanted the field for himself. However, the directors refused to drop Walter, whose association with Salzburg was of long standing, and who was extremely popular in foreign countries, especially among the English. Moreover his dismissal would have severely weakened the Festival's international drawing power, and would have upset the musical balance. Walter, Krauss and Schalk (though the latter was ailing) were to divide up the programme between them.

There was some question as to the extent of Reinhardt's participation in 1931. It was feared that, since many fewer Germans were expected to attend the Festival, Reinhardt's plays would be poorly attended. Nevertheless, the directors agreed that Reinhardt's presence was vital, whatever the risks. He had hoped to secure finance for the construction of a provisional roof over the Riding School so that he could put on his long postponed production of *Faust*, but this proved impossible. Instead Reinhardt produced *The Servant of Two Masters*, Goethe's *Stella* and von Hofmannsthal's *Der Schwierige*, all of which received spectacular reviews, although, as feared, none of the performances sold out. [9]

Advance sales were low, and it was one of the rainiest of summers. By great good fortune, the Festival authorities had, for the first and last time, arranged for rain insurance. If 0.04 of an inch of rain fell between five and seven in the evening during a performance of *Jedermann*, after two consecutive rainy days, the insurance company would pay 6000 Schillings. This happened on 13 August, and the Festival was duly reimbursed. However, overall cost of the insurance had been 15,000 Schillings, so the Festival was still out of pocket, though they did gain some extra publicity. [10]

Reinhardt laid on one spectacular production for his friends, at his own expense, at Leopoldskron, where he had had an outdoor theatre constructed. In late August he presented *Twelfth Night* with Alexander Moissi, Helene Thimig and a rising young Viennese actress, Paula Wessely. The Lord of Leopoldskron had taken this project very seriously indeed. Rehearsals had gone on for weeks, and he had engaged Paumgartner and members of the Vienna Philharmonic and

Chorus to perform suitable seventeenth-century music in the background. The players were to enter by sailing across the lake at Leopoldskron to the stage as though from a shipwreck, but as they disembarked, dark storm clouds gathered, and soon rain fell in torrents. The 250 guests were forced to scurry back into the castle, where they were wined and dined until five o'clock the next morning. Gusti Adler wrote that all Reinhardt's 'enthusiastic fans' wanted to shake his hand at the reception.

> The next day [Reinhardt's] hand was painfully swollen; he said that each of these friends had put into the pressure of the handshake everything stored up through years of silent admiration.

The garden theatre at Leopoldskron was never used again; Reinhardt did plan to perform other plays there, but they always fell through. After 1938 it was left to decay, and today nothing is left; but for those few feverish weeks in 1931 it had been the very centre of his existence, the set for his last great dramatic fantasy in Salzburg.[11]

The musical and operatic elements of the programme for 1931 fared better than the theatrical, despite the critically well-received, but poorly attended La Scala productions. Schalk's increasingly poor health (he died that September) forced the directors to divide his operas between Krauss and Walter, and to ask Sir Thomas Beecham to give an orchestral concert at the last minute.

Walter's *Orfeo ed Euridice*, with a ballet staged by the Austrian dancer Margherita Wallmann, was the hit of the Festival. Walter had persuaded Kerber to travel to Munich to engage the choreographer, and the result of the collaboration had been stunning. Walter by all accounts, was one of the few world class conductors of our century not touched by a severe case of megalomania. After one of the performances of *Orfeo* Wallmann complemented him on his conducting. 'I conducting? I completely forgot to conduct, I was admiring the *mise en scène*.'[12] That Walter had scored an overwhelming success must not have been lost on his detractors, including Krauss.

Casts were stronger than in the late Twenties, and included such internationally known singers as Franz Volker, Emanuel List, Lotte Lehmann, Richard Mayr, Lotte Schöne and Viorica Ursuleac (the Romanian soprano who was also Krauss's wife), Koloman von Pataky and the French soprano Germaine Lubin, all of whom contributed to the integration of the drama and the music. According to the eminent French critic, Emile Vuillermoz, the programme approached 'absolute

A History of the Salzburg Festival

perfection'; there were no *prima donnas* on the stage, only performers who were dedicated to serve the glory of the composer.[13] Paul Stefan too was satisfied, especially since Salzburg had successfully invited several foreign companies and orchestras to take part. He had initially feared that musical anarchy might result if too many operas were scheduled, but decided that Salzburg had at last overcome the greatest crisis in its history, and was as 'indisputably' grounded as Bayreuth; it was finally self-sufficient and had gained Austria untold prestige; music-lovers all over Europe, and even in America, where the music was transmitted over 83 radio stations, had been able to savour segments of the Festival.[14]

In their secret internal analysis of 1931, the directors admitted that at one point cancellation had been considered, but after the first ten days of the Festival, attendance had increased. Critics, even the usually hostile Viennese, were happy. Festival visitors could be counted on to spread the word that Salzburg was a 'spiritual oasis', a 'land of bliss'. Certain measures were put forward to protect the 1932 Festival from the consequences of the Depression: a shorter season of only four and a half weeks, fewer operas and concerts and closure of the Landestheater, which was rented at great cost. Max Reinhardt's contribution would consequently be limited to *Jedermann* and a possible reprise of *The Great World Theatre* either in the auditorium of the old University or the Kollegien Church. The directors were aware that Schalk's death had impoverished the Festival and that a new permanent third conductor must be found; it might also be necessary to find a new actor to play *Jedermann*.[15]

For the Festival had only been over for a week when a sudden scandal had erupted around the popular figure of Alexander Moissi, who had played *Jedermann* at every performance since the beginning. Moissi was writing a novel in which he wished to describe a live birth. In order to get his facts right, he had asked the head of the Salzburg Hospital, Hofrat Dr von Karajan (whose son had just begun his conducting career) if he could be present at a birth, and Dr von Karajan had given permission. The woman in question was given a certain sum of money for her agreement (though she later denied this). Within days the story was leaked to the press, and became a local *cause célèbre*, especially for the Nazis and certain conservative Catholic women's organizations. Moissi had his defenders, notably the CSP's organ, the *Volksblatt*, and the Socialist *Wacht*, both of whom were used to criticizing each other but for once were in agreement that everything had been blown out of

62

proportion and that the Nazis were using the incident to vent their anti-Semitism (they accused Moissi of being Jewish, which he was not) and to weaken the local government.[16] In any other big city, such an event would not have even been reported, for there was nothing illicit, immoral or criminal in Moissi's behaviour. The *Eiserne Besen* revelled in the 'scandal'. It called for Salzburg women to 'rise up' and throw out the people who were responsible for allowing 'Moses Moissi' into the hospital. His action, they claimed, was an example of 'his degenerate race and he should never again be allowed to perform in public'.[17]

The Viennese press found the incident almost laughable. The *Allgemeine Zeitung* cited the rumours that Moissi would not be asked to return in 1932, then suggested that the Festival directors should 'muster up their courage' against such 'prejudiced provincialism' and renew Moissi's contract.[18] Meanwhile, Salzburg Catholic women's organizations were demanding that the actor be dismissed and Moissi was subject to 'stink bomb' attacks in February 1932, when he portrayed *Jedermann* at the Raimund Theatre in Vienna. This made him decide to hold a press conference which he had previously refused to do. No, he was not a Jew; his family had been Roman Catholic for generations. All the fuss was caused by anti-Semitic, anti-Reinhardt feeling in Salzburg.[19] Finally, in April, Kerber and Puthon announced that, because of the 'pressure' from the Archbishop of Salzburg (Rieder's successor) and from local women's organizations, Moissi would not return.[20] The directors had caved in, and Moissi would never act in Salzburg again. An era had ended.

This hurt Reinhardt deeply. It was not therefore surprising that he used the excuse that he was creating a new Berlin production of *Jedermann* to withdraw from his commitment to producing *The Great World Theatre* in Salzburg for the coming August. By the time summer came round, however, he was prepared to go through the motions of coaching Paul Hartmann in the title role of *Jedermann* for 1932; nevertheless he left most of the work to his assistant and spent little time at Leopoldskron. His absence was noted. The *Neue Freie Presse* thought that he was too big a man to abandon Salzburg; he should not hold a grudge, for only a small group of 'haters' was responsible. Reinhardt should return to the place to which he was bound by 'a thousand artistic connections'.[21]

The scandal had brought to the surface much prejudice and provincial stuffiness, and continued to embitter local politics for months; it also put the directors in a very uncomfortable position.

Ticket sales were slow in the early months of 1932, and they could find no third conductor, so had to divide up the musical chores between Fritz Busch and Richard Strauss. The latter decided to introduce his opera *Die Frau ohne Schatten* to Salzburg. Written in 1919 and based on a story by von Hofmannsthal, who also wrote the libretto, it is not the most approachable of Strauss operas; the story is highly complex, shrouded in mysticism and needs an eye-catching production if it is to be a success. Yet Lothar Wallerstein, one of the first opera stage directors to achieve fame, did his best, and the *Christian Science Monitor* agreed that his imagination had saved the Salzburg production from disaster; other critics were less kind. *La Rampe* found it a 'calamity, burlesque and incomprehensible', with a libretto so

> frankly detestable that I am astonished, 13 years after its première, that a musician of Strauss' intelligence in the literary and dramatic field could have wasted . . . his talent . . . on a subject of no interest whatsoever.[22]

Critics were generally hard on the Festival of 1932. Lotte Lehmann was pictured as being past her prime, Walter's tempi in *Orfeo ed Euridice* were too slow, Busch's reading of *Entführung* too prosiac, Strauss's *Fidelio* under-rehearsed. The programme was 'unimaginative', and some reviewers felt that the directors were pandering to the increasingly 'snobbish' clientele.[23] This was not altogether fair. Any programme that included Weber's *Oberon*, *Die Frau ohne Schatten* and *Orfeo ed Euridice* in addition to Bach's B minor Mass (the first time that the master had been so honoured in Salzburg) could not be characterized as banal. None of these operas was a crowd-pleaser, and all depended on sensitive conducting, strong performances and creative staging. It was, moreover, only natural that Salzburg should wish to retain the ever-popular *Rosenkavalier* and *Fidelio* in its repertoire as well as the Mozart operas, for these were the mainstays of the Salzburg 'idea'.

Perhaps the critics of 1932, having heaped so much praise on the previous year's offerings, were at a loss for new things to say. They tended therefore to search out weaknesses and to allow themselves a certain nostalgia for Salzburg's imagined past. It is simpler for the critic to find fault than to praise; it is likewise more pleasurable to the lay reader to see his own nostalgic tendencies confirmed by critics. The 1932 Festival received less praise than it was due; other years perhaps received more praise than they deserved. One visitor slipped into the city on a quiet early August afternoon, spent an afternoon walking around in the old quarters, then returned to Berchtesgaden; Joseph

Goebbels noted in his diary how 'beautiful and colourful' was the town, full to the brim with famous people.

Five months later Adolf Hitler came to power, and within weeks, two pillars of Salzburg, Max Reinhardt and Bruno Walter, were no longer welcome in Germany. Bruno Walter was almost literally chased out of his homeland in March, a few days after a concert with his Leipzig Gewandhaus Orchestra had been cancelled through the intervention of Nazi officials. Reinhardt's treatment was less brutal. In late February 1933 he directed a performance of *The Great World Theatre* in Berlin after which he left the country, never to return. Within weeks the Nazis had seized his theatres, which were heavily in debt, and imposed a heavy tax demand on Leopoldskron, employing an old and obscure tax treaty with Austria as a pretext.[24]

The Nazi offensive against Jewish artists, especially those with world-wide reputations, had a certain haphazard quality during the first months of the régime. 'Purification' required the creation of a huge and complex apparatus, and this could not be put in place overnight. But for those with eyes to see, the early months of Nazi rule were proof enough that Hitler would give no quarter and intended to eradicate Jews from their prominent place in German cultural life. All 'degenerate' art was banned, not only the works of Jewish composers such as Mendelssohn, but also those of Schoenberg and his followers.

In May 1933 the Austrian Chancellor, Engelbert Dollfuss, outlawed the Nazi Party. German reaction was immediate: a tax of 1000 Marks was imposed on any German citizen who wished to travel to Austria. This reprisal seems to have been conceived in haste, without a clear notion of how it would be implemented or whom it would affect. The German Consul in Salzburg wrote in July to his Foreign Office in Berlin to say that German students had applied to participate in an international conductor's course given by the Mozarteum during the Festival and pointed out that very few of these music students had received tax waivers; most had not. The Consul went on to explain that those students who attended would be given free tickets to general Festival rehearsals, a teaching programme centred on German music and close personal contact with such world-renowned conductors as Paumgartner, Walter, Krauss and Maynhard von Zallinger, director of the Cologne Opera.[25]

The German Foreign Ministry passed on this information to Goebbels's Ministry of Propaganda, and asked if a precise policy had been formulated concerning Germans going to Salzburg. Was it purely a 'discretionary' decision? If it were deemed 'useful' to allow some German students to attend the Salzburg course, then should a waiver be granted to all? The Ministry responded that, since so many individual German artists had refused to take part in the 1933 Festival, 'I see no necessity to suggest that Germans should take part in the Salzburg conductor's course.'[26] On the other hand, the Ministry of Propaganda allowed that the Foreign Ministry could use its 'discretion' where it saw fit. This 'discretionary' power to grant a waiver on the tax was indeed employed often during the next three years, though much less frequently for Salzburg than for Vienna, Graz and other Austrian cities. Essentially, it was the ordinary German tourist who suffered. German artists who would lend prestige to the Reich were allowed to perform in Austria, even during the years of heightened tension between the two countries. In 1935, for example, the soprano Erna Sachs received permission to perform a concert in Graz. When she sang 'Heil deutsche Nachtigall' the theatre stood as one and gave the Nazi salute, at least according to her husband, who proudly relayed the news to Goebbels at the Ministry.[27]

Salzburgers realized that the new tax spelt ruin for their Festival. Indeed it was to reduce the number of Germans attending in 1933 to 800, and many of those had slipped across the border from Switzerland. But more trouble was to come. On 27 July Sigrid Onegin, who was to sing the key roll of Orpheus, and Wilhelm Rode, who was to play Pizarro in *Fidelio*, abruptly cancelled 'for political reasons'. Rode added that he would come to Salzburg 'next year, for a purely German festival'. At the same time, Hans Pfitzner gave up his conducting assignment, using the same excuse. They had all been ordered not to attend by the Nazis, who saw the 1933 Festival as a particular challenge, as its major attraction was to be Reinhardt's long-awaited production of *Faust*, and two of the featured conductors, Walter and Otto Klemperer, were also emigré Germans.[28] The only exception to this policy was Richard Strauss, who was allowed to come to Salzburg. His fame, his associations (and no doubt his willingness to accommodate himself to Hitler) evidently made him untouchable.

The Festival began in a tense atmosphere; German visitors were rare, major artists had cancelled, giant swastikas and fireworks blazed into the night sky from the hills beyond the border near Berchtesgaden, Nazi planes dropped propaganda pamphlets and loudspeakers blared over the border at Freilassing. And then there were the makeshift bomb attacks, which caused no loss of life, but added considerably to the tension. Salzburg became an armed camp, as police and local Heimwehr units guarded all the major Festival locations.[29]

The programme for 1933 was the most eclectic ever performed. Walter, as a direct challenge to Bayreuth, conducted *Tristan und Isolde*, as well as *Oberon*, *Orfeo ed Euridice* and *Zauberflöte*. Krauss, besides giving two Mozart operas, repeated *Die Frau ohne Schatten* and *Rosenkavalier*. But the great novelty of the festival was the premiere of the Vienna version of Strauss's *Die aegyptische Helena*, alas the least fruitful result of the composer's long collaboration with von Hofmannsthal.

The major event in 1933 was not however in the Festival Hall, but in Max Reinhardt's theatre. Von Hofmannsthal had written as early as 1919 that *Faust* belonged to the Salzburg programme. Reinhardt had wanted to produce it in 1926, but since there was nowhere to stage it he had chosen *Turandot* instead. Throughout the late Twenties, Reinhardt, von Hofmannsthal and Clemens Holzmeister had discussed ways and means of presenting *Faust*, but had never been able to find an acceptable format. In 1932, Holzmeister, in what would prove to be an act of genius, had suggested that the Riding School should be the locale for the play, and throughout the winter and spring preparations were made at great expense, although there was no money to spare for a roof or even an awning to protect against the rain.

Reinhardt conceived a most eloquent production, returning yet again to the idea of the medieval mystery play, always dear to his heart, while Holzmeister reversed the notion of the city as stage and transformed the backdrop of the Riding School into a city which bore more than passing resemblance to medieval Salzburg. Faust's celebrated study, Auerbach's cellar and Marguerite's prison were all in different parts of this city, and the scene moved from one section of the giant set to another. Reinhardt used voice overlays to increase the sense of realism, and in many respects the production resembled a modern-day *son et lumière*, except that actors and actresses appeared and spoke, and were not replaced by recorded voices. There was no curtain between the stage and the audience, for Reinhardt wished, as always, to make the spectator feel a sense of participation, to narrow the gap between the audience and the players. He himself believed that the whole notion of Faustian striving, of Faust's mystical romanticism, must seem very foreign to a modern audience; in order for the play to work, the spectator must perceive and feel the human side of the story. His production was therefore an attempt to highlight this aspect of the play at the expense of the philosophical and literary preoccupations of the young Goethe, who, when he wrote the first part of *Faust*, was substantially affected by the pessimism of the *Sturm und Drang* movement. Reinhardt also relied heavily on symbols associated with the old mystery plays: an angel hung over the city, the voice of God wafted down from a church tower, and the prologue seemed literally to come from the heavens. Years before, when Reinhardt and von Hofmannsthal had discussed *Faust* in considerable detail, von Hofmannsthal had thought that the production should be aimed at the more educated section of the audience, whereas Reinhardt had always wanted *Faust* to touch all men, whatever their intellectual background.[30]

The brilliant and compelling production of 1933 could not, however, succeed on its own; *Faust* needed performers of the highest quality. Reinhardt chose Paula Wessely, already under contract with him in Vienna, to take the role of Gretchen; Edward Balser performed the title role and Max Pallenberg was Mephisto. Balser and Wessely were just beginning long and distinguished careers, and their performances in Salzburg won them world-wide fame. Pallenberg, Reinhardt's wonderful comic lead in the 1923 Leopoldskron production of *Le Malade imaginaire*, had last acted in Salzburg in the ill-begotten *Turandot*. He now created a splendidly jocular devil.

After three and a half weeks of intensive rehearsals, the première of *Faust* was set for 17 August 1933. There was no roof on the Riding School but the massiveness of the set made it impossible to recreate the production in the Festival Hall in case of rain; therefore only cursory rehearsal time had been spent there. Reinhardt gambled that his luck of 1920 would hold. He lost. As one reviewer put it,

> The first few scenes held the rapt attention of an audience assembled on the uncovered benches. A few raindrops made a diversion, and evening wraps were held closer. A steady shower could not be ignored, umbrellas made their prosaical appearance to obscure the line of vision, and the weaker among the spectators here and there slipped out. A few thunderclaps and a cloudburst ended the matter. The full-dress première of *Faust* was no more.[31]

Margherita Wallmann, who had prepared the dance scenes, was dejectedly sitting alone in the Riding School as the rain came down. Suddenly she heard a voice. 'Don't look so sad; I'll come back for the second performance to see your *Walpurgisnacht*.' It was Chancellor Dollfuss, who did indeed attend the second brilliantly successful (and dry) performance.[32]

68

Bernhard Paumgartner had composed the musical background for the play, which was conducted that first summer by Herbert von Karajan, aged twenty-four. It had been Paumgartner who had persuaded him to give up a promising career as a pianist in order to focus his immense talents on the art of conducting.

Faust was the undeniable hit of the summer; while only fifty-two per cent of the seats were filled for other events, *Faust* sold out for every performance. Pallenberg had been the subject of anti-Semitic agitation, but had refused to step down; his determination to continue heightened the emotion of the audience and won him much sympathy.[33] Critics were generally enthusiastic, though some thought his Mephisto was insufficiently menacing and that Reinhardt had sacrificed the clarity and majesty of the words for spectacular effect. One Nazi critic went further, accusing Reinhardt of 'disfiguring German art because of his racial compulsions'. His production was 'sinful'.[34] The majority of reviewers, however, eschewed their old complaints about Reinhardt, and praised the magic of his vision, the splendour of the setting, the majesty of the performance.[35] Until now, Salzburg had seen old productions of his from Berlin or Vienna, or lesser plays such as *Victoria* or *The Servant of Two Masters,* perhaps to show how these too could be convincing if they were given sensitive productions, but now at long last he had created something entirely new for Salzburg; he had taken up the formidable challenge presented by *Faust* and conquered this problematic masterpiece, which was at the centre of German theatrical tradition, giving it new life.

Caught between excitement and danger, between the cacophony of Nazi loudspeakers and sublime singing, the 1933 Festival was an emotional experience for all who attended. Bruno Walter's interpretation of *Tristan* was not only an opera, it was the conductor's way of throwing down the gauntlet to Bayreuth. One critic noted that, although he did not personally care for Walter's reading of the score, the audience were swept away with emotion; at the end of the third act, everyone in the house was weeping.[36]

Richard Strauss was praised, most of all, for coming to Salzburg at all. The *Prager Presse* noted that Strauss, in open defiance of the 'world of the swastika', could be seen walking in public with the 'non-Aryan' Bruno Walter. The Berlin *Vossische Zeitung*, which still retained some editorial independence, also praised Strauss, although its critic found difficulty in understanding the obscurities of *Die Frau ohne Schatten* and *Die aegyptische Helena*.[37]

Critics from New York, London, Paris and Prague all described Salzburg, in this time of strife, as a 'window' on Austria. They depicted the Festival-goers, whether from England, France, Hungary, Czechoslovakia, Italy or the United States, as true friends of Austria, whose attendance was as much a political as an artistic statement. France was suffering from 'Austromania', wrote one. Others mentioned that the foreign press had encouraged its readers to go to Salzburg to express solidarity and sympathy with Austria. Paul Stefan viewed the Nazi boycott as 'ridiculous', since the German Empire was turning its back on the supreme manifestation of its own artistic heritage.[38]

Despite the general euphoria, some journalists realized that Nazi sympathizers had only put their swastikas out of sight temporarily; the 'unexpected success' of the Festival should not allow people to forget that there was great misery and discontent in Austria. Numerous Austrians were leaving for Germany, there perhaps to prepare a *coup d'état* against their homeland. The rest of Europe stood by . . . silently. Salzburg had proved that Austria, 'throughout the years . . . [had] accomplished its international mission, which had always been to mediate between civilizations and races. . .'. But could Austria continue to play this part? It was doubtful. Many young Austrians were intrigued by Nazism. The situation was grave.[39]

As if to underline the uncertainty, Stefan Zweig announced in October that he would be leaving Salzburg. He had been subject to a police search, and the experience had given him a stark vision of the future. He left the city in the spring of 1934; he returned briefly for a few short visits in the ensuing years, but the tie was broken. He spent his final years restlessly travelling from place to place, from Europe to America and finally to Brazil, where he took his life in 1942. In his autobiography, *Die Welt von Gestern* (The World of Yesterday), he described these years in Salzburg, when Austria was the 'artistic Mecca' of Europe. 'Those blessed years of peace' had meant much to him, because 'faith in the world, in humanity, had again become possible.' He recounted the names of those whom he had entertained at his villa on the Kapuzinerberg: H.G.Wells, Jacob Wassermann, James Joyce, Emil Ludwig, Franz Werfel, Paul Valéry, Arthur Schnitzler, Maurice Ravel, Richard Strauss (for whom he wrote the libretto of *Die schweigsame Frau*), Alban Berg, Bruno Walter, Béla Bartók, Arturo Toscanini.[40] With Zweig's departure, Salzburg was reduced to one local celebrity, Reinhardt. And he too, despite the huge success of *Faust*, was looking to America and Hollywood for his future, and spending less and less time at Leopoldskron.

70

Meanwhile the Festival directors counted the ticket stubs for 1933; suspicions were confirmed. Only 56,000 seats had been sold, 16,000 less than the previous — bad — year. The German 1000-Mark exit tax had had its intended effect, and visitors from elsewhere could not make up the difference. During the Festival the directors had twice been forced to ask for emergency subsidies from Vienna, which were only grudgingly given.[41]

At a meeting of the *Aufsichtsrat* in late January 1934, a crucial decision was made: the Festival would continue. Both Chancellor Dollfuss and Education Minister von Schuschnigg assured Rehrl that Salzburg would receive governmental backing whatever the circumstances, and 100,000 Schillings was immediately guaranteed for the forthcoming year. The Austrian government now realized that Salzburg was not only a source of foreign currency, and a symbol of Austria's cultural excellence, but also a living example of Austria's independence which had to be preserved at all costs.[42]

During the early Thirties the Festival organizers began to broaden programmes, occasionally to ask foreign artists to appear and to encourage the formation of Salzburg societies throughout Europe. These Salzburg societies, it was hoped, would popularize the Festival and increase its audience, but they eventually tended to make life extremely complicated for the directors, with their demands and their squabbles.

A Salzburg travel agent, Hilda Sperrs, helped to found both the London Salzburg Society in 1931 and *Les Amis de Salzbourg* in Brussels in 1932; the French *Société des Etudes Mozartiennes* had been founded independently in 1930. These societies organized trips to Salzburg for their members and occasionally sponsored fund-raising events in order to help students attend the Festival. In the summer of 1932, Frau Eva von Wünscheim was in Salzburg running a sale of Austrian handicrafts for the Viennese charity 'Austrian Women's Help', when she met Hilda Sperrs, and asked if she might meet some members of the London Salzburg Society. Soon friendships were formed, and that fall von Wünscheim went to visit some members of the Society in London. Her enthusiasm for Salzburg was infectious, and she was asked to set up a 'Vienna Section' of the Society, so that English members could be kept abreast of events in the capital city.[43] The following year she went to Rome, hoping to create another group there. The Austrian press attaché, when informed of her visit, sought support from the Conte di San Martino, President of the Accademia di S. Cecilia, but San Martino

71

said that he was to 'too lethargic' to become involved. Frau von Wünscheim refused to be deterred and tried to find other lovers of Mozart and of Salzburg, but she left without obtaining any firm commitments.

The Austrian attaché was not surprised. Italians, he surmised, with the notable exception of the Crown Prince, were not interested in Mozart, still less in Gluck, Wagner or Strauss; when people went out, they preferred to hear their own composers. He also feared that the formation of such a society might harm relationships between Austria and Italy, which remained tense due to the Italian occupation of the south Tirol. He did not think that the Italian government would wish to help advertise a foreign festival which would drain needed currency from the country. Moreover the highly nationalistic Italian press could be counted upon at best to ignore, at worst to criticize, such a society. Perhaps it was better that Frau von Wünscheim did not succeed.[44]

Frau von Wünscheim's enthusiasm for Salzburg knew no bounds, and for the next three years she became a self-appointed roving ambassador for the Festival. During the 1933 Festival she ran a special 'club' for the various members of the national Salzburg Societies in the luxurious Hotel Europa, gave tea parties and sponsored a number of chamber music concerts. She also managed to convince the Brussels and Paris Societies to affiliate with the London and Viennese sections, which had affiliated the year before. Now her letterhead read: 'President of the Austrian section', not 'Secretary of the Viennese section', and Dollfuss and Rehrl were named as honorary presidents. She had also collected membership fees in Vienna, and continued to advertise Austrian handicrafts. This did not please some English members, who, goaded on by Frau Sperrs, became openly hostile. Many had little love for Dollfuss, did not like the way in which Frau von Wünscheim had appropriated the title of President, and were concerned how membership funds were being spent.

In London that autumn the Salzburg Society split into two factions, and a new British Empire Salzburg Society, under the presidency of the former Vice-President of the London Society, was founded; meanwhile the old London Society accused von Wünscheim of misusing membership funds. She fought back, and used her influence to convince the Brussels Society to write an extremely disagreeable letter to the Londoners, who were accused of persecuting her. Brussels renounced its affiliation with London.[45]

All of this may seem unimportant, a mere storm in a teacup, a story of high society intrigue, injured egos and pathetic grabs for power. But it was not unimportant to the Austrian government, for the war of words between the contending factions could only serve to harm the Festival whose preservation was the sole *raison d'être* of these groups. Although a truce between the English Societies arranged by Ambassador Franckenstein, held through the summer of 1934, it began to unravel in the autumn. Frankenstein found himself in an extremely unpleasant situation, with both Societies asking him for his patronage. When the old London Society threatened to initiate legal proceedings against Frau von Wünscheim, Frankenstein had had enough. He went to the Vice-President of the British Empire Salzburg Society, explained his position and persuaded him to drop Frau von Wünscheim from his board, if it were found out, after a thorough check of her past, that she had used her position for illicit financial gain. The Ambassador then wrote to the Austrian Foreign Office, and asked them to do a thorough check on the lady's background. The Foreign Ministry agreed. They had already discovered that the registered Vienna Section of the Austrian Section of the Salzburg Societies had never been incorporated, nor had Dollfuss ever consented to be a patron. Unfortunately the final report is missing, but there can be little doubt of its conclusion. In July 1935 Rehrl wrote to the Foreign Ministry to convey the following information: the Austrian Section had been dissolved by court order. No one should have anything to do with Frau von Wünscheim.[46]

The last thing the Festival needed was this kind of petty and unproductive conflict. The next year a New York group set out to form an American Salzburg Society. The Austrian Consul in New York discouraged the enterprise through bureaucratic delay, while publicly claiming how delighted he was. He wrote privately to the Austrian Foreign Office that the Consulate was well able to publicize the Festival itself without help, and it could also advise on transport; an American Society would only duplicate its efforts.[47] The last functioning Society to be formed, in Hungary in 1934, had a limited success. The Austrian Ambassador in Budapest acted as its patron (after deterring the Hungarians from dealing with the ever-active Frau von Wünscheim), but wrote to his superiors that the Society had little freedom of action, since the Hungarian government did not want its currency to leave the country. In 1935 the Austrian Trade Minister suggested to his colleagues in the Ministry of Education that the Festival should perform Kodaly's *Psalmus Hungaricus* under Toscanini, as this would bring Hungarians to Salzburg. But the direction turned down the idea for lack of funds.[48]

The Czechs never formed a Society, but they became an increasingly prominent part of the Salzburg summer scene. In 1935 the Austrian Ambassador to Prague, after an 'unofficial' conversation with the Czech Prime Minister, suggested that, to encourage Czech visitors, the Prague Symphony Orchestra might be invited to the Festival. He doubted that the Sudeten Germans would object. Here politics and culture became hopelessly intertwined. On the one hand, Austria was cultivating relations with Czechoslovakia; on the other, the Sudeten German minority made up a sizeable contingent of Czech Festival-goers, and elements of this minority were seeking integration into Hitler's Reich. Inviting a Czech orchestra might antagonize them. A series of interchanges between Prague, Vienna and Salzburg then took place. Various correspondents in Prague argued that, in fact, Sudeten Germans were proud of the Czech Philharmonic, and would welcome its being invited to Salzburg. Nazi sympathizers there were, but, in any case, they would never attend the Festival. But the Festival directors would not be moved, despite the pleas from their own Foreign Ministry. The official argument was that, if Salzburg invited a foreign orchestra (which Salzburg had in fact done in 1931) then there would be a never-ending series of requests from other orchestras, requests that the Festival could not fulfill without losing its unique character. The real reasons went unmentioned. The Vienna Philharmonic could not abide competition, and the appearance of the Budapest Philharmonic in 1931 had been less than a success.[49]

In theory, the inclusion of foreign musicians was a good publicity strategy, but in practice this often lead to conflict, unless the artist was clearly of world-class quality. Otherwise the singer, and it was usually in the operatic area that controversy arose, would perforce replace an Austrian, and the nation had more than its share of top-grade talent. Delicate and complex negotiations inevitably ensued. Sometimes other nations wished to show solidarity with Austria by suggesting that their own national ensemble come to Salzburg, but the directors wanted to keep an Austrian flavour to the Festival programme and so tended to be very wary.

Each country in Europe had its own relationship with Salzburg, and that relationship to some extent was controlled by the shifting political sands of the period. Italy was a complex case. In March 1934, for example, Chancellor Dollfuss travelled to Rome for a meeting with Mussolini; their political discussions are of no interest here, but, in an intriguing aside, Mussolini mentioned that he was writing a play called

Giulio Cesare; might Dollfuss suggest that it be performed at Salzburg? Upon returning to Vienna, the Chancellor wrote to the Italian Foreign Ministry to say that Viennese cultural circles were awaiting with 'excited expectation' a draft of the play, and hoped it could be presented at the forthcoming Salzburg Festival. Dollfuss also asked if it might be possible to engage Beniamino Gigli, Italy's foremost tenor, to sing in *Don Giovanni*, which was to be given that summer for the first time in the original Italian. The Under Secretary of the Italian Foreign Office, Suvich, responded that the play would not be finished until the autumn, but that the *Duce* would like to see it produced in 1935. He also promised to persuade Gigli to come to Salzburg in 1935, for 'his presence will contribute to the success of the Salzburg season'. Needless to say, Mussolini's play never saw the footlights of Salzburg. Gigli *did* perform — in 1936 — but presented only a programme of arias. It is tantalizing to imagine what effect a play by Mussolini would have had in Salzburg. But at its inception Dollfuss supported the idea — as long as Gigli was part of the package — and let his Minister of Education know this in no uncertain terms.[50]

There was one country, however, where a combination of factors resulted in a close working relationship with Salzburg. This was France. Since the mid-Twenties, the French press had sung the praises of Salzburg. Negative reviews of the Festival were rare. Furthermore, France had an official government cultural policy aimed at increasing French involvement in Salzburg. This meant constant pressure on the Salzburg authorities to include French works on the programme and to invite French artists to perform. Robert Brussel, a scholar and journalist, headed an association, under the joint patronage of the Ministries of Foreign Affairs and of Education, called *Action artistique*, which was directly responsible for French relations with the Festival. Brussel was ably supported by Gabriel Puaux, who became French Ambassador to Vienna in 1933, and was a keen observer of cultural events and an active supporter of French interests in Salzburg. Finally, France's unofficial representative in Salzburg, the Marquise de Peyrebere, acted as the conduit between Salzburg, Vienna and Paris. She had lived in Salzburg since the mid-Twenties, wrote gushing reviews of the Festival for the French press (under the pen name of Etienne Gary) and knew everyone who counted in the Festival and provincial administrations. In Paris, the local Society was renamed the *Association Mozart-Paris-Salzbourg* in 1933; it contained more than 600 members, whose names read like the *Almanach de Gotha*. The

Association's activities went much further than the arrangement of summer trips to the Festival. It held concerts and lectures and sponsored publications about the works of Mozart. Unlike the other Societies, it made a real and continuing contribution to spreading the Salzburg 'idea'.[51]

The official French attitude towards the Festival was a mixture of self-interest and, after 1933, a desire to give cultural support to the broader concept of Austrian independence. Puaux later wrote, 'The Salzburg Festival formed one of the key aspects of Austria's system of self-defence.'[52] Puaux, Brussel and Peyrebere worked tirelessly to convince the Festival directors to hire French artists and perform French works. They had close contacts with Clemens Krauss, and in 1933 suggested he ask a French singer to perform one act of Paul Dukas's *Ariane et Barbe-Bleue* at the forthcoming Festival. Krauss refused, allegedly because he had never heard the soprano's voice.[53] The more probable reason was that he, the head of the Vienna State Opera, had not been invited to perform in Paris the year before.

For the next five years a pattern developed in which the Marquise de Peyrebere would discuss possibilities with the Festival authorities and relay these to Paris, where the Education Ministry and the Foreign Office, working through Brussel, would decide how much French involvement should be requested. After 1933 the French were not always discreet in their suggestions. In 1936, Peyrebere, who seems on occasion to have acted on her own, was negotiating simultaneously with Reinhardt and Walter; she tried to convince Reinhardt to stage, in the form of a mystery play, Paul Claudel's *Annonciation*. She wanted Walter to promise to conduct *Pelléas et Mélisande*. Both said that they would 'consider' the projects; neither came to fruition.[54]

Though the Salzburg authorities never had the slightest intention of putting on French operas, they did welcome the interest of the French, for Rehrl realized that the French cultural presence at the Festival, though marginal at best, had strong symbolic importance. Rehrl himself received the rosette of the Legion of Honour, as did several Salzburg notables, including Lotte Lehmann.

One reason why the Festival directors were so unwilling to allow more than a token representation of foreign works and foreign artists in their programmes was that with the arrival of Toscanini in 1934, there was no need to worry about Hungarian, Italian or French sensibilities; the maestro filled the seats. Moreover, his involvement became so total, his power so awesome, and his aversion to competition so great, that no one dared to oppose his wishes.

Arturo Toscanini was in his mid-sixties when a series of people and events persuaded him to come to Salzburg. He was the most popular, the most sought-after conductor in the western world. The mannerisms, the poor eyesight, the temper tantrums, the total recollection of musical scores (then rare), the fury and excitement of his performances, all were part and parcel of a persona who became a legend early in a lifetime that was to span nine decades. Toscanini was already a star at the turn of the century; by the 1930's, as chief conductor of the New York Philharmonic, he commanded a unique place in a world already blessed with many great conductors.

In 1930, in Bologna, Toscanini had refused to play the fascist hymn *La Giovinezza* and had been set upon by party members. After this he had refused to conduct in Italy, although he continued to spend his holidays on the island of San Giovanni in Lago Maggiore. Mussolini abhorred him and ensured that he was continually subjected to major and minor irritations, including having his phone tapped. Erich Leinsdorf, who then worked with the maestro, does not think that pure idealism caused Toscanini to refuse to conduct in Italy for, as he says, 'there was only room for one dictator in that country.'[55] Whatever the real motivation, Toscanini's stand was perceived as a gesture of defiance against a brutish state, and it made people reconsider their views on the relationship of art and politics.

Barely three months after the Bologna incident, Toscanini realized a life-long dream and conducted at Bayreuth. He returned again the following year. There was no Festival in 1932 because of the Depression, but during that year Toscanini decided not to return to Bayreuth because of differences with the Festival administration. When Winifried Wagner heard this, she travelled to Paris in the spring of 1932 in order to make Toscanini change his mind. She promised him that he would conduct *Die Meistersinger*, an opera dear to his heart, and gave a tentative assurance that Wilhelm Furtwängler, his great rival, would be absent.[56]

Toscanini was in New York when Hitler came to power in January 1933. Six weeks later he received a letter from the pianist and conductor, Ossip Gabrilowitsch, mentioning Hitler's persecution of Jewish artists and asking Toscanini if he would make some gesture. On 1 April Toscanini signed a telegram to Hitler protesting against his treatment of the Jews; among others, conductors Serge Koussevitzky and Fritz Reiner also signed. The Nazi reaction was immediate; all records of artists who sent the offending telegram were forbidden in

Germany.[57] Hitler then asked Winifried Wagner to write to Toscanini personally to persuade him to come to Bayreuth. Toscanini's response was somewhat equivocal. He loved Bayreuth, he longed to conduct *Meistersinger* and *Parsifal* there, but he would like to see some change in Nazi attitudes towards Jewish artists. No change in the Nazi position occurred.

In late May, conductor Fritz Busch went to visit Toscanini at San Giovanni. Busch, though not a Jew, was horrified by the turn of events in Germany, and left Germany later that year for Buenos Aires. (Eventually he was to become one of the founders of the Glyndebourne Festival.) However in May 1933 Busch was trying to find out exactly where Toscanini stood with regard to Bayreuth. To sound him out he mentioned that Heinz Tietjen, *intendant* of the Berlin Opera, had presumed that Toscanini was not coming and had asked Busch to come to Bayreuth in his place; but of course, Busch pointed out, that was out of the question. Busch's firm stance seemed to galvanize Toscanini to take a decision that he dreaded. On 5 June he informed Bayreuth that he would not come to conduct in 1933. His telegram read, in part:

> The lamentable events which have wounded my feelings both as man and as artist have not up to this moment changed, despite my hopes. It is my duty today to break the silence that I have imposed upon myself for the last two months and to inform you that for my, for your, and for everybody else's tranquillity it is better not to think any more of my going to Bayreuth. . . .

Time magazine lauded Toscanini's decision, and remarked that Bayreuth would be hard put to find a replacement of his stature. The most likely choice, Karl Elmendorff, was 'a man of mediocre talent who in past years had turned out stupid performances shoddily rehearsed'.[58]

In the event, Richard Strauss accepted the offer to conduct the opening *Parsifal* in Bayreuth that summer, as he had filled the breach in Leipzig after Bruno Walter's forced departure. Strauss was naïve and ambitious, moreover he desired the accolade that conducting at Bayreuth would bring, so he seized the opportunity when it was offered to him. The Nazis had created a political atmosphere which caused the older generation of Toscanini, Walter, Busch and Klemperer to depart. As a result rising young conductors such as Clemens Krauss, Karl Böhm and Herbert von Karajan were given their chance. A whole generation of German musicians, replacing those who had left, would eventually be politically tainted, even though in general they did not view themselves as political people. The truth was that they profited from the Nazi régime and became beholden to it.

Toscanini's renunciation had far-reaching ramifications. In New York, Dorothy Thompson, Sinclair Lewis's wife, sent a telegram to Dollfuss:

> Since Toscanini has refused to conduct in Bayreuth thereby winning applause of art and freedom lovers throughout the world many of whom are choosing Salzburg this year in place of Bayreuth, cannot Austrian officials arrange that he could conduct in Salzburg. . . . This comes from a sincere lover of Austria.[59]

The telegram was given to the Minister of Education, Kurt von Schuschnigg, for action. He declined to take the matter further because the Festival programme was already prepared, and he doubted that Toscanini would come to Salzburg at such short notice. When asked, the Salzburg Festival directors said that Toscanini demanded too much rehearsal time, and that his being invited would be an affront to Bayreuth — although no doubts had hindered them the year before when they had tried to enlist Toscanini's participation. Perhaps they feared that if he came, the Nazis would withdraw those German artists who had already signed contracts. Whatever their motives, they declined to invite him.

Meanwhile the Polish violinist Bronislaw Hubermann and his son went to visit Toscanini at San Giovanni. Hubermann had been in the forefront of international opposition to Hitler, and had refused to set foot in the Reich after 1933, even when his good friend Furtwängler invited him.[60] When Hubermann had learned of Toscanini's refusal to go to Bayreuth, he wrote the following letter to the maestro:

> An artist can only give what he possesses as a man. Your action, with the artistic solidarity and moving words which accompanied it, has given an example to the world, which will understand from now on where the sources of Arturo Toscanini's inspiration come from: the depth of the human heart.[61]

Hubermann now suggested to Toscanini that he should 'go to Vienna. By giving concerts there [you would] complete the positive action that you have undertaken by your great refusal to conduct at Bayreuth.' Toscanini immediately agreed. Hubermann then went to Vienna, where the Minister of Foreign Affairs assured him that the government was doing everything in its power to get a firm commitment from Toscanini. The minister himself was going to write to him personally: Hubermann was asked to send a telegram as well.[62]

Soon afterwards, Toscanini agreed to come. He would give two concerts with the Vienna Philharmonic in their home town, and then would take the orchestra to Budapest. Hugo Burghauser, bassoonist and manager of the orchestra (which was an autonomous corporation) acted as the liaison between the Philharmonic and Toscanini; the two struck up an immediate rapport, perhaps because Burghauser was half Italian. This was just as well, for initially most of the Viennese musicians were fearful of a man with such an aggressive reputation.[63] However by the time of the first concert, on 24 October 1933, orchestra and conductor had adapted to each other. After the second Viennese concert they took the short trip to Budapest, where they scored another triumph. As they were saying their goodbyes, Burghauser casually remarked on the success of their collaboration and asked if it might be possible to continue it the next summer in Salzburg, where Toscanini could conduct the same programme that he had given in Vienna. The maestro's response, an immediate and unequivocal 'Si', was transmitted by Burghauser to Kerber. The wheels were in motion.[64]

Although Hugo Burghauser had only held the position of manager of the Philharmonic for less than a year, he had been well aware of the symbolic meaning of Toscanini's presence in Vienna; he knew that it underlined Austria's quest to remain an independent entity and he fully recognized it as propaganda value. He had already suggested to the Austrian Theatre Administration that the State Opera should perform in France and Holland under Bruno Walter the following year, because such a trip would have 'considerable artistic and propagandist value' and he saw that if the Berlin Philharmonic were going to Paris, then the Viennese must perform there too.[65] Although buffeted by the winds of Viennese politics, and subject to the petty whims and irritations of Clemens Krauss, who disliked him, Burghauser had friends in high places and was quick to piece together political nuances.

Hubermann and Burghauser had, each in his own way, contributed to Toscanini's decisions to come first to Vienna, and then to Salzburg in 1934. Both understood the value of symbols, and the Italian conductor was an outstanding symbol if ever one existed. Burghauser specifically wanted to use Toscanini's presence to strengthen Austria's image of independence. Hubermann was prepared to fight Hitler on all fronts, and Toscanini was one element of that battle. Their later histories are of interest. Hubermann founded the Israeli Philharmonic in 1936, and later that year welcomed his friend Toscanini there for a series of concerts. In March of 1938 Hubermann was in Vienna, preparing to give a concert, when he made the wise decision (which few took) to leave the city barely twenty-four hours before the *Anschluss*. Burghauser stayed in Vienna until 1939, though he was dismissed from his position by the Nazis. He then left for New York, where be became first bassoonist for the New York Philharmonic.[66]

5

Toscanini Triumphant

1934–8

Arturo Toscanini agreed to repeat his Viennese concerts at Salzburg in 1934, and to add an all-Wagner evening with Lotte Lehmann as soloist; Wilhelm Furtwängler, director of the Berlin Opera, was also to make his first appearance in Salzburg, and would give two orchestral concerts; Bruno Walter would conduct *Don Giovanni* in the original Italian with Ezio Pinza in the title role;[1] Richard Strauss planned to conduct several operas and concerts, and was to be honoured on the occasion of his seventieth birthday by having four of his operas performed, including *Elektra*, to be conducted by Clemens Krauss. The programme was superb; prospects for the summer looked excellent.

In May, however, rumours abounded; Hitler was said to be concocting secret plans to sabotage the Festival.[2] Then the British Consul in Munich passed on to the Austrian authorities the information that he had heard that the SS were planning to smuggle bombs across the border from Freilassing, with the collaboration of some local people, and were planning a 'serious bomb outrage'.[3]

In fact Hitler's plans for Salzburg were less grandiose but just as effective. The head of the Austrian Section of the NSDAP, now based in Munich, wrote to Dr Goebbels, the Minister of Propaganda, in early May saying that Furtwängler should not be allowed to perform at the Festival, for 'he would represent an important propaganda victory for Austrian tourism; our party comrades should use every means to boycott him'. The actor Werner Krauss and Richard Strauss should likewise be forbidden to take part.[4] A high functionary of the German Broadcasting Corporation also complained that allowing German artists to perform in Salzburg would only strengthen Dollfuss's moral and economic position. Even worse, many Jewish artists were on the programme.[5]

82

On 16 May 1934 Goebbels made up his mind, and nine days later Furtwängler and Strauss received identical letters from Walter Funk, head of Section VII of the Ministry of Propaganda, telling them that their participation in the Festival 'runs counter to the Führer's policy and [Dr. Goebbels] asks you to refrain from going there for political reasons.'[6] Strauss and Furtwängler dutifully followed orders. Strauss wrote to Salzburg claiming illness, Furtwängler cited overwork: neither mentioned the real reason for his cancellation.[7] In the event, Strauss did spend an evening in Salzburg that summer, not as a conductor, but as a private citizen; he attended the performance of *Elektra* and took a bow. It was to be his last appearance in pre-Nazi Salzburg.

At the beginning of the year, the Festival directors had asked the government to provide a guarantee against any losses that might be incurred. Negotiations were dilatory until cancellations and rising tensions in the country finally convinced the government that the Festival was indeed in danger. In mid-June a hasty agreement was signed between state, province and city; if 'outside events' caused the Festival to lose money, all three would make up the deficit, with the government responsible for fifty per cent of the losses.[8] A few days after this agreement Salzburg suffered another blow; Max Pallenberg announced that he would not play the part of Mephisto in *Faust*, because there were too many Burgtheater actors already in the production. This sounded spurious. Unfortunately he was never able to explain, for he died the next day in an air crash in Czechoslovakia.[9]

In 1933 Chancellor Dollfuss had dissolved Parliament and created a one-party Christian corporate state. On 25 July 1934, three days before the opening of the Salzburg Festival, Dollfuss was assassinated, part of a bungled Nazi attempt at a *coup d'état*. Kurt von Schuschnigg became the new Chancellor and Puthon immediately wrote to tell him that ticket sales had come to a halt, that hundreds had cancelled; he needed money at once. The government complied, but demanded that a very close watch be kept on revenue.[10] After a delay of eighteen hours, the 1934 Festival began, with Krauss honouring the fallen Chancellor by conducting a moving rendition of the Funeral March from Beethoven's Third Symphony. The house was not sold out, and the following days saw no increase in attendance. The government demanded that the directors make bi-weekly reports on gate receipts. After two weeks the intake was fifty per cent below that of 1933, which in any case had been a difficult year.[11]

With the Festival launched a new fear arose. Would Toscanini honour his commitment? Many thought not, but the maestro sent a telegram to Burghauser in early August. He would come.[12] By mid-August attendance began to increase dramatically. Salzburg was crowded again, thanks in part to foreign press reports which asserted that the crisis was over, that calm had returned. The major French newspapers urged their readers to go to the Festival, not only to help out the Austrian economy, but to assert their support for Austrian independence.[13]

The July crisis had a deep effect on Reinhardt. At the time of Dollfuss's assassination, he had been in Venice, staging a Shakespeare play. He then had to postpone his return to Salzburg for five days, because the border had been closed. According to Gusti Adler, the night before his departure, Reinhardt slept not a wink.[14] He pondered, silently. Helene Thimig later wrote that those five days in Venice had profoundly marked her husband. 'From the outside we suddenly saw things that we never could have seen had we been inside the country.' Reinhardt had always been reserved about discussing his fears for the future of Austria or of Europe, and had tended to believe Rehrl when he had assured him that Austria would stand up to Hitler. Now Reinhardt saw Austria for what it was, a nation hopelessly divided, and an easy prey for its voracious neighbour to the north.[15] Nevertheless he took the train back to Salzburg on 1 August, and, surrounded by bodyguards provided by Baron Puthon, went straight to the Riding School to begin work on the first rehearsal of *Faust*. At the première six days later, the audience gasped as a shadow carrying a rifle entered the theatre. There was momentary panic, until someone realized that it was not a Nazi terrorist, but a local Salzburger who had, on his own initiative, decided to become Reinhardt's bodyguard. The audience tittered; it was like a scene from a comic opera as the slightly drunken 'guard' inspected the premises.[16]

Immediately after the Festival, Reinhardt left for America where he staged the 1927 Salzburg version of *A Midsummer Night's Dream* on the west coast; he also signed a long-term contract with Warner Brothers to direct a film of the play. Jack Warner, who had been his guest at Leopoldskron the previous summer, had consistently urged Reinhardt to leave Salzburg and come to Hollywood, because he felt that Austria had become a dangerous place to live.[17] At the end of 1934 Reinhardt made his decision, and applied for American citizenship. Though he would return to Salzburg the following three summers, though Leopoldskron would resound with laughter and conversation, Reinhardt's status had changed. His world was now America, Salzburg was his escape from that world. Carl Zuckmayer pictured the scene better than anyone.

> For in this world of doomed enchantment politics were underplayed — because everyone knew that in the long run he would not be able to escape their iron grip. It was somewhat like Versailles in the days of the Bastille, only more alert, more aware, intellectually more lucid, as is only proper for an élite devoted to the Muses. For it was just such an élite which set the tone in Salzburg and that gave those days and nights their unique glory.

And the playwright remembered a comment of Reinhardt's, uttered at a late hour: 'I heard Reinhardt say almost with satisfaction: "the nicest part of these festive summers is that each one may be the last." After a pause he added: "You can feel the taste of transitoriness on your tongue." '[18]

Festival-goers in 1934, and in the following years, may have been less sensitive to that world of 'doomed enchantment' but they could not avoid the sense of danger, of menace, which lurked behind the often forced gaiety of the locals. The emotion that followed Dollfuss's assassination, and the relief when normality returned, were constant themes for the critics. Audiences too were caught up in the charged atmosphere.[19]

Despite Goebbels's attempts to sabotage the Festival, there was much to see and hear. Joseph Mengelberg and Felix Weingartner replaced Furtwängler, and Krauss took over the conducting duties of Strauss. As Time put it, the audiences 'showered flowers on Mengelberg, applauded Weingartner and Clemens Krauss, shouted themselves hoarse over Bruno Walter, and the roar that they gave Toscanini sounded like nothing so much as a Yale Bowl demonstration.'[20]

Walter and Toscanini were undoubtedly the heroes of the hour. Despite their different temperaments and conducting styles, they were also friends, unusual among conductors of the first rank. Each attended the other's concerts. Toscanini was hailed with such enthusiasm that he was unable to get the Philharmonic to take a bow; they too were applauding vociferously. The maestro had brought to Salzburg a dynamism that it had never before experienced; shortly after the close of the Festival he announced that he would return the next year, to conduct *Fidelio*.[21]

The most stirring words written about 1934 came not from a music critic, but from the pen of novelist François Mauriac, who had talked with many Austrians, and reported their words:

> Tell everyone that we are at the end of our resources, that we are paying heavily for being at the centre of the battlefield of Europe, that Austria can no longer pay the costs.

He added his own views:

> Salzburg hears Hitler breathing . . . a few kilometres from the town. . . . These sublime diversions here, are they but a great festival which the old world is offering during its final agony? Travellers who come here from all over the world to hear Mozart feel . . . this same anxiety, an anxiety, moreover, which deepens their pleasure.

He then quoted an anonymous poem:

> Let us love what we will never see twice
> Ah, who can see twice your grace and tenderness.

To Mauriac, the greatest enemy of Germany ('this furious and stupid Goliath') was Mozart, whose music 'is simple, measured and spiritual. . . . It is his music which reminds Austrians at every moment that they are not Germans.' Mozart's music, he said, would enable Austria 'to save her soul'. He hoped that one day Germany might be saved from this 'horrible drunkenness'. For her to live again, she needed Austria, for Austria was preserving German culture; when Germany came back to its senses, then Austria would return that legacy to her.[22] Mauriac put into eloquent words both the fragility of Salzburg, and her new mission.

In sum, the 1934 Festival, born in the worst crisis of Austrian history, could only be considered a success; attendance figures were, at fifty-three per cent of capacity, barely about those of 1933; but the last three weeks had seen a marked improvement, thanks to Toscanini.[23]

Toscanini, however, was a master at provoking crises — as well as resolving them. In October he let it be known that the following year he wished to conduct, along with *Fidelio*, a performance of Verdi's *Falstaff* in Italian. He would only come to Salzburg if he could do both operas. This caused great consternation: Erwin Kerber was the most upset. It was he who had been the unofficial artistic director of the Festival for the past few years, since the Artistic Council had ceased to function, and he still believed that it was his duty to preserve the Salzburg 'idea' and the artistic consistency of the programmes. For him Verdi had no place in the Festival; he had even been sceptical about *Tristan*, but at least it was the work of a German composer. Once the door was opened to Verdi, would not the French, the Czechs, the Poles ask equal billing? Moreover, Clemens Krauss was preparing a new production of *Falstaff*, to be sung in German, for the 1934–5 Vienna season. A conflict with Toscanini seemed inevitable.

At the meeting of the *Aufsichtsrat* Kerber alluded to Krauss's growing animosity towards Toscanini. The press had reported that Krauss was furious to have been eclipsed by Toscanini and Walter during the 1934 Festival. Kerber also pointed out that Krauss had even told an American visitor that he hoped to be in a position to forbid all 'foreign' singers from performing at Salzburg in 1935; this was a direct reference to Walter, who had brought a number of Italians, including Pinza, to sing *Don Giovanni*. Kerber feared an explosion if Toscanini were given his way. But he was overruled by the other members. The Minister of Education, Hans Pernter, wanted Toscanini at all costs and insisted that the maestro's demands should be met.[24] In truth, Kerber's fears were realized. Within weeks a conflict erupted over which conductor would bring *Falstaff* to Salzburg. The final decision was made by Chancellor von Schuschnigg in late 1934; he chose Toscanini.[25]

Toscanini was indeed a feather in Salzburg's cap, but his presence caused problems. In October 1934, the Italian composer Vittorio Gnecchi proposed creating a society, the *Amici de Salisburgo* in Milan if Salzburg would again play one of his religious compositions as they had done the year before. The Austrian Consul in Milan thought that this sounded like a fair exchange, since the composer had many important connections with the local aristocracy and had helped recruit them for previous Festivals. But Toscanini did not like Gnecchi, and when he had been at La Scala he had refused to play Gnecchi's works.[26] Rather than upset Toscanini, Baron Puthon decided to try to deter Gnecchi with a delicate compromise. He told the composer that it would be impossible to put his work on in Salzburg unless the composer managed to have a piece by Salzburg's own Joseph Messner played in Milan. However, this ruse was accepted, and Gnecchi's aptly titled *Missa Salisburgensis* had therefore to be put on in 1935. It was slipped into one of the usually poorly attended church concerts in the hopes that Toscanini's ire would not be raised. The *Amici de Salisburgo* was set up in due course, but never became active.

Later, the Italian *Società per la propaganda musicale* wrote to the Austrian government, suggesting that Italy's second ranking conductor, Bernardino Molinari, was prepared to bring his Augusteum Orchestra to Salzburg to give a couple of concerts, which might increase Italian patronage. This request was turned down by the directors, who wished in no way to antagonize Toscanini; they responded that there was 'no possibility' that Molinari could be invited.[27]

Clemens Krauss was as imperious and stubborn as Toscanini, and he too continued to make trouble. In November of 1934 he decided to take the Vienna State Opera on a South American tour the following summer, which would mean that he would not be in Salzburg until the second week in August. The young conductor Josef Krips had quickly to be asked to replace Krauss for the first two performances of *Rosenkavalier*. When Toscanini arrived in Vienna in late October to conduct a performance of Verdi's *Requiem* in honour of Dollfuss, Krauss did everything he could to make the maestro unwelcome, and went so far as to try to ruin his rehearsals.[28]

Throughout the autumn Krauss had been negotiating with the government for a renewal of his contract with the Vienna State Opera. The fact that the Minister of Education was only willing to allow him a one-year extension reflected the conductor's highly controversial image. For over a year the Philharmonic had been hopelessly divided, and Burghauser led the anti-Krauss faction. In early December Krauss travelled to Berlin, where Furtwängler had just resigned as Director of the State Opera there. While Krauss was in Berlin he had conversations with Goebbels and Goering.[29] Then the bombshell hit. The Viennese press picked up a dispatch from Berlin. It read:

> Minister President Goering has named the Director of the Vienna State Opera as Director of the recently vacated post of Director of the Berlin Opera.

The Viennese reacted characteristically. After having criticized Krauss for months, indeed for years, because of his 'vanity' and 'ambition', the critics now accused him of 'desertion', and said that it was Krauss who had engineered Furtwängler's resignation. Krauss, the Viennese, was making not an artistic, but a political decision. He was throwing his lot in with the Nazis and turning his back on his homeland. To make matters worse, there seemed to be no obvious successor for him in Vienna. No one expected Furtwängler to emigrate. Walter was not available. The post was finally given to Felix Weingartner, then aged seventy-one, who had had a long-standing relationship with the Philharmonic.[30] His new general administrator was Erwin Kerber, who now held concurrently the two most important posts in the Austrian musical bureaucracy.

Krauss compounded the damage he had caused by taking along to Berlin several of his top stars, including his own wife, Viorica Ursuleac, tenor Franz Volker and baritone Karl Hammes. He had effectively fragmented the Vienna ensemble which he had forged during the past five years. This was perhaps his most destructive legacy. The entire affair left a collective bad taste in Vienna, and Krauss would never regain his popularity there.

These events in turn affected the Salzburg Festival, although, since it was early December, the directors had ample time to develop a modified programme for 1935. *Rosenkavalier* would be the only Strauss opera performed that year; Weingartner, Erich Kleiber, Sir Adrian Boult and Josef Krips would be asked to complement Walter and Toscanini.

Nazi attitudes towards Salzburg, though fundamentally hostile, went through various stages between 1935 and 1938, reflecting the see-saw relationship between the two countries. For example, after the July *putsch* the German press was ordered to go softly on Austria, to report all cultural events, and to avoid undue provocation.[31]

The *Völkische Beobachter*'s summary report on Salzburg illustrates the new tactic. The critic 'M.M.' knew Salzburg, its history and development. To be sure he found much which annoyed him in the 1934 Festival: the lack of local Salzburg productions, the tendency to play the same popular works year after year, a reluctance to feature such prominent German composers as Bach, Liszt and Bruckner and the perpetual discomfort of the Festival Hall. And there was never a mention of Walter's or Reinhardt's presence. Yet most of these inadequacies had been mentioned in earlier years by other reviewers. The only bow to Nazi ideology was the conclusion: once a 'German peace' returned, then Salzburg would evolve into a truly German Festival.[32]

By 1935 the tone had changed. The *Stuttgarter N.S. Kurier* wrote of the 'jüdische *Faust*', and said that 'Goldmann-Reinhardt' was all technique and no soul. It mocked the 'young women' who attended a performance they did not understand, and lit up cigarettes at its conclusion. If anyone wanted to experience a true German 'people's theatre' he need only come to Germany. In Austria, the theatre was 'foreign' to the people (*Volk*).[33] The *Beobachter* too, had ceased to be on its best behaviour. In a hostile review of Kerber's *Ewiges Theater*, a book published in Munich in 1935 which included short essays from Salzburg's major luminaries, the Nazi organ could only opine that it was 'unbelievable' that a German publishing house could produce a book in which three of the seven essays were written by Jews (Walter, von Hofmannsthal, Reinhardt).[34] On the whole Nazi reviews of the Festival were rare between 1935 and 1937; the Ministry of Propaganda chose to ignore rather than to provoke.

This is known because the minutes of the 'Cultural Press Conferences' inaugurated by the Ministry of Propaganda in the summer of 1936 are available. In fact their title is misleading, for they were not press conferences, but weekly meetings in which a functionary of the Ministry told representatives of the German press exactly how they should treat all cultural events, from scholarly publications to music festivals. The system was created at the same time as the July 1936 Agreement between Germany and Austria which, on the surface at least, lessened the tensions between the two countries. The 1000-Mark tax on those travelling to Austria was lifted. Germany conceded Austrian independence, the German press was allowed to appear in Austria, and Austrian Nazis could wear Nazi insignias. Goebbels saw the agreement as a means for extending Nazi influence in Austria — nothing more. And he wrote in his diaries that one important area where he hoped this influence might be increased would be the Salzburg Festival.[35] But in the end the Agreement had little effect on Salzburg. German attendance remained sparse, and only two German artists, Werner Krauss and Wilhelm Furtwängler, were allowed to perform at the 1937 Festival.

At one of the 'Cultural Press Conferences' which took place in March, journalists were ordered to treat the Festival with the greatest 'reserve'. No reports of individual performances were to be allowed. A brief summary article must suffice. Toscanini's involvement must be played down as much as possible, since he was 'an enemy of the régime'.[36] One reason for this 'reserve' was the Nazi hope, never realized, that the July Agreement might lead to greater cultural liaison between the two countries. This was not to be. Negotiations on press, literary and musical exchanges dragged on throughout 1936 and 1937, but the Austrians were loath to allow outright Nazi propaganda material into the country, and the talks led nowhere.[37]

Nazi attitudes to the question of which German artists would be allowed to perform in Austria were inconsistent. Herbert von Karajan had received permission to conduct in a 'private capacity' in Salzburg during the 1934 Festival (though an Austrian citizen, he then lived, and conducted, in Germany).[38] Later, in October, when Paul Hindemith asked for permission to conduct in Vienna, his request was denied.[39] Even Furtwängler had to write endless letters and wait months before permission was granted for him to conduct at the Vienna State Opera later in the same year. When he finally did receive permission, he was warned against conducting operas staged by Jews, particularly by

Lothar Wallerstein or Dr Herbert Graf.[40] Within the Ministry of Propaganda itself there was some confusion as to the 'correct' attitude to take towards Austria. In one exchange, in late 1934, a functionary suggested that, since Franz von Papen was now the German representative in Vienna, and was trying to improve relations between the two nations, was it not time to change the policy of not allowing German performers to go to Salzburg? His superior rejected the proposal.[41]

Occasionally the Nazis granted exceptions to the rule. In his memoirs the actor Werner Krauss claims that, in 1937, he went personally to Goebbels and asked him if he might perform Mephisto in Salzburg. Goebbels seemed to think it a good idea, and gave immediate permission. The name of Reinhardt was not mentioned, though both knew that they were discussing the 'Jewish' *Faust*. Krauss did not ask questions, and went off to Salzburg, making his first appearance there since 1921.[42]

An interesting sidelight to this story concerns Nazi policy towards Vienna, where there was an outspoken National Socialist minority. The German government on occasion would allow its artists to perform in the Austrian capital. In 1935 Hans Knappertsbusch, though not a warm supporter of the régime, received permission to conduct three concerts in Vienna. Later the following year, the Ministry of Propaganda became embroiled in a dispute which involved a certain Leopold Reichwein, a friend of Goebbels, an ardent Nazi and the musical director of a private Viennese organisation called the Vienna Concert Society (*Wiener Konzerthaus Gesellschaft*). Every year Reichwein would conduct eight to ten concerts which were boycotted by Viennese Jews and others and supported primarily by Nazi enthusiasts. In mid-1935 the Concert Society asked Reichwein to limit the number of concerts he gave and suggested that he invite a German conductor to take over two or three of them in his place. He was not pleased about this idea, and turned down the Ministry of Propaganda's suggestions of Hans Knappertsbusch or Carl Schuricht, because they were both, according to Reichwein, tepid supports of the Third Reich. Later on that year, Karl Böhm wrote to the Ministry of Propaganda offering to conduct the Society's concerts. (Böhm, an Austrian from Graz, had lived and worked in Germany for the last decade; when Fritz Busch decided to emigrate, leaving the general directorship of music in Dresden open, Böhm had accepted the job). Böhm now assured the Ministry that he had

many supporters [in Vienna], especially National Socialists; I believe that

91

these concerts could be a great advantage in terms of propaganda for Germany.

After infinitely laboured and complicated negotiations, during which the Concert Society threatened to remove the stubborn Reichwein from his post, the German government agreed to allow Böhm to go. He gave the concerts in February of 1936.[43] Two years later, Karl Böhm stepped on the Salzburg podium for the first time. His association with the Festival would last for more than four decades.

Direct Nazi provocation against Salzburg, as distinct from critical newspaper coverage or the refusal to allow most German artists to perform there, was relatively rare during the period between 1935 and 1937. There were no more repetitions of German planes flying over and dropping leaflets or blaring propaganda from loudspeakers. Bomb attacks too almost ceased, though a small bomb did go off at Leopoldskron in 1937; Reinhardt, who was sitting in the park reading a book at the time, is said to have looked up, made a face, then returned to his reading.[44] The German representative in Vienna, Franz von Papen, did his best to improve relations between the two countries; he made a tour of Salzburg province in 1936, and attended the 1937 Festival. Though secretly trying to curry favour with Hitler — and to destroy Austrian independence — von Papen was superficially the soul of amiability. At a reception given at Salzburg that summer, he graciously allowed that Frau Bruno Walter might prefer to have another partner at her table. Meanwhile, he was doing his best to foster Nazi support in the province.[45]

A potentially devastating threat to Salzburg, which in fact never materialized, emerged from a conversation which occurred between an unnamed German journalist and the Austrian Consul in Cologne. The journalist said that he intended writing an article for the *Saturday Evening Post* which would appear in the spring of 1936 and would say that there was an active homosexual community in Salzburg, and that such people gathered at the Café Bazaar during the Festival with the expressed intent of seducing young foreign visitors. The purpose of this article, he frankly admitted, was to frighten Americans enough to prevent them coming to Salzburg. The Consul took the journalist's words seriously. He himself had been in Salzburg the previous summer and had heard of one or two incidents of this kind.[46] The government too was moved, and with Teutonic thoroughness asked for, and received, a voluminous report from the Salzburg police on all homosexual incidents, both in and out of the Festival period, during the past two years. The police promised to clean up Salzburg; the article never appeared.[47] But the Government reaction suggests its extreme sensitivity to any publicity that might have affected the vital American market.

In truth the Nazi offensive had now become more an irritant to the Festival authorities than a real threat; the extreme tension of 1933 and 1934 had lessened. Whatever Goebbels said or did, whatever the controlled press wrote, nothing seemed to stem the throngs of visitors from abroad who came to Salzburg to celebrate their heroes, Mozart, Reinhardt, Walter and Toscanini.

Once Toscanini had committed his talent and efforts to Salzburg, he transformed the Festival. Mozart and Reinhardt took second place; the maestro's word was law. The Festival directors squirmed and complained in private but there was no hope of preserving the original Salzburg 'idea' for it had been displaced by another: Salzburg as Toscanini's anti-Fascist and anti-Nazi showcase. But hidden behind that laudable symbol was another: Hollywood-on-the-Salzach (as one discontented critic put it), or Salzburg seen as the home of the stars and the snobs.[48]

Beginning with the 1935 Festival, Salzburg began to enjoy an embarrassment of riches. The major operatic and orchestral concerts were invariably sold out. In that and the following two years, Toscanini conducted over forty per cent of the time; only once did he play before empty seats, and even then ninety-eight per cent were full.[49] Overall attendance jumped from fifty-three per cent in 1934 to eighty-nine per cent in 1937. Festival-goers now streamed into Salzburg not only from Eastern and Western Europe, but from Japan, India and the Middle East. It was a sparkling crowd, overflowing with famous personages. Edward VIII came, incognito, in 1936, then appeared the following year as the Duke of Windsor; after diplomatic negotiations the Crown Prince of Italy attended the 1936 Festival, as did Admiral Horthy, the Hungarian Head of State;[50] President Roosevelt's son, John, and his mother, Sara, were fêted in 1937; then there were celebrities, like Marlene Dietrich, who caused a small scandal by dressing as a man in *Lederhosen*. The Salzburg newspapers resembled extended social columns, and described who ate with whom, the latest fashions and recreational habits of the famous. Once a columnist suggested, with no apparent irony, that a polo field should be created, so that the English would have something to do in their spare time besides visiting the Mirabell Casino which was only too happy to relieve them of their spare cash. Every night crowds of the locals would gather outside the Festival Hall to stare at the Rolls Royces and Packards as they unloaded their famous visitors.[51]

Erwin Kerber had many misgivings about the direction in which Salzburg was heading. He had dedicated his entire working life to keeping the Salzburg 'idea' alive; now Toscanini's authority was so great, that Kerber was at times reduced to the role of errand-boy. Although, as he once told his nephew, Tassilo Nekola (who after the War became General Secretary of the Festival), whatever he personally thought of Toscanini, he had made the Festival successful. The problem was that Toscanini would eventually leave. Could Salzburg survive his departure? Had it become too dependent on one man?[52]

The maestro did not spare Salzburg his well-known temper and stubbornness. In 1935 he would conduct *Fidelio* and *Falstaff* or nothing; the Festival directors, prodded by the government, caved in. The next summer, when Toscanini saw the set for the third act of *Falstaff*, he was horrified. He demanded that it be rebuilt immediately, and it was, at great expense. Equally expensive that year was his *Meistersinger* production, but the directors accepted Toscanini's designs. They nearly had a collective heart attack when he wrote saying that he would not come if he were not allowed to stay in the house he had occupied the previous year; the house had been sold meanwhile. Kerber was given the job of persuading the new owner to vacate the premises for the summer, which he did. Fear that Toscanini might fail to appear thoroughly alarmed the directors; the Ministry of Education became involved, and Bruno Walter travelled from Vienna to San Giovanni to plead with the maestro.[53] These were the major crises; although Toscanini had a fond relationship with the Vienna Philharmonic, here too there was never the certainty that rehearsals would go smoothly. Tenor Anton Dermota, hired by Kerber in 1935, recalls that, at one rehearsal, Toscanini had thrown down the piano score in mid-phrase and stormed out of the hall. The frazzled orchestra and singers had no idea what had irked him; when he finally returned, he said nothing, and continued as before.[54]

There was a lighter side, of course. Toscanini and Reinhardt were close friends, and the maestro was a constant guest at Leopoldskron. He also spent much time with Stefan Zweig and his circle, during the few visits the writer made to the Festival after 1934. Probably his closest friend and collaborator in Salzburg was Lotte Lehmann; Bruno Walter was a near second, for although they were of vastly different temperaments, both on and off the podium, they maintained a relationship of mutual admiration. But Toscanini's real love was Salzburg itself, and he was determined to dedicate his not inconsiderable energies to serving the Festival.

The Festival Hall had been a subject of contention since 1926. The seats had not become any softer over the years (though it was possible to hire seat cushions), the stage was still cramped and singularly inappropriate for grand operas such as *Tristan*, *Rosenkavalier* and *Meistersinger*. Backstage was a shambles; there was no advanced technical apparatus for scene changes, and the singers' dressing rooms were extremely small and uncomfortable. After the 1936 Festival, Toscanini decided that the time had come to reorganize the whole place along modern lines, and that he would lead the campaign. Lotte Lehmann also became involved, and at the beginning of 1937 she gave a series of charity concerts in the United States to help raise funds for the project. The government was slow to respond, but in March of 1937 agreed to pay half the costs (estimated at about 3,000,000 Schillings) if the city and province would pay a quarter between them, and Toscanini the remainder.[55]

Reinhardt now seemed to have become the Festival's elder statesman. Though he continued to direct *Faust* and *Jedermann*, his major activities were in the United States. The Warner Brothers' production of *A Midsummer Night's Dream*, featuring among others the teenaged Mickey Rooney as Puck, had its première in the autumn of 1935. Critics generally praised the film, though there was a distinct undercurrent in their writings which suggested that they appreciated the man, Reinhardt, more than his work. One discordant voice was Karl Kraus, Reinhardt's old enemy, now in the last year of his life. *Die Fackel* had not had a good word to say about the stage director for three decades. Kraus's last edition, in 1936, included a thirty-page tirade against Reinhardt and his film entitled 'The Great Humbug'. Kraus found Reinhardt's work anachronistic and superficial, full of style but without content.[56] He exaggerated as usual to make his point, but he was probably close to the truth, for Reinhardt did not seem to have a 'feel' for the new medium. He had gone far over budget and although it was a *succès d'estime*, there were no box-office receipts to match. Further plans in Hollywood fizzled out, and from 1935 to 1937 Reinhardt spent much of his energy (and other people's money) on the brilliant but ill-fated New York production of Franz Werfel's *The Eternal Road*. Despite good reviews and packed houses, the play lost a fortune, thanks to the huge production costs.[57] America now viewed Reinhardt as just another European refugee, not as the all-conquering European theatre director.

He still returned each year, however, for those few summer weeks in Leopoldskron where Toscanini was a constant visitor; although the conductor's German was non-existent, and Reinhardt's English halting, the two giants had an empathy beyond words.[58]

Critics of the time were unanimous on one point: Toscanini could do no wrong. His *Falstaff* of 1935, his *Meistersinger* of 1936, *Fidelio* and the orchestral concerts all received rave notices. Otto Strasser, who had the good fortune to play with Toscanini throughout these years, wrote that, despite the cramped stage, and the last-minute changes in cast, the *Meistersinger* of 1936 was perhaps his greatest musical experience.[59] Audiences, critics and even the orchestra were hypnotized by the fire and excitement of Toscanini's interpretations. Usually the maestro was known for his absolute and religious dedication to the written score, but in 1935 he relaxed his standards in *Fidelio* out of sympathy for Lotte Lehmann, whose voice was now incapable of reaching the high notes. He transposed her major arias down a half-tone, and no one seems to have minded.[60]

Walter was overshadowed, but remained faithful to the Mozart repertoire, where his interpretations were universally praised. He also conducted his beloved *Tristan* in 1935 and 1936 as well as *Orfeo ed Euridice* and two operas seldom heard, Carl Maria von Weber's *Euryanthe* and Hugo Wolf's *Der Corregidor*. That neither of these was successful with the public proved what was already known, that Festival audiences had little taste for the unusual. In 1936, after Weingartner's brief and unhappy interlude with the Vienna State Opera, Walter was chosen to replace him. He was delighted to occupy the post of his great teacher, Gustav Mahler.[61]

Early in 1935 Pierre Monteux was asked to come to Salzburg, but when he received an early copy of the Festival brochure he found that his name was in black print, not in the red reserved for Toscanini, Walter and the other conductors who had been engaged. Monteux threatened to cancel, but was finally persuaded to come when the definitive programme was published and he received what he felt was his due. Toscanini was not the only sensitive conductor.[62]

1936 was a great year, for as well as Monteux, Weingartner, Artur Rodzínski (a favourite of Toscanini's) and Erich Kleiber, there was the superb Straussian, Hans Knappertsbusch. In 1937 Wilhelm Furtwängler also came. With the exception of Weingartner, who shared the Mozart conducting assignments with Walter in 1935 and 1936, all were well received.

Furtwängler's performance of Beethoven's Ninth Symphony in 1937 has become legendary, not so much because of his interpretation, but for the 'interview' he had with Toscanini after the concert. Furtwängler had never conducted in Salzburg before. He was a proud and vain man, like Toscanini. Their meeting after the Ninth was private. There were no witnesses. Later it emerged that Toscanini had confronted Furtwängler with a choice: Bayreuth or Salzburg. According to Furtwängler, he told Toscanini that he preferred conducting 'neither at Bayreuth nor at Salzburg'. When informed of the incident, Goebbels found Toscanini's challenge an 'enormous insolence'. He could not tolerate the 'arrogance' of the *émigrés* and if Toscanini put pressure on Vienna to keep Furtwängler away from Salzburg, then he would allow no German artists to enter Austria.[63]

The enmity between Furtwängler and Toscanini continued until Furtwängler's death in 1954. Erich Leinsdorf recalls that Furtwängler asked him that summer, after a rehearsal of the Ninth, what Toscanini had had against him? Leinsdorf was only twenty-five at the time, and as a protégé of Toscanini, he could only answer in meaningless monosyllables. Only later did he realize that, as is human nature, the older man feared the younger — Furtwängler's reaction to the later rise of Herbert von Karajan was to be similar.[64]

Toscanini's last operatic première in Salzburg, *Die Zauberflöte*, was not the happiest occasion for him. The costs of the production made the Festival directors shudder, but they were becoming inured to this. The maestro's interpretation was a shock to many visitors who were used to Walter's contemplative and moving reading of the score. Toscanini chose to vary his tempi, and some of the opera's most sublime moments, like Sarastro's 'In diesen heiligen Hallen', went by in a flash. Erich Leinsdorf, who worked on the opera with Toscanini as *répétiteur*, admits that the performance was a 'disaster'.[65] At the time the critics were kinder. Such was Toscanini's mysterious and magical power over his listeners, that no reviewer ever seemed to voice any but the mildest of rebukes.[66]

Critics in general wrote less about Hitler's threat to Salzburg in the late Thirties than before; no crises of the magnitude of those in 1933 and 1934 threatened the Festival. Perhaps the excitement of the crowds and the banners lulled people into a false sense of security. The only overtly

97

political review of Salzburg between 1935 and 1937 came from the pen of Thomas Mann, who, like François Mauriac, saw Salzburg in a larger context. Mann wrote in 1935:

> It was delightful to witness the tremendous success of the Salzburg season — politically delightful, for the vexation over in Germany was enormous, and the *Völkischer Beobachter* asserted that the Austrian government chartered 300 automobiles and had them driven around with foreign licence plates. . . . everything smacking of happiness and prosperity immediately hurts Nazism. It has to be night when Hitler's star shines. . . . The best of all was the *Fidelio* under Toscanini and with Lotte Lehmann. People have a feeling for that opera now, we all agreed that it would be perfect as the festival opera for a certain day [the day that Hitler would be overthrown].[67]

What did bother the critics was Toscanini. All adored him, but many feared that his presence was bringing in large numbers of people who had loyalty only to their 'hero', not to Mozart or to the Salzburg 'idea'. Salzburg was also losing its intimacy now that the crowds were so huge. By 1937, most artists fled the city after their performances, so as to avoid being hounded for autographs at the Café Bazaar or the Hotel Europa.[68] Of course the musical 'snobs' had invaded Salzburg before, but never in such great numbers. They had always been scorned, though in truth the Festival would not have existed without them. They even had defenders, such as the French critic who claimed that it was indeed the 'snobs' who created evolution in art, for they were the innovators, and thus a 'precious auxiliary' to a Festival. Another Frenchman, a frequent visitor to Salzburg, Emile Vuillermoz, expressed the doubts of many when he wrote that the 'atmosphere' around Toscanini was ruining Salzburg, which was becoming the 'Hollywood of music'.[69] Prominent London critics also feared for the future. Toscanini had become so dominant, so irreplaceable, that his inevitable departure would kill the Festival. If Salzburg realized this before it was too late, and engaged artists and created programmes which would appeal to the coming generation, then and only then could the Festival be saved.[70]

These words were written in the last week of August 1937, at the end of the last of the 'golden years', though only a few sensed this. Bruno Walter was one. He met with his French friend, the writer Jacques Foschotte, at the Café Glockenspiel on the Mozartplatz. The conductor remarked that 'God only knows if this will be our last meeting in Salzburg. I may be wrong, but I hear everything falling apart, and no one dares to do anything; but there may still be time.'[71]

On 15 August 1937 Rehrl gave a vast reception for the Festival artists at the Residenz. The guest list suggests the awesome array of talent and dignitaries that Salzburg had gathered together. Reinhardt, the lone founder who remained, was flanked by Knappertsbusch, Walter, Toscanini and the actors and actresses whose careers he had made, such as Helene Thimig (now his wife), Werner Krauss, Paula Wessely, Edward Balser and Paul Hörbiger. Then the singers: Maria Reining, Lotte Lehmann, Alfred Jerger, Erich Kunz, Alexander Kipnis. The Archbishop of Salzburg was present as well as an array of ambassadors including Franz von Papen, Baron Franckenstein from London and representatives of many of the old Austrian families, the Schwarzen-bergs, the Windischgrätz and the Fürstenbergs. The Salzburg *Chronik* remarked that there was nowhere else in the world that such a gathering could take place:

> That this is possible in Salzburg is irrefutable evidence of what a powerful role our Festival plays.[72]

A few days later, Reinhardt, Toscanini and Walter met, away from the glare of the crowds, to discuss the rebuilding of the Festival Hall which was to be completed in time for 1938. Quick scene changes were to be made possible and both operatic and theatrical directors would be able to employ solid scenery. Toscanini presented ten tightly written pages detailing the problems and their remedies; he hoped that with a modernized stage and improved facilities, the forthcoming Festival would outshine all the previous ones.[73]

The Salzburg Festival of 1937 ended on the final day of August. On the last evening Walter conducted *Figaro* in Italian. Pinza, Mariano Stabile (who had made such a hit in *Falstaff*) and Esther Rethy starred; Wallerstein directed and Margherita Wallmann was the choreographer. The sets were by Alfred Roller, who had died two years before. In the Residenz, Bernhard Paumgartner conducted a Mozart serenade, a divertimento, an early symphony and a group of occasional orchestral pieces which he had reworked into a suite. Toscanini had conducted fifteen times in the past five weeks and he ended with *Die Zauberflöte*. As the evil Queen of the Night was crushed, as the sun shone on the last chorus of Herbert Graf's production, so ended Salzburg's most exciting and well-attended Festival in history.

Slowly the hotels began to empty and Salzburg returned to its quiet self. Plans for the next summer were well under way. Toscanini's duties were to be prodigious. He would conduct twelve operatic performances (*Tannhäuser*, *Zauberflöte*, *Meistersinger*, *Fidelio* and *Falstaff*) and two concerts. Walter was committed to *Figaro*, *Così fan tutte*, *Don Giovanni* and *Orfeo ed Euridice*, Knappertsbusch to *Rosenkavalier*.

What was not on the Festival plan for 1938 was a project that had become very dear to Reinhardt, a new production of *Die Fledermaus*; it would be his first staging of an opera in Salzburg. That summer he had mentioned this to Toscanini, who was unenthusiastic. The maestro was not sure that the opera was 'appropriate' for a Festival programme. Reinhardt thought that Toscanini could be convinced. After the Festival was over, he went to Vienna to sound out Kerber and Chancellor von Schuschnigg, who were both amenable. The only objection came from Walter, which worried Reinhardt, for the Director of the Vienna State Opera had great power. Reinhardt then sailed for America feeling depressed and hurt; the press had not mentioned him at all in their 1937 Festival reports.[74] Publicity counted in America, as did the appearance of success.

Upon his arrival in Hollywood, Reinhardt learned that his projects for future films had been turned down by Warner Brothers, who found them too costly to produce. In a letter to Gusti Adler, he vented his bitterness towards Hollywood. It seemed that his alienation increased his desire to return to the scene of past triumphs. Perhaps, he suggested, Salzburg might be interested in putting on *The Great World Theatre* again. The Archbishop would surely not object, and the work was appropriate given the difficult times that Europe was experiencing.[75] By December of 1937 Reinhardt learned that, because of Walter's objections, *Die Fledermaus* was impossible. He was furious, and wrote that he was sure that Walter had his own plans to bring a Viennese production of the work to Salzburg; his antagonism was a 'hostile provocation'. Then, uncharacteristically, Reinhardt launched into a long tirade against the 'weak' and 'intriguing' Walter. Toscanini himself had said that Walter was a 'weak artist, a weak man', whose renown was due not to his talent, but to the pity of those who had been revolted by Walter's treatment by the Nazis.[76] Reinhardt was not by nature addicted to self-pity, but now, in his mid-sixties, though his mind was always filled with ideas and projects, it was becoming increasingly difficult to realize these dreams. Financial resources were running thin, and Hollywood had turned its back on him. He even wrote to Mrs Sara Delano Roosevelt, whom he had entertained the previous July in Leopoldskron, and asked her support for a new project: he planned to give festival performances in the Yosemite Valley and the Pilgrimage Theatre in Los Angeles. People would flock to these performances, he said, as they had to the Olympics in ancient Greece. He concluded:

> Culture is shifting from east to west, and while Salzburg shimmers in a marvellous sunset glow, the sun is rising over the Pacific.[77]

The 'sunset glow' was turning to night, but the world of Salzburg ignored the portents as the ticket orders flooded in. By February of 1938 twice as much money was coming in for tickets as in the previous record year.[78] The day after these figures were reported, Chancellor Kurt von Schuschnigg met Hitler in Berchtesgaden. In New York Toscanini was preparing to give a concert to raise funds for the rebuilding of the Festival Hall. When he heard the news of the meeting, he rushed off a telegram to Salzburg.

> Because of the changed situation, must cancel my participation in the Festival.[79]

Rehrl's immediate response was to demand a clarification, and to assure the conductor that the situation 'had not changed' in Austria. Toscanini made no reply. Bruno Walter then sent him a telegram, urging him to reconsider, as did Lotte Lehmann. Walter had been assured by the Austrian authorities that press reports were 'greatly exaggerated' and that the Salzburg season would not be affected by the new situation. From San Francisco, Lehmann too thought that the press should not be believed, that the situation was too unclear to serve as a basis for action.[80] Toscanini wrote back to Walter that it was 'useless' for him to reply to Rehrl because his decision was 'definitive'. No compromise was possible.

The news hit the world, at least the cultural world, with as much force as had Toscanini's refusal to conduct at Bayreuth five years earlier. A headline from a French Egyptian newspaper told the story: 'Without Toscanini, Salzburg will no longer be Salzburg.' The rich who had made Salzburg unique, who went there to hear Toscanini (when they were not at cabarets or gambling for high stakes at the Mirabell Casino), would never come back. They needed a star. 'Art is condemned . . . by the rigours of politics.'[81]

Panic reigned in Salzburg. Rehrl met the Ministers of Finance and of Education on 25 February, and obtained their agreement to back all losses to the Festival caused by Toscanini's departure.[82] Rehrl knew that the situation was critical. Already the Austrian Foreign Minister, Guido Schmidt, had received a dispatch from his ambassador in the

Hague, describing the 'great consternation' felt by Festival lovers in Holland and Belgium; there was a real danger that many would not attend the forthcoming Festival.[83]

Franz Rehrl's last official act in support of an undertaking which had consumed so much of his energy over fourteen years was to write a letter to the new Minister of the Interior, Artur Seyss-Inquart, reminding him that the Salzburg Festival had become an 'Austrian event'. The Festival must take place in an atmosphere of 'peacefulness'. At the moment the foreign press was claiming that the Berchtesgaden meeting would create political unrest and violent demonstrations. Rehrl hoped that the Minister would reestablish order and security as quickly as possible, so as to ensure the success of the Festival.[84] Gabriel Puaux reported that, after von Schuschnigg had been forced by Hitler to admit Seyss-Inquart into his Cabinet, the Chancellor had remarked that there was no danger, since Seyss-Inquart liked Mozart.[85] He may well have liked Mozart, but, as the internal architect of Austria's demise, he obviously loved the Führer more. At the same time, Kerber in Vienna was throwing the dice to save the forthcoming Festival. He convinced Furtwängler to return to Salzburg, to conduct a series of operas and concerts. This news did not please Hitler. Furtwängler was immediately informed by the head of the General Chancellery, Fritz Wiedemann, that 'The Führer is against [your] participation in the Salzburg Festival.'[86]

On 11 March 1938 Nazi troops marched into Austria. Bruno Walter was out of the country; Kerber helped his daughter to escape.[87] Reinhardt was in California, Zweig in England. Toscanini was rehearsing the NBC Symphony Orchestra. When he heard the news, he exploded over some trifling offence, dismissed the musicians, locked himself in his dressing room and wept.[88] Annette Kolb, who herself fled Vienna, concluded her chronicle of the magical summers of 1935 to 1937 *Abschied von Österreich*, with the words:

> Should I describe more of the summer of 1937 . . . it is past, it is no more, everything is blown away, lost, finished.[89]

6

The Nazis Move In

1938–45

Salzburg fell to a bloodless Nazi *coup d'état* on the evening of 11 March 1938; it was a long day. In the morning Chancellor von Schuschnigg had spoken to the nation on the radio, prayed for God to spare Austria, and resigned. President Miklas, however, refused to appoint Seyss-Inquart to replace him, and there existed no central authority in the state. In Salzburg Governor Rehrl had kept close to events, and was prepared to call in the army for support, but he could get no direct answer from Vienna. In the late afternoon a Nazi demonstration broke out in front of the Residenzplatz. Exhausted, the Governor returned to his home for dinner. Then at 8.30 in the evening Anton Wintersteiger, a local Nazi leader, received word from his German masters that he should take action; half an hour later he walked into Rehrl's empty office and proclaimed himself provisional *Gauleiter*. At the same time local Nazis took over all the major city and provincial government buildings, the radio station, the newspaper offices and the local barracks. They met no resistance whatsoever.[1]

Early the next morning, German troops crossed over the frontier; only three Austrian soldiers manned the gates, and all raised their arms in the Hitler salute. Later, as the troops marched down the narrow and elegant shopping street of Salzburg, the Getreidegasse, they were met by rousing cheers and a proliferation of German flags. As if by magic the Fatherland Front had disappeared without a trace. Whether out of fear, opportunism or conviction — or a mixture of all three — Salzburgers welcomed the occupiers with enthusiasm. The next day Rehrl formally gave up his office. As the local leader of the Fatherland Front he could expect no quarter from the conquering Nazis, and he received none. He had dedicated sixteen years of his life to the province, had seen it grow and prosper under his leadership, through ingenuity and guile he had done more than any other man to save the Festival in the Twenties. He

103

had also been responsible for building the road to the Grossglockner (Austria's highest mountain) which had become a popular tourist attraction. Most of all, Rehrl, through his moderation, had managed to spare Salzburg from the bloodshed and political conflict that had raged throughout other areas of Austria. Now he was shunted aside. In May the Nazis arrested him; for the next seven years the former Governor, whose health began to fail, would spend part of the time in jail, the rest in internal exile. He was finally liberated from a Berlin prison in May 1945, a broken man.[2]

Once Austria was occupied by German troops, the Nazis installed the entire apparatus of National Socialism; propaganda, arrests, Jew-baiting, all worked like clockwork, since the process had been refined in Germany itself. Salzburg, the gateway to Austria (but no longer Austria's window to the world) was the first stopping point for Nazi leaders who now arrived from Germany. Heinrich Himmler paraded through the streets in late March; Hermann Goering followed on 2 April, and Adolf Hitler arrived two days later, welcomed by huge crowds and a sea of swastikas. April 10 was chosen as the day when Austrians would have a 'free choice' to vote for or against union with Germany. In Salzburg, 158,058 voted for the *Anschluss*, 463 voted against it (0.29% of the total).[3] The other provinces followed suit and voted their nation out of existence. The *Salzburger Zeitung* gushed that 'only a Beethoven, Germany and Austria's favourite son, would have been capable of expressing in music the joy that has been raging through Austria.'[4]

On 30 April Salzburg had the dubious honour of being the only city in Austria to witness a book-burning. Twelve hundred volumes were taken to the Residenzplatz and put to the flames. The authors so honoured included Stefan Zweig, Josef-August Lux, Arthur Schnitzler and Franz Werfel.

In May Friederich Rainer was named *Gauleiter*, replacing Winter-steiger, who became his deputy. Rainer was an excellent organizer, and within the next six months he completely reorganized the adminis-trative structure of the area. One of his first actions was to take a long hard look at the plans for the forthcoming Salzburg Festival.[5] Ticket cancellations were flooding in from abroad now that the streets resounded to the crash of jackboots and the shouts of 'Heil Hitler'. Problems abounded: there were casts to be re-hired, without emigrés; the breach left by the departure of Walter and Toscanini had to be filled; the Festival had to be made more 'German' and yet still remain international; plays to replace *Faust* and *Jedermann* had to be chosen at short notice, and payment had to be arranged.

The last issue caused great complications, for as there was no longer an Austrian state as such, it was now necessary to negotiate directly with the Ministry of Propaganda in Berlin. Most of the singers and actors were in Vienna, while the conductors were in Germany. All this, just when Austria was itself going through a period of total political reorganization, imposed extraordinary difficulties. Although Baron Puthon and Erwin Kerber still held their positions, real decision-making was now in the hands of Nazi functionaries in Salzburg, Vienna and Berlin. A key figure in this process was Kajetan Mühlmann, the State Secretary for Culture in Seyss-Inquart's Cabinet. Mühlmann had a long association with Salzburg, having been the chief public relations officer for the Festival between 1926 and 1932. After his departure from the post he had become an active Nazi, and had been selected to sit in on the 12 February interview between Hitler and von Schuschnigg in Berchtesgaden as a 'representative' of the Austrian Nazis. In Salzburg, Albert Reitter, a former lawyer, had been elevated to the post of Provincial Governor, though his powers were limited; he was now told to organize the 1938 Festival. He had only four months in which to do so.

There was little need to purge the Festival Society's personnel. Puthon was already a venerable character and was approaching his seventieth birthday; his role was reduced, though he retained his title. Kerber too was spared. His vast experience and musical reputation in Salzburg and Vienna protected him, though it was common knowledge that he was cool towards the Nazis.[6] None of the hated Jews and emigrés remained in Salzburg, so persecution took the form of renaming streets and squares, destroying pictures and busts . . . and in desecrating von Hofmannsthal's grave near Vienna. Only one Festival figure suffered more than symbolic punishment: Bernhard Paumgartner. Shortly after the *Anschluss* he was fired from his position as Director of the Mozarteum. The story is instructive, for it demonstrates how, in the atmosphere of a small town, the Nazi takeover could unleash all kinds of hates and personal jealousies.

In April 1938 the Chorus Director of the Mozarteum wrote a strongly worded letter to the German General Staff representative in Salzburg in which he defended Paumgartner, pointing out that the Director of the Mozarteum had been dismissed because of the attacks of petty and envious people who had floated vicious rumours that he was a Jew, which were patently false. The letter also said that Paumgartner himself was apolitical, although his son had been an 'illegal' SA member who had fought in Corinthia during the 1934 *Putsch*; his father-in-law, Peter Rosegger, had been a well-known writer on 'folkish themes'; Paumgartner had always wanted to conduct more Mozart in Salzburg; it had been the Jewish influence which had hindered him; he should be allowed to resume his job. Seventy party members signed this letter.[7]

In May the Secret Police issued a report on Paumgartner, no doubt inspired by the controversy which surrounded his firing. In this report he was pictured as a 'political charlatan' who had changed his party and his religion to meet prevailing fashion; he no doubt would have been fired earlier, if it had not been for his connections with Rehrl and other government officials. Moreover it was pointed out that he had had an affair with one of his students, and had shown her a nude picture of his wife; he had also consistently tried to dismiss Nazi sympathizers from the staff of the Mozarteum, and had almost ruined the institution through mismanagement. True, his son was a confirmed Nazi, but his father had disowned him. He should not be rehired, nor should his operas be performed.[8]

The next month Frau Paumgartner wrote a pathetic letter directly to Goebbels, begging the Minister to reinstate her husband. He was a 'pure Aryan', his son an avid Nazi, her own father an intellectual precursor of National Socialist ideology; the jealousy of a few Salzburgers had caused all the trouble.[9] The Minister did not bother to answer. Given the stark criticisms of the Secret Police report, it may seem surprising that Paumgartner escaped arrest, but his old friend and collaborator, Mühlmann, intervened and suggested an 'Austrian solution': a compromise which effectively swept what dirt there was under an inconspicuous rug. Paumgartner was given a small state subsidy and encouraged to carry out musical research in Florence, where he spent a peaceful war. When he later returned to Salzburg, his prestige and power were enhanced; his enemies had unwittingly done him a favour.

If there was no real purge in Salzburg, this was not the case in Vienna. The lynchpin of the Festival had always been the Philharmonic, some of whose most prominent members were Jewish. Within days of the Nazi occupation all Jewish artists in the orchestra had been dismissed or forced into retirement. The most prominent of these was Arnold Rosé, whose career with the orchestra stretched back to 1881; for over fifty years this violinist (who was Mahler's brother-in-law) had led a world-renowned quartet, which had performed many times in Salzburg. Rosé and certain of his colleagues were fortunate, for they eventually made their way out of the country to England; others ended their lives in concentration camps. Otto Strasser recalls how Kerber, who was given the distasteful task of dismissing friends with whom he had worked for decades, invited each one individually to his office to render his personal appreciation for his years of service to the orchestra.[10]

If Salzburg's history was being obliterated, if the names of streets were changed, if a bust of Goebbels replaced that of Rehrl, if Reinhardt's 'Faust City' was being dismantled, there still remained an enormous paradox for the Nazis: how could they at one and the same time destroy a tradition and also encourage it to continue? How was Salzburg to change and yet to remain the same? The bureaucrats at the Ministry of Propaganda did not pose the question in those terms. They claimed that they were replacing the 'decadent' with pure German art. In fact they were imitating that which they despised. Heinz Hilpert, Reinhardt's former assistant at the Deutsches Theater, had been encouraged to remain in Berlin by Reinhardt himself, and had become General Manager of the theatre under the Nazis.[11] Now he was commissioned to come to Salzburg to direct a production of Goethe's *Egmont* at the Riding School. 'Faust City' would be reconstructed and become 'Egmont City'. Erich Engel was asked to direct a production of *Amphitryon*, a minor play by Heinrich von Kleist, in the Cathedral square in Reinhardt's style. In the end the play was put on in the Festival Hall, since expenses were too great for an outdoor production.

By May there were signs of panic, since the final Festival programme had not been published, and the promised subsidy to reconvert the Festival Hall had not been received from Berlin. Almost half of the impressive pre-March ticket sales had been cancelled, mostly by Americans and English. The lack of coordination between Berlin, Vienna and Salzburg slowed down negotiations with artists and conductors. Reitter complained to Mühlmann that the 50,000 Reichsmarks that had been promised to shore up the Festival would not be enough; a huge deficit seemed probable, given the cancellations and the Festival's inability to publicize the unfinished programme.[12]

There was considerable confusion in Berlin about how the Salzburg Festival should be put over to the general public. Goering had consulted Kerber and Mühlmann in Vienna back in April, and had then announced that Salzburg 'would have its German character again'. He did not mention when Salzburg had lost its German flavour, because he could not; in Nazi terms the Festival had never had strong German characteristics. Goering went on to say that Germans, not Jews and emigrés, would create a new Festival. There would no longer be 'English and American ladies discussing lipsticks and powder during the prelude to *Meistersinger* who were only woken from their dreams of bathing and flirtation by the last chord of a symphony.' These ladies had gone to Salzburg 'not to hear music, but to buy clothes labelled "from Austria" '. The new Festival would be a festival of the 'German soul'.[13]

Goering might scorn the international public, the snobs who had given Salzburg its unique flavour, but the Ministry of Propaganda was not at all sure that Salzburg should now turn its back on such people. On the other hand, bringing in foreign visitors meant ceasing to discuss the 'German soul'. The Cultural Director of the Ministry of Propaganda, Rainer Schlösser, decided that it would finally be best just to stress the international character of the programme and the efficiency with which the Germans ran a festival. In a message to journalists at a Cultural Press Conference on 18 May 1938, Schlösser admitted that it had been difficult to turn a completely Jewish programme 'on its head', but he thought that there would probably be a large number of curious foreigners who would come to see how 'we', the Germans, ran such an affair. Reporters were told not to dwell on the past but on the future, and not to become involved in arguments with foreign reporters. This seems to have silenced the German press, because at several subsequent press conferences Schlösser requested greater coverage.[14]

At the beginning of July, almost an entire press conference was dedicated to the Festival. Schlösser reported that it was now certain that few foreigners would attend the Festival. Nevertheless the press should continue to stress Salzburg's international aspect. The Festival would not be 'purely German' although it would be a means for showing German art to the world. Foreigners had stayed away from Bayreuth in 1933, but they had returned in later years; the same was sure to happen with Salzburg. In the recent past Salzburg's standards had not been particularly high; there had been little rehearsal time, and with a few exceptions, operatic performers had been mediocre. Despite the lack of preparation 1938 would certainly attain the level of the previous year and would send an artistic, cultural and political message to the world. Journalists should in no case give the impression that the Reich was worried about slow ticket sales abroad. They should, however, continue to promote the international flavour.[15]

The final programme published in June was a back-handed tribute to what had gone before. The concert and operatic repertoire had little to do with the 'German soul' and was essentially unchanged from 1937, except that *Così fan tutte*, *Orfeo ed Euridice*, *Elektra* and *Zauberflöte* were dropped. Wilhelm Furtwängler was to replace Toscanini as conductor for *Meistersinger*, Vittorio Gui (who had conducted orchestral concerts at the 1933 and 1934 Festivals) was to take over *Falstaff*; Hans Knappertsbusch's new responsibilities included *Tannhäuser*, which had already been programmed before the *Anschluss*, *Figaro* and *Fidelio*. There were to be two new faces on the podium: Karl Böhm, the director of the Dresden State Opera, chosen to conduct *Rosenkavalier*, *Don Giovanni* and an orchestral concert, and the well-known Swiss pianist, Edwin Fischer, who was both to conduct and play in a Mozart–Haydn concert. Otherwise the programme included the usual serenades, the C minor Mass and various orchestral concerts featuring the works of Beethoven, Mozart, Brahms, Debussy, Ravel, Respighi, Weber, Schubert and Bruckner. This repertoire was squarely in the Salzburg tradition. Operatic casts had changed somewhat, and there were a few more singers from Berlin, but most of the major artists from 1937, including Ezio Pinza, Mariano Stabile, Alfred Jerger, Maria Reining, Esther Rethy and Elisabeth Rethberg, were back. Some of the singers making their Salzburg debut — Set Svanholm in *Tannhäuser*, Paul Schöffler as Don Pizarro in *Fidelio* and Maria Cebotari as the Countess Almaviva in *Figaro* — were eventually to have distinguished musical careers.

In terms of content and level of artists engaged, therefore, it could be argued that the Nazis had very little impact on the 1938 programme; they had denied the Salzburg tradition and then followed it. The theatre programme *did* change, but the way in which this was done was in itself an admission of Reinhardt's genius. It flattered by its very imitation even if, as the critics pointed out, the imitation lacked the spirit of the original. To be sure, the built-in excitement of Toscanini's presence was missing, but then many in pre-*Anschluss* Austria had worried that the maestro was becoming excessively dominant.

But if Salzburg was not a celebration of the German soul, if its programme and performers were almost identical to those of the previous years, it was, in the crassest terms possible, a propaganda tool for the Nazi régime. The city was festooned with swastikas. To replace the foreign visitors, Goebbels had brought in thousands of Germans, who visited Salzburg as part of their 'strength through joy' summer vacations; they were often workers of modest means, and they received cheap tickets, subsidized by the Ministry of Propaganda. In a sense these middle- and working-class Festival-goers brought Salzburg closer to its original 'ideal' than ever before. In reality many of these people had little interest in music or opera. They were mere tools in the hands of the Ministry of Propaganda who could now brag about Salzburg's contribution to the 'Volk.' To the limited number of foreign correspondents who visited the 'pure Aryan' Festival, these crowds were tantamount to a perversion of the Salzburg idea. Many remarked on audiences who drank beer, wore peasant clothes, talked during the performances and seemed to know little about what they were hearing.[16] The only 'international' aspect of Salzburg was the large number of Italians present, which reflected the 'pact of steel' between Mussolini and Hitler.

Hitler himself had been invited to attend by the Vice Chancellor of the Ostmark, Edmond Glaise von Horstenau, who hoped that the Führer's presence would show that he had forgiven Austrians their sins. Hitler had said that he might come, but did not wish to attend the opening or receive any publicity.[17] No doubt the Czech crisis kept him away. Instead Goebbels, as patron of the Festival, was present at the opening, a performance of *Meistersinger*; later he sat in the Café Bazaar, with Rudolph Hess and other SS dignitaries, at the very tables which had once been occupied by Moissi and Walter.

It is not easy to describe the quality of the 1938 Festival, since most Western critics were so overwhelmed by the new atmosphere that their reviews of concerts or operas were often cursory. Willi Schuh, the musical scholar, found it wanting in most areas; the Nazis had proclaimed a 'new era' but had repeated old operas and performed new plays which were, unconsciously, inferior tributes to the absent Reinhardt; the 'Ayran' directors had only copied their predecessors; operatic productions were little changed from 1937 save for *Meistersinger* and that lacked distinction, though Svanholm and Rethberg sang gloriously; Gui's *Falstaff* was no match for Toscanini's despite the similarity of the cast. Schuh's most serious complaint, however, concerned the nature of the Festival itself: it lacked joy. 'Unfortunately even the beauty of the streets and the architecture has been drowned in a sea of swastikas of every size.'[18] The Nazis had brought nothing to Salzburg, excepting a celebration of themselves, and a rebuilt Festival Hall by Bruno von Arendt which had its Führer *loge* and reminded many of a cinema. Salzburg had become the background for the Nazi's own form of theatre, which had served to destroy Salzburg's ineffable atmosphere. The French composer George Auric also felt the change. Salzburg could continue to produce excellent programmes, but the true Mozart, whom Bruno Walter had 'rediscovered', was lost. The only feeling left was a 'poignant melancholy which. . . penetrates the hearts of "free men".'[19] A critic from the American *Saturday Review of Literature* noted that, though the Nazis could not insert propaganda into Verdi or Mozart, they did 'modernize' *Egmont* to their own ends. The play deals with the revolt of the Dutch against the Spanish Count of Alba. Werner Krauss, who played the Count, was wearing make-up which left no doubt as to the modern day 'dictator' he was portraying — von Schuschnigg.[20]

A few critics praised the 'new' Salzburg. The reviewer from the *Journal des Débats* found that Salzburg had returned to its earlier 'simplicity'; for him the charm of the city increased in direct proportion to the decrease in tourists. Nevertheless he too was put off by the ever-present swastikas, which reminded him of an earlier excursion to Bayreuth.[21] Madame Peyrebere continued to write as if nothing had happened. Since her main goal of gaining entry for Debussy and Ravel into the Salzburg programme had been satisfied, she had no words of criticism for the Nazis. To her the change of régime merely served as an illustration of the 'eternal value' of French art, which was appreciated by all, whatever their political allegiance.[22]

When the accounts were settled, the Festival, which had cost 900,000 Reichsmarks to produce, had a gaping deficit of almost half a million. Most of this was covered by the Ministry of Propaganda, which had already spent more than 300,000 RM to bring in holiday-makers, members of the Hitler Youth, women's organizations and adherents of various political associations. Other direct subsidies (including a small amount from the city) evened accounts. The Nazis were paying dearly for 'their' Festival.[23]

At the end of September 1938 journalists at a Cultural Press Conference were told that they should no longer mention Salzburg; personnel changes were taking place; once these had been accomplished, they would be informed.[24] The *Gauleiter*, Friederich Rainer, was now made Director and told to choose the Artistic Council and prepare the 1939 programme.[25] In truth his power was limited; he depended on Kerber's advice from Vienna, and the ultimate decisions were made by Schlösser and Goebbels. Furtwängler actually discussed the 1939 programme with Hitler. The original proposals put forward suggested that seven operas be performed, one of which would be a new production of *Zauberflöte* staged by Gustav Gründgens and conducted by Herbert von Karajan.[26] To please the Italians, it was thought that *Il Barbiere di Siviglia* and *Falstaff* might supplement a programme of *Rosenkavalier*, *Don Giovanni* and Weber's *Der Freischütz*. Negotiations continued into January. Rainer and Kerber wanted to bring back Clemens Krauss and add *Fidelio*. In the end *Zauberflöte* was dropped, Furtwängler did not appear and Krauss, now Director of the Bavarian State Opera in Munich, returned for the first time in five years. The theatrical programme, which was originally projected to include plays by Shakespeare, Molière, Raimund and Goldoni, ended up with only two, *Much Ado About Nothing* and the *Le Bourgeois Gentilhomme*, both directed by Hilpert.[27]

The Nazis were much less interested in selling Salzburg to the outside world than they had been the year before. The German press was instructed to put Salzburg on the same level as festivals in Munich, Düsseldorf, Frankfurt and Heidelberg. The focal point of interest had shifted to Bayreuth. The Minister of Education's suggestion that a conference of German scientists be held during the last ten days of the Festival, to include lectures, exhibitions and propaganda material — whose goal was to bring foreign intellectuals to Salzburg — came to nothing.[28]

The 1939 Festival was overshadowed by growing international tension over Poland. Primarily a German event, although a scattering of Italians was present, its major surprise was the arrival of Hitler, who came to hear *Don Giovanni* on 9 August and returned on the 14th for *Die Entführung aus dem Serail*. The local press was enraptured by the Führer's presence and that of his entourage: Friederich Rainer, Martin Bormann and Albert Speer. During the interval Hitler left his box, and appeared above the alcove of the Festival Hall, where he was greeted by cheers and Nazi salutes. After the performance, the singers gathered beneath his *loge*, and were handed a laurel wreath covered by a swastika and a personal note of appreciation from the Führer. Then he left for Obersalzburg (presumably to work on his plans for war), through streets packed with his cheering followers.[29]

Two days later it was suddenly announced that the September programme had been altered so that the Vienna Philharmonic could give *Meistersinger* in Nuremburg during the Nazi party rally. But before August was out, people had begun to drift away as rumours of war increased. Otto Strasser's landlady woke him on 1 September with the news that shooting had begun; he took the first train back to Vienna to get his ration card.[30]

Several hundred miles away, in the Swiss town of Lucerne, another festival was taking place with Arturo Toscanini, his son-in-law Vladimir Horowitz, Bruno Walter, Alexander Kipnis, Fritz Busch and Sir Adrian Boult. Jacques Foschotte and his old friend (and now *émigré*) Paul Stefan spent the last days of August listening to concerts conducted by this formidable group of Salzburg alumni, reminiscing about the Salzburg that they knew and loved, and gossiping about absent friends like Stefan Zweig. Hearing Toscanini's last concert, on 20 August, had left almost a palpable taste of Salzburg in their mouths. For here was yet another imposing demonstration that artistic freedom was not dead. That festival ended on 29 August.[31] Soon however, Europeans were no longer listening to the strains of Verdi, Beethoven or Mozart, but to the martial airs of war.

The outbreak of war ended all plans for the 1940 Festival. It was thanks to the initiative of the Vienna Philharmonic that the tradition was kept alive at all. In the early summer, the orchestra took upon itself the responsibility of performing a series of concerts; continuity would be preserved, even if no operas could be staged. The orchestra dug into its own private funds as a 'guarantee', then signed contracts with Böhm, Knappertsbusch and Franz Léhar. The latter's music was alien to the Salzburg 'idea', but the orchestra hoped that his popularity would help sell seats in Salzburg. They need not have worried. Every concert was sold out, and Furtwängler appeared in a 'special performance' which included symphonies by Beethoven and Brahms, as well as 'Siegfrieds Tod' from *Götterdämmerung*.[32]

With most of Europe subject to the 'New Order' in 1941, Goebbels decided to relaunch the Festival, though on a smaller scale. His purpose was part of a larger strategy: he wished to boost morale by putting on as many cultural events as possible.[33] Though the Minister of Propaganda made an appearance during the 1941 Festival, he made no claims as to its 'international' character. Most of the audience, and this was true of the subsequent war years, were soldiers on leave and munitions workers. None of the Nazi notables attended after 1941. They presumably had other matters on their minds.

The 1941 Festival lasted only three and a half weeks and presented four operas: *Rosenkavalier*, *Don Giovanni*, *Figaro* and *Zauberflöte*. Though Salzburg was very much overshadowed by Bayreuth, standards evidently remained high, because Karl Böhm and Hans Knappertsbusch had collected an excellent group of young singers who were eventually to have sparkling careers. Reviews of the wartime

Festivals are inevitably suspect, given that a critic would be foolhardy to attack an 'official' Nazi event. It appears, however, that *Zauberflöte* was the high point of 1941. It was directed by Heinz Arnold from the Dresden State Opera, and produced specifically for Salzburg, in itself an unusual event.[34] The cast included Ludwig Weber, Alfred Poell and Maria Reining. Goebbels was present at its first performance, together with his wife. The Minister remarked in his diaries that the atmosphere was very different from 1939: some of the audience were made up of war wounded. He could not help being envious of 'peaceful' Salzburg, so far from the theatre of war. Yet he suspected that Salzburgers would probably feel better about themselves if in fact they had to experience the war at first hand.[35]

After 1941, with Germany at war in the east, the 'island of tranquillity' that was Salzburg became more precarious. Nazi interest in the Festival declined, and the German press was now instructed to restrict its coverage: reviews should only be published after the Festival was over, and journalists should stress that it was primarily for deserving munitions workers, the wounded and soldiers on leave. Since travel conditions were difficult, it made little sense to publicize an event which ordinary citizens could not hope to attend. In 1943 the Ministry of Propaganda even took the name 'Festival' away from Salzburg. It was now called the Salzburg Summer of Music and Theatre.[36]

Three men kept traditions and standards going during these difficult years: Krauss, Böhm and Fischer; each in his way maintained the old ideals and so enabled the Festival to return to greatness after the war. Fischer's contribution was less important than that of the other two. In 1942 and 1943 he presented a series of concerts with his own chamber ensembles and acted as director of the Salzburg Summer Academy at the Mozarteum. The Summer Academy tradition went back to 1929; now Fischer revived it and brought in such artists as Anna Bahr Mildenburg (Hermann Bahr's widow), the pianist Elly Ney and the violinist Vasa Prihoda. Young artists from all over occupied Europe came, in great numbers.[37]

Krauss's role was vital. At the end of 1941, Goebbels, at a meeting in Munich, had decided to make him the Artistic Director and *Intendant* of the Festival, the first time in history that one man had been given both artistic and administrative control in Salzburg. Goebbels hoped that Krauss would change the practice of simply bringing in Viennese productions and would encourage Salzburg to develop 'its own style', especially with regard to Mozart and possibly Gluck, despite the added

e founding fathers: (from top left to bottom right) Max Reinhardt, Hugo von fmannsthal, Richard Strauss and Franz Schalk.

The first performance of *Jedermann* in the Domplatz in 1920.

Alexander Moissi as Everyman, being stalked by Death (Armand Zäpfel), 1928.

Max Pallenberg as Argan (on right, reclining), with Raoul Lange as Dr Purgon and Hansi Niese as Toinette, in Molière's *Le Malade imaginaire,* Schloss Leopoldskron, 1923.

Max Reinhardt (on left) with Lady Diana Manners and Duff Cooper in the park of Schloss Leopoldskron in the early Twenties.

Clemens Holzmeister's 'Faust City' in the Riding School 1933.

Werner Krauss in 1937, when he was given permission by Hitler to come to Salzburg to play Mephisto in *Faust*.

runo Walter (on left), Thomas Mann and Arturo Toscanini at the Festival in 1935.

he opening of the 1938 Festival: a scene from the third Act of *Die Meistersinger*.

Clemens Krauss, who dominated the Festival during the war years.

Karl Böhm, whose accomplished career at Salzburg spanned forty-three years.

Hitler at the Festival in 1939, attending a performance of *Die Entführung aus dem Serа*

lisabeth Schwarzkopf as the countess in *Figaro*, 1952.

ilhelm Furtwängler, the undisputed
aestro of the postwar Festival until his
ath in 1954.

Herbert von Karajan at Salzburg in 1957:
the return of the exile.

The new Festival Hall, opened in 1960.

Von Karajan rehearsing *Der Rosenkavalier* for the 1983 Festival.

costs that this would entail. Certainly Krauss's career had been a rocky one. His personality and undisguised ambition produced strong reactions; one either loved him or hated him. He had left Vienna under a cloud in 1934 and had managed to alienate the Berliners as well; finally in 1936 he had found a happy home as Director of the Munich Opera, but he remained unsatisfied. Krauss had written a personal letter to Hitler after the *Anschluss* asking to be appointed head of the Vienna State Opera which, according to him, had become mediocre.[38] His wish had not been granted; though he had friends in high places, he also had enemies. In 1940 it had been decided to convert the Mozarteum into a national musical institute with Krauss as director.[39] Though he scarcely appeared at the new institute, he now had a foothold in Salzburg. Then the summons came from Goebbels; at the same time, Erwin Kerber, the inspiration behind a decade of Festivals, was replaced by a Nazi functionary. He left Vienna a broken man, his long career at an end. Though his name (and that of Puthon) remained on the Salzburg prospectus, his only role was as director of the local theatre. He died in February 1943.[40]

Krauss completely dominated the Festivals of 1942–4, and converted them into showcases for the works of his close friend and collaborator Richard Strauss. *Gauleiter* Rainer made sumptuous rooms ready for the *Intendant* in Schloss Leopoldskron, now reserved as lodging for visiting potentates.[41] He engaged the best artists available to stage Strauss and Mozart operas. In 1942 Walter Felsenstein came from Berlin and Stefan Hlawa from Vienna to put on a new production of *Figaro* which boasted a cast including Hans Hotter, Erich Kunz, and Gustav Neidlinger, an imposing group of singers. Felsenstein is today recognized as one of the geniuses of operatic stage production; his *Figaro* came alive as he stressed the drama of the individual characters against the 'fantastic' sets provided by Hlawa.[42] Krauss also engaged Rudolph Hartmann, with whom he collaborated in Munich, to stage Strauss's *Arabella*, with Ursuleac in the title role. Strauss, Mengelberg and the Swiss Ernest Ansermet conducted the orchestral concerts.

The following year Krauss produced and directed a new production of *Zauberflöte* for Salzburg. This was the first Festival performance which saw the conductor also take the responsibility for staging an opera. It was an unusual production, in that the roles of Papageno and Papagena were played by actors, Paul Hörbiger (Paula Wessely's husband) and Gusti Huber. Krauss wished to stress the ' *buffo* ' quality of Papageno and Papagena, and to perform the opera in the spirit of its first Papageno, the distinctly unvocal Schikaneder. It is difficult to discover from the reviews of the time (which were hardly objective) whether this approach worked or not. In any case, it has never been repeated.

The assassination attempt on Hitler on 20 July 1944 coincided with Goebbels' decision to close down all festivals in the Reich in order to concentrate on total war. Three operas had been planned for Salzburg: *Così*, *Zauberflöte* and the world première of Strauss's *Die Liebe der Danae*. Though the Nazis were now antipathetic to the ageing composer and had refused to recognize his eightieth birthday with any celebration,[43] Krauss wanted to honour his friend, and had promised him that he would lead the first performance. *Danae* had been completed in 1940, but never performed, due to the extreme difficulty of staging a work nearly as complex as *Die Frau ohne Schatten*. Rehearsals had begun, but, because of allied bombings, the production was in trouble. Sets had been destroyed and travel was perilous. Then came Goebbels' specific order cancelling the Festival. *Gauleiter* Gustav Scheel appealed to the Ministry of Propaganda, and asked that at least this important first performance be allowed. After some discussion, the Ministry permitted the general dress rehearsal to take place, as well as a concert by the Berlin Philharmonic with Furtwängler (the first time the Berliners had ever come to Salzburg). On 14 August, Furtwängler conducted a performance of Bruckner's Eighth Symphony, a work very much in keeping with the mood of the time.[44] Two days later Hartmann and Krauss presented *Danae*. At one of the last rehearsals Strauss quietly told the orchestra, after hearing his beloved music from the third act, 'I hope we will see each other again in a better world.' At the performance itself, Strauss, in tears, received a standing ovation and was called back many times. He made no speech.[45] A young soldier from Graz found himself in Salzburg that day; his name was Albert Moser. A friend told him that he had an extra ticket for *Danae* that evening, and they attended this 'downgraded' première together.[46] Moser is today President of the Salzburg Festival.

Karl Böhm restricted himself to several orchestral concerts during 1942, then in January 1943 he was named Director of the Vienna State Opera. He immediately engaged Oscar Fritz Schuh and Caspar Neher, both Germans, to direct his operatic productions. Therein was born a collaboration which outlasted the war, and enabled the Vienna State Opera to maintain the highest standards. He also nurtured a new generation of singers, including Anton Dermota, Irmgard Seefried,

Wilma Lipp, Walter Berry, Erich Kunz and Hilde Güden among others, who would delight audiences for the next two decades. Neither the destruction of war nor the privations of the first years of peace would diminish the accomplishments of this extraordinary concentration of talent which Vienna produced, Salzburg exposed, and the world enjoyed.[47] It may seem extraordinary that, in a period of crisis, Vienna was able to develop this exquisite combination of ensemble singing, creative stage production and orchestral excellence. Perhaps the crisis itself was responsible. With their world circumscribed by war, it had been impossible for singers to gain international reputations; they had had to sing and work together. However ambitious they had been, they could go no further than the stage of the Vienna Opera; incapable of being seduced by an international career, the demands of which might have served only as constraints, they had been left to hibernate under the undisputed talents of Böhm, Neher and Schuh which had allowed them time to develop and mature their talents.

While Böhm kept Austrian musical talent alive in Vienna, Salzburg remained quiet. People hoped that its beauty would spare it from the fury of the approaching armies, but as the Soviets raced across Europe from the east and the Americans pushed in from the south and west, Salzburg became an important communications pivot. The Allies feared that Hitler might retire to his Alpine redoubt in a final defensive gesture. Between October 1944 and April 1945 about six thousand bombs landed on Salzburg destroying Mozart's house and most of the Cathedral. On 4 May 1945 the United States Army entered the undefended city.

7

Renewal

1945–9

When American soldiers entered Salzburg in May 1945 they came officially as 'liberators' of a nation that had been Hitler's first conquest; this was in consequence of the policy outlined in the Allies' Moscow Declaration of 1943. The reality was rather different. National Socialism had had deep roots in Austria, even before the *Anschluss*, and the extraordinary majority obtained by the Nazis in the plebiscite only underlined this fact. Furthermore, Austrian resistance had been moderate: most opponents of the régime had fled, been imprisoned or remained silent.

The Allies did not turn a blind eye to Austria's Nazi past, but they were willing to accept the fiction of her liberation. Active Nazis were to be subject to punishment and political purges were ordered, but the country was not required to pay reparations nor was it treated as a defeated enemy. Instead every effort was made to help Austria economically in order that she might build a democratic future.

However the Americans were not the only ones occupying Austria. The French, British and Soviet troops each had a section of the country, and all four were present as occupying powers in Vienna, which now became the city of turmoil and intrigue so dramatically depicted in Graham Greene's *The Third Man*. Medicine, food and lodging were at a premium, long-distance travel was almost impossible; the Allies had to recreate a state which had not existed as an independent unit for seven years.

There was no common Allied cultural policy and no subject which caused more disagreements during the immediate post-war period. Soviet commanders ordered cinemas and theatres to reopen so as to boost civilian morale while Supreme Headquarters Allied Forces in Europe (SHAEF) prohibited musical performances until a full reconnaissance had been made of all facilities and personnel; it was hoped that eventually non-Nazi-inspired works would be allowed to be performed, but the Soviet example forced their hand.[1]

On 1 May, within a week of their entrance into Vienna, the Soviets allowed Clemens Krauss to conduct the Vienna Philharmonic; a few weeks later the head of the American Information Service Branch arrived in Salzburg to discuss the possibility of putting on a limited Festival in three months' time. The citizens proposed that Baron Puthon and Joseph Messner be made responsible, but the Americans chose an Austrian-born member of the occupying forces, Otto von Pasetti.

Von Pasetti had a complicated past. After a youth spent in Austria and Italy, he had drifted to the United States in the early Thirties, where he had launched himself in various careers, including that of a tenor; none of these worked out. Then, like many another Austrian opposed to Hitler, he had joined the American army. He had entered Austria in 1945 and had been posted to Vienna to deal with communication problems, but his background and flair for languages had made him a natural choice for the Salzburg post. He had never attended the pre-war Festival, but he was strongly committed to reviving Austrian culture and was determined to make his presence felt and to create a success.

The American occupiers had definite ideas as to the nature of the post-war Festival: as one high-ranking diplomat suggested, it was to be a means of getting the Austrians to work on 'their cultural salvation as a proof that liberation means something more than stagnation'.[2] It was initially hoped that Toscanini and Walter would be able to come; when they were not available, efforts were made to entice Jascha Heifitz and Yehudi Menuhin, but this again turned out not to be possible.[3] Von Pasetti realized that reviving Austrian morale and self-esteem through Austrian artists untainted with the brush of Nazism was going to be difficult. He once wrote that he might have to seek out musicians in the wilds of the Salzkammergut, since in Salzburg itself most potential performers had belonged to the National Socialist Party.

Von Pasetti was under great pressure to succeed, not only from his superiors but from the people of Salzburg themselves. He also believed that the Americans must 'compete' with the Russians, who had already opened up Viennese cultural life. The revival of the Festival would have a symbolic meaning for Austrians and Americans alike, for had it not been the American love affair with Salzburg which had made the old Festival such an extraordinary event?[4]

Puthon now proposed that Knappertsbusch and Böhm be asked to conduct. Von Pasetti flatly refused, on the grounds that the former was a German, the latter a 'good Nazi'.[5] But in truth von Pasetti's choices were limited. Given the generally chaotic state of communications, it was impossible to check on everyone. There was no organized 'denazification' programme in operation. The forthcoming Festival had therefore to be a makeshift affair, based on the availability of artists. Close scrutiny of their past history was out of the question. The sole opera that the Festival authorities could mount was *Die Entführung*, as these were the only sets available in Salzburg. The principal singers engaged — Maria Cebotari, Julius Patzak and Ludwig Weber — had all performed at Salzburg during the Nazi occupation. The Americans made all travel arrangements for the performers. In one case, the Czech conductor Felix Prohoska was literally smuggled into Salzburg in the back of a lorry by a friendly British officer, since travel between Allied zones of occupation was forbidden.

The opening of the Festival, on 12 August 1945, signalled an important step forward in Austro-American relations. For the first time artists, administrators and local dignitaries mingled with the Americans over drinks;[6] up to that point there had been an official 'non-fraterniz-ation' order. The audience at this inaugural concert, conducted by Prohoska, was almost entirely made up of US Army personnel from the Second Corps, which occupied Salzburg. A few British, French and Russian officers were also present. Baron Puthon and General Mark Clark made welcoming speeches; then Esther Rethy sang an operatic excerpt from Léhar (she was another veteran of the Nazi Festival) and the Mozarteum orchestra played two works by Johann Strauss and a Mozart serenade. The following three weeks saw a production of *Die Entführung*, von Hofmannsthal's *Der Tor und der Tod*, several evenings of *Lieder*, orchestral concerts, the first Salzburg appearance of the Vienna Boys' Choir and two church concerts conducted by Messner. Two-thirds of the seats went to the armed forces, one third to Austrians. It was very definitely a khaki Festival. Even the *Stars and Stripes*, the US Army newspaper, admitted that many of the soldiers were somewhat out of their element. 'Some [at an orchestral concert], perhaps associating "festival" with a merrier type of entertainment, looked a little bored.'[7]

The importance of the 1945 Festival is that it took place at all. Three months after the fall of Austria, in a Salzburg bursting with refugees and bristling with American troops, where food and shelter were at a premium, the city had managed to clear up most of the bomb wreckage and mount a semblance of a Festival. The slow and agonizing process of reconstruction was beginning. The non-fraternization order had been abandoned and Americans now enjoyed an easy familiarity with the people of Salzburg. In the United States three of the Festival performances were broadcast across the nation. Continuity had been preserved.[8]

The course of the history of Austrian denazification is linked very closely with the progressive cooling of relations between the Soviet Union and the United States. Between 1945 and 1947 denazification was a major preoccupation; after that it became of secondary importance, as the Americans focused their energies on strengthening the general Austrian antipathy towards the Russians; the Cold War had begun.

In the autumn of 1945, as the administrative structure of the occupying powers became formalized, the United States began to develop a coherent cultural policy. This policy had three themes: denazification, the development — on every level — of Austrian cultural life in the occupied zone, and thirdly, the introduction of American artists, theatre and music into the mainstream of Austrian life, so as to publicize American values and cement good relations between the two countries.

Accomplishing these goals simultaneously proved to be virtually impossible. The issues were unclear: it was one thing to judge a Keitel, a Streicher or a Goering; it was another to make a firm judgement on the role of a singer, a musician or an actor. For example, Paula Wessely had been discovered by Max Reinhardt (like many Austrian and German actors and actresses) and had never publicly or privately disavowed her debt to him. However, after the German occupation in March 1938, she had urged her fellow citizens to vote for the *Anschluss*. She had continued her acting career throughout the war, and had appeared in a film, made in Italy, which had been of an obviously propagandistic nature. She was also Vienna's most popular and beloved actress. Another case, that of Herbert von Karajan, bedeviled the authorities throughout this period. It was clear that he had been a Nazi Party member, but after his marriage in 1942 to a woman who was one-quarter Jewish, he had fallen out of favour, and his conducting opportunities had been sharply curtailed. Thus he had neither been lionized nor severely persecuted. Clemens Krauss was known to have helped Jews leave Austria in 1938, but he had also been considered Hitler's favourite conductor, and had had close relations with the Nazi hierarchy. He had made many enemies in the past decade, and now this

121

came back to haunt him. Wilhelm Furtwängler's case was the most complex. He had made the point that 'where Beethoven is played, freedom exists' and had claimed that the artist is beyond politics. This was a man who won the eternal respect and love of his Jewish secretary and Jewish members of the Berlin Philharmonic, whom he had protected, and who had noisily resigned from the Berlin State Opera and the Berlin Philharmonic when his artistic freedom had been endangered. Goebbels found him sometimes 'intolerable' but adored his conducting, and appreciated Furtwängler's willingness to perform throughout Germany and occupied countries during the war. Furtwängler was an extremely proud (and vain) man, and would never admit that he had made an error. To the Austrians he was something of a hero: the Vienna Philharmonic still viewed him as their wartime protector.[9]

Two other artists with close Salzburg ties, Karl Böhm and Werner Krauss, were in a somewhat less ambiguous position. Böhm had written compromising statements, Krauss had appeared in the most famous of Nazi anti-Semitic films, *Jud Süss*, and had never hidden his Nazi sympathies.[10] But perhaps performing in films, conducting, singing or acting on the stage were normal functions of artists, and were rather more innocent pastimes than sending people to concentration camps or conspiring to wage war. All these stars — and others — had their defenders, some of whom came even from the ranks of Austrians who had suffered at the hands of Nazi occupiers. One was Egon Hilbert, a survivor of Dachau, who would shortly come to dominate the Austrian cultural scene.

The Americans for their part could never settle on a consistent denazification policy. At first they and their Russian, British and French allies directed the process, developing a 'point' system which led to the creation of Black, Grey and White lists. Sanctions against an artist would increase in relation to that artist's point count: if he or she had been a Party member, that was worth three points; belonging to an affiliated organization earned one; membership of the SS earned five, of the Gestapo eight. If an artist accumulated eight points, that meant banishment for life; fewer than three points allowed him or her to perform freely. Between the two extremes was the Grey list; artists in this category might be subject to banishment for a limited period.[11] All artists were forced to fill out a questionnaire specifying the organizations to which they had belonged. Looking back from the safe perch of hindsight, one sees that these questionnaires were not unlike those that the Nazis passed out to many of these same artists in 1938 to insure that they were Aryans and politically reliable.

The American authorities soon became aware that the point system was absurd. How could one possibly assess 'guilt' based on a swing of one point to another. There was a second fundamental problem, too, and this provoked much debate. Should one punish well-known artists, whose visibility had made them particularly vulnerable, more than lesser figures who, even if they had collaborated, were not famous and therefore had contributed little propaganda support to the régime? Yet, if the stars had given more aid to the enemy, was this not because they were the generators of cultural excellence? If they were banned, would not the artistic dynamism that the Americans wished to establish in Austria be damaged? Furthermore, with the possible exception of Clemens Krauss, all of these performers were highly popular. Banning them only served to anger the public, and turn it against the occupiers.

The American theatre officer in Vienna, Henry Alter, like von Pasetti an Austrian emigré, saw these contradictions. In November 1945 he reported that, by the present criteria for denazification, ninety per cent of Austrian artists would be denied the right to perform.

> European artists have always considered it their privilege to be honoured and flattered by the existing governments without giving them true allegiance and without . . . ever acquiring a political conscience.

Alter agreed that the present generation had collaborated with the Nazis through vanity, government pressure and a lack of political awareness, but unless the authorities wanted to deny art to the people, they would have to revise the denazification measures, which were 'limping along' and often being implemented on the basis of 'intangible' evidence. To be sure, if an artist had bought a requisitioned home or denounced others, he should be disqualified. Otherwise he should not be persecuted. Even now, concluded Alter, the policy was being pursued in a highly inconsistent manner in Vienna. 'Popular' artists were being allowed to perform on an exceptional basis, while lesser ones were banned.[12]

Clearly the denazification programme was unpopular and unworkable, especially now that Austria was in the process of recreating its own democratic institutions. In the autumn of 1945 the Allies decided that the Austrians, not the occupiers, should control the process. The Allies would retain ultimate right of veto, that was all. The Austrian government therefore created a special commission to considered denazification in the cultural realm under Felix Hurdes, Minister of Education.

Once the Commission was formed, the whole tenor of the denazification process changed. Much of this was due to Egon Hilbert, who as
the head of the *Bundestheaterverwaltung* (State Theatre Administration)
played a vital role in the new body, and quickly emerged as the most
dynamic character on the Viennese cultural scene. His background did
not predispose him to such a role. Hilbert had been a minor official in
the Austrian mission to Prague in the Thirties; then he had spent five
years in Dachau, where he became a leader among the prisoners and a
privileged inmate. Once liberated, he dedicated all his pent-up energies
to re-establishing Austrian cultural life. As head of the State Theatre
Administration, he was the chief officer for all state-sponsored cultural
affairs, and he was immediately made a member of the Directorium, the
small body which ran the Salzburg Festival. If Hilbert harboured
bitterness for his wartime treatment, he kept it to himself. His was a
single-minded campaign to bring Viennese theatre, music and opera
back to pre-war levels, which of course had important ramifications for
Salzburg. He wanted the best, and, as a member of the Hurdes
Commission, campaigned privately and publicly to clear practically
every artist who came before him. The single exception was Werner
Krauss. While Americans, Russians, French and British (who had the
final say on Commission recommendations) continually squabbled
about who should and should not be cleared, Hilbert kept up the
pressure. He was a small man with a high-pitched voice, a workaholic
who often held important meetings into the small hours of the early
morning (like Max Reinhardt), long after the end of the evening
performance at the Burgtheater or the Theater an der Wien. Hilbert
ruffled the feathers of his superiors, irritated everyone, but in the end
was respected. Von Pasetti especially distrusted him, found him
unstable and remarked that there must have been something tarnished
in Hilbert's Dachau experience, because he even 'had the key to the
armoury' there.[13] But Hilbert's greatest distinction was, perhaps, that
years later he became one of the few men who ever managed to dominate
another Austrian of equally determined temperament, Herbert von
Karajan.

Probably the best-publicized scandal of the denazification years
occurred during the preparations for the 1946 Salzburg Festival.
Hilbert and Paumgartner (who had returned from Switzerland that
spring) now took on the major administrative duties, and planned to
invite von Karajan to conduct no less than ten times, a predominance
which would have rivalled that of Toscanini in 1937. In March 1946 the

Hurdes Commission cleared von Karajan after Alter had interviewed him, and had elicited further details regarding his relations with the Nazis.[14] Von Karajan maintained that, while conducting a performance of *Meistersinger* in Hitler's presence in 1940, Bockelmann, who sang the principal role, had been noticeably drunk. Hitler had not been amused and had refused to attend any more of the conductor's performances. From then on his activities had been restricted. Alter urged von Karajan's reinstatement.[15] Once cleared, the conductor began painstaking rehearsals of *Don Giovanni*, *Figaro* and *Rosenkavalier* in Vienna. But in May, the Russian representative on the Inter-Allied Commission began to have doubts. So did von Pasetti; an early supporter of von Karajan, he now changed his mind. He thought that the former Nazi had altogether too much power in Salzburg; Josef Krips, the anti-Nazi, who had suffered during the war (and now conducted most Vienna Philharmonic concerts), had far fewer performances scheduled for the 1946 Festival than von Karajan. Even in June, when it seemed likely that von Karajan would be banned, he was still doing all the preparatory work for the operas, auditioning singers, working with the chorus, rehearsing the orchestra. In addition to this, von Pasetti was concerned that Ernest Ansermet and Edwin Fischer, who were also scheduled to appear, had voluntarily conducted in Salzburg (and elsewhere) during the German occupation, although they were both Swiss.[16]

Despite Puthon's strong support for von Karajan (he threatened to cancel the Festival if the conductor was not allowed to perform) it was the Americans who made the final decision, and when in mid-June, at the demand of the Russians, von Karajan was officially banned for another six months, there was no question, on the American side, of cancellation.[17] The Festival would go ahead and rely on other conductors. But the long and tortured negotiations that had preceded the ban came to a bizarre end. Indeed von Karajan did not conduct at the 1946 Festival. But, up to the very last moment he continued to add finishing touches. The new Theatre and Music Officer in Salzburg, Ernst Lothar, who had replaced von Pasetti in June, wrote a strong letter to Baron Puthon at the beginning of August demanding that von Karajan cease his activities. But even this did not work, though the conductor stayed out of the limelight.[18]

There is no need to follow the stories of Furtwängler, Schwarzkopf, Böhm, Clemens Krauss and the others in such detail. By the end of 1947, all were given clearance. Even Werner Krauss was eventually given permission to perform again. Von Karajan was finally allowed to perform in Austria in the summer of 1947. By then, thanks to Walter Legge and his new Philharmonia Orchestra, von Karajan was already an international figure. Though he took no part in the 1947 Festival, the way now seemed clear for him to resume his activities in Salzburg.

Denazification was also a burning issue with regard to the Vienna Philharmonic, for the orchestra was the jewel in the crown of Austria, and here too complications arose as to the players' pasts. About forty of the orchestra's members had joined the Nazi Party, and the concert master, Wilhelm Jerger, had been politically active. But the Vienna Philharmonic, more than any individual, was at the absolute centre of the Austrian cultural tradition. If a quarter of its members were banned because of their (often formal) membership of the Party, who would replace them? Would the quality of the orchestra be damaged? The occupying powers wrestled with this problem in 1946 and 1947, and then more or less gave up. In the end, only thirteen members were forced to retire, and some of these rejoined the orchestra later. Oddly, the Russians were at first more forthcoming than the other occupying powers. Shortly after the liberation they told Krips that, given the importance of the orchestra in the Austrian cultural scene, it should remain intact, despite the presence of former Nazis. The Allied Denazification Bureau, after long and heated debates, agreed, with the exception of the thirteen who were retired. They could not bear to break up what the British representative called 'Austria's greatest cultural asset'.[19]

Thus, after two years the denazification programme, full of false starts, contradictions, misinformation, disinformation and special pleading, came to an end. The Americans had been much less thorough in Austria than they had been in Germany. Once the decision had been made, in late 1945, to allow Austrians to take the lead, the Americans were relatively powerless to influence events. For Austrians such as Hilbert had little taste for dishing out punishment, especially to artists. They were far more interested in recreating a vibrant cultural life. In essence, despite a number of inconsistencies along the way, the occupying powers came to agree with this point of view.

In the city of Salzburg itself, on the political level, the Americans did not grant the local people power over the denazification process until 1947. Two reports made in 1948 suggest that the Americans were right to do this, for the people of Salzburg seemed loath to punish their fellow citizens, the courts were allowing proceedings to drag on, and people were covering up for their friends; many former Nazis were drifting back into city and provincial administration; many officials were 'openly opposing' all denazification activities.[20] A series of polls run by the Gallup organization that year suggested that, of all the major cities in Austria, Salzburg was the least inclined to punish former Nazis. Twice as many people in Salzburg (nineteen per cent) than in Vienna or Linz thought that the 'Jews were worth less as a race than the Aryans'. A third question related to people's perceptions of Jews. Half of the Salzburgers interviewed (thirty-eight per cent in Vienna, which had had a large Jewish population) agreed with the statement that 'The Nazis went too far, but something had to be done to keep them [the Jews] in their place.' One out of four people in Salzburg (versus half of the Viennese) believed that *all* Nazi measures taken against the Jews were wrong. Generally half of all Austrians (here Salzburg had similar percentages to Vienna and Linz) thought Nazism 'a good idea, which in practice worked out badly'.[21] It is not surprising that the Americans were sceptical about Salzburg's commitment to denazification. But what is surprising is that, in the final analysis, the Americans did little to countermand Salzburg laxity. But then by 1948 the Cold War had begun, Poland and Czechoslovakia had fallen into the Soviet camp and the city of Berlin was being blockaded by the Russians.

Otto von Pasetti left his Salzburg post in June 1946 and was replaced by Ernst Lothar, who had been trained as a lawyer in Vienna, but had made his reputation as a novelist and manager of Reinhardt's Theater an der Josefstadt in the mid-Thirties. His great-uncle was the famous Austrian critic Eduard Hanslick, Wagner's *bête noire*, so his Viennese connections and his administrative background were excellent. Lothar had escaped from Austria at the time of the *Anschluss*, had become an American citizen, and returned with the US Forces as an officer. The American authorities in Vienna saw him as 'one of the most able Austrians of American origin', and wanted him placed 'where he can do the most good'.[22] Lothar recounted that, when taking the train from Vienna to Salzburg for the first time since the day he left Austria, he felt a gnawing sense of fear and anxiety. But as the train pulled into Salzburg, as the mountains, castles and towers came into view, he felt a great sense of relief. Then he heard the church bells which 'rang away the hate of the banners we had seen as we fled Vienna in 1938'.[23]

The serenity of the Salzburg scene which seduced Lothar was misleading. He had stepped into a highly charged and difficult situation. Von Karajan's banishment had just been announced, Walter was not available and rumour suggested that Toscanini had no intention of stepping in at the last moment to replace the 'Nazi' conductor, so Krips and Prohoska were engaged instead.[24] In his memoirs Lothar claims that he first allowed, then disallowed, von Karajan's behind-the-scenes participation in the Festival.[25] Von Pasetti, meanwhile, had stayed on in Salzburg until the end of August; in a series of reports he continued to discuss the von Karajan affair. He, like Lothar (and many others who have dealt with the maestro), was in two minds. On the one hand, von Karajan's guile ran roughshod over the whole spirit of denazification. On the other, it was he alone who had taken almost total artistic responsibility for the three operas — *Don Giovanni, Rosenkavalier* and *Figaro* — that were being performed. Paumgartner had been away from Salzburg for most of the spring. Puthon dealt only in administrative matters, and Hilbert's attentions were drawn to Vienna. Von Pasetti was full of admiration for von Karajan's contribution — but furious that the conductor could make such a sham of denazification policy. Von Pasetti was also unhappy that Furtwängler, whom he had earlier interviewed in Switzerland, and whom he admired, was not allowed to perform. In his view, the German conductor was far less compromised than von Karajan.[26]

In spite of the last-minute changes and the behind-the-scenes controversy over von Karajan's role, the 1946 Festival was a creditable effort, though well below the standards of 1937. Major administrative decisions were still made by the Americans, who made all travel arrangements for the performers. Some had to be smuggled across the border from Germany, since it was technically illegal for a German to change zones. The practice developed of 'arresting' German performers in Freilassing, then bringing them over to Salzburg for 'observation'.[27] After the Festival was over, they would be returned to their homeland. Occupation forces, as in 1945, filled the majority of the seats. Lothar appreciated the American troops, whose 'naïvety' charmed him; their enthusiasm was nonetheless real despite their lack of musical education.[28] The remaining seats went to Austrians and a sprinkling of French, Italians, Russians and Swiss who had to make do in a city where it was nearly impossible to find a free room. Many stayed in villages outside Salzburg. There were strong evocations of the past. Heinz Hilpert revived *Jedermann* in the original Reinhardt production, and also staged another Reinhardt (and Salzburg) classic, Goldoni's *The Servant of Two Masters*. Lothar Wallerstein was scheduled to return to produce *Figaro*, but was unable to come. Schuh replaced him. General

Clark and Chancellor Figl were present for *Der Rosenkavalier*, and the atmosphere was much more festive than in the previous year, with excellent casts including Hans Hotter, Maud Caunitz, Ludwig Weber, Ljuba Welitsch, Anton Dermota, Hilda Güden and Karl Dönch. Soprano Irmgard Seefried made her Salzburg début in *Figaro*.

For the Americans, the 1946 Festival had achieved its goals, Reinhardt's legacy had been highlighted, and despite the impossibility of drawing an international audience, a number of non-Austrians had performed. The Festival directors, especially Puthon, had not been enthusiastic about inviting outside artists, but they had been overruled. Grace Moore sang a *Lieder* recital, and Yehudi Menuhin, Charles Munch (an *émigré* but an American citizen) and Sir John Barbirolli performed in orchestral concerts. Forty-six performances were given and eighty-five thousand tickets sold, some for as much as 900 Schillings, twenty-five times their face value, and greater than a local citizen's average monthly wage.[29] Yes, Salzburg was returning to normal.

Though Oscar Fritz Schuh had been given a last-minute opportunity to direct *Don Giovanni* in the 1946 Festival, he had been unimpressed with the direction the Festival was taking. For him the Festival had been 'without meaning'. All it seemed to have done was to tell outsiders 'we are still here; we exist.'[30] It looked backward, not forward. Others too were beginning to question aspects of the Festival. In a country where cupboards were bare, where religious fervour had been undermined by seven years of Nazi rule, the pious invocations of *Jedermann* seemed somewhat archaic. Many critics, especially Salzburg critics, began to question whether *Jedermann* was relevant.[31] And yet *Jedermann* was the sole remaining link with Reinhardt and von Hofmannsthal, those almost mythical figures who had formulated the Salzburg 'idea' in the first place. Did their old ideas, their old concepts have any relevance in post-1945 Europe? Could Salzburg still aspire to be the home of the 'good Europeans' after all that had taken place? Indeed did the term itself retain any meaning in the post-war world?

While such ideas were being discussed and debated, the new personalities on the Salzburg scene — Schuh, Neher, Gottfried von Einem and Hilbert — gradually hammered out a more modern framework for the Festival with a positive forward-looking orientation. The veterans Paumgartner and Puthon showed surprising openness to the new suggestions, and were far less conservative than many local critics who could have been their grandchildren.

For the next twenty-five years Schuh collaborated closely, directing both plays and operas. Even after he ended his formal association with the Festival in 1970, he continued to direct Salzburg street theatre and the festival in Hellbrunn until shortly before his death in 1984. He described his plans for Salzburg in a short volume which appeared in 1951, entitled *Salzburger Dramaturgie*. In this he explained that the old world, the pre-1945 world, was dead: it could not be resurrected. But a new creative phoenix might arise out of the chaos. In the particular context of Salzburg, this meant three things to Schuh: the development of a critical awareness of contemporary music and opera which would reflect the spirit of the times; secondly, a determination to create opera exclusively for Salzburg, avoiding dependence on Viennese productions. The Riding School was unique; it resembled no other stage, anywhere. As Reinhardt had used the 'city as a stage' for *Jedermann* and *The Great World Theatre*, so the creative *régisseur* would use the Riding School for opera production. And thirdly, Salzburg must rededicate itself to creating a true Mozart 'style'. Schuh and Neher (who as a young man had worked with Bertolt Brecht and at the Kroll Theater in Berlin) had laboured for years to develop Mozart productions which fully integrated the drama and the music, but whose clarity would allow the audience to get to the heart of Mozart's genius.[32] Here Schuh was harking back to the old Salzburg ideal, but one that had only on occasion been realized.

His good friend, Gottfried von Einem, had not yet reached his thirtieth birthday, but in some ways he had had a lifetime of experience. Von Einem, though an Austrian, had spent most of the previous decade in Berlin, where he had studied composition with Boris Blacher. He came from a family of diplomats, and his mother had been on close personal terms with Goering. As a result von Einem had been able to observe many of the top Nazi officials at first hand, both before and during the war. In 1942 he had been sent to Bayreuth to act as a *répétiteur*. Later he had been arrested for his anti-Nazi beliefs — which subsequently stood him in good stead with the occupying powers. Von Einem's first major operatic composition, *Dantons Tod (Danton's Death)*, was entered on the 1947 Salzburg programme, with the blessing of Paumgartner and Puthon. Neher and Schuh were engaged to design the costumes and sets and to direct the production. This was the first time that a contemporary opera was to have its première in Salzburg. With the exception of Strauss's works, only one other modern opera had ever been performed before, Paumgartner's *Die Höhle von Salamanca*, in 1928, and this by a guest company, the Leningrad Opera Studio. But the originality of the event went beyond the fact that it was the opera's world première. *Dantons Tod*, based on Georg Büchner's early nineteenth-century play, deals with revolution, and more specifically, with how the revolution 'eats its children'.[33] It shows how the loftiest of intentions can lead to horror and destruction, how a group of rational individuals can become a bloodthirsty mob. As such the opera spoke directly to a generation in Austria, and throughout Europe, who had witnessed a revolution which had destroyed what idealism it contained at the moment of its realization. *Dantons Tod* was played out against a background of stark realism and few stage props, with Paul Schöffler in the title role. The opera had a powerful effect on audiences then, and it has been performed over a thousand times since. It not only propelled its young author into the forefront of contemporary Austrian composers, but also led to his being chosen as a member of the Directorium of the festival. For the next four years he would be the *de facto* artistic director of Salzburg, and he would use that position to propagate his consuming interest in contemporary music. His influence is still felt.

Egon Hilbert was the administrator, not the creator. He put together casts, arranged financing for operatic productions, engaged artists, all at whirlwind speed. Though he was more of a worker than a writer, he did jot down his views on the new Festival in 1947. His goal was neither to deny Austria's cultural tradition nor to wallow in it. The Festival must be the synthesis of old and new, of tradition and progress. Salzburg must take risks, must encourage new composers and new artists who would become the standard-bearers of the future. This was her new mission.[34]

Paumgartner had been closely involved with the Festival since its inception. He had not always been happy with Salzburg's direction, especially during the Thirties, but he made his complaints public only long after the war, in 1965, when he wrote that year's introduction to the Festival's official almanach. For him, the true golden age of Salzburg had been between 1921 and 1934. This age, he wrote,

> was succeeded by a period of unrest and turmoil just before World War II that witnessed, in the opinion of many, deviations from the Festival's true line in favour of somewhat hastily improvised mediocrity, such as the inclusion of Wagner in the programmes (due largely to the personal ambitions of certain individuals) and the transplanting of routine repertoire productions from Vienna to Salzburg.[35]

For him the creative period began and ended with Reinhardt, especially the productions of *Jedermann* and *The Great World Theatre* which created a Salzburg style consistent with the version of the founders. Paumgartner was at once a great musical scholar and a mediocre composer. As such he welcomed the idea of a new post-war beginning, and was fully aware that the world around Salzburg was not static. New festivals were being instigated elsewhere; film, radio, records, modern production techniques and the development of all forms of mass communication were forcing Salzburg to examine its past and prepare for the future. The coming generation must be part of the process, must reinterpret the past in its own way.[36]

Ernst Lothar, during his two years as Theatre and Music Officer, gave effective backing to von Einem, Hilbert, Schuh and Paumgartner. He perceived the necessity for Salzburg 'to avoid a rigid adherence to conservative programmes which would lead to a routine contrary to the very idea of a festival, which must be the unique'. He too was sceptical about *Jedermann's* lasting powers and in the summer of 1947 approached Carl Zuckmayer about writing a new play to replace it.[37] Lothar's real powers were less than von Pasetti's. Austrians ran the Festival; it was the American role to facilitate, not direct. But given Lothar's connections, and his considerable background as a critic, writer and administrator, his influence was far from negligible. As an Austrian he still harboured a love for his country and, by 1948, he had decided to renounce his American citizenship and continue his career in the Viennese theatre. But his debt to America was great, and his main activity during these years was to bring American theatre to Austria. A number of American plays were performed in Salzburg (and Vienna) under his aegis. He had more limited success in convincing the directors to engage American artists — and play American compositions — at the Festival. In fact most of the artists who performed in the 1947 and 1948 Festivals (Otto Klemperer, Charles Munch and Artur Rodziński, among others) were naturalized Americans rooted in the European tradition. Lothar tried very hard to convince Bruno Walter to return. Walter promised that he would come back to Salzburg, but at a later date.[38]

Lothar also tried. and failed, to convince Richard Strauss to allow the world première of *Danae* for the 1947 Festival. Strauss would only agree if Clemens Krauss was allowed to conduct, and this was out of the question.[39] The 1947 Festival was a marked improvement on that of the previous year. Helene Thimig now took over the production of *Jedermann*, as Hilpert was forced aside. She brought in Attila Hörbiger for the title role and Ernst Deutsch to play Death. Krips conducted *Così* and shared the assignment for *Figaro* with Otto Klemperer. Klemperer had agreed to conduct *Dantons Tod*, but illness forced him to cancel his performance. The young Hungarian brought in to replace him, Ferenc Fricsay, made a sensational début. It would be fair to say that his eventual meteoric rise was thanks to his Salzburg appearance in 1947. In place of *Danae*, Böhm and Günther Rennert collaborated on *Arabella*. The most conspicuous 'return' was that of Furtwängler, who was engaged for two orchestral concerts, one with Yehudi Menuhin as soloist. Von Karajan had still not been cleared by the denazification tribunals, although he had been invited to Switzerland to conduct. He took no part in Salzburg.

The 1947 Festival brought together singers who would enrich the Salzburg scene for more than a decade. Elisabeth Schwarzkopf had been banned in 1946 after having been accused of making misleading statements about her past on three separate questionnaires, but, assisted by the advantages of her extraordinary popularity in Vienna, and the general inclination to allow most artists to resume their activities, she was cleared in 1947. She now made her Salzburg début as Susanna in *Figaro*. Sena Jurinac sang Dorabella in *Così* and the Swiss soprano, Lisa Della Casa, performed the trouser role of Zdenka in *Arabella*. She would later make the title role her own. Festival attendance was slightly down from 1946: fifty per cent of the audience was Austrian, a combined twelve per cent were British, French, Swiss, Italian, Hungarian, Yugoslav or Russian, and thirty-eight per cent (again mostly soldiers) were American. The ambitious programme brought a corresponding increase in the deficit, which at 400,000 Schillings was thrice that of 1946. It was covered by subsidies from the city, province and federal governments.[40]

Von Einem's entry into the Directorium in the autumn of 1947 had an immediate effect on future programme planning. The composer was determined to seek out contemporary operas and have them performed in Salzburg. He also wanted to augment the number of modern orchestral and chamber works. He realized that these innovations would not receive immediate public approval, but hoped that, through repetition and exposure, the basically conservative Salzburg audience would eventually come to accept, and even appreciate, the modern.[41] Such ideals were not shared by his close 'acquaintance' Herbert von Karajan, who did not agree with von Einem's championship of modern music, and opposed the staging of *Dantons Tod* in Salzburg. The conductor was not concerned about consistent guidelines for the Festival. To him, the Salzburg repertoire should reflect the availability of the best singers and conductors. Almost any opera could be a success with an ideal cast. To von Einem, this was heresy. Von Karajan seemed to want to introduce an 'international star parade' to Salzburg, to trot out old war horses with the sole purpose of satisfying the public.[42] There was more here than a debate over Salzburg's 'mission'. Von Einem had become a close field of Furtwängler, who, for whatever reasons, loathed von Karajan. Yet both conductors wished to play a major role in Salzburg's future. Von Karajan, through his contact with Walter Legge at EMI, was gaining increasing international prestige with the New Philharmonia Orchestra. During the next years his involvement — or non-involvement — with the Festival was to be a subject of endless gossip. He had already informed Paumgartner in 1946 that, if he did work in Salzburg, he planned not only to conduct but to have a 'certain influence' over Salzburg's artistic direction.[43] To von Karajan, a 'certain influence' meant domination, and he could not achieve it as long as Furtwängler and von Einem were in a position to obstruct him.

The 1948 Festival profited from an unstated 'truce' between the two proud and arrogant conductors. Lothar had left his post to become director of the Theater an der Josefstadt; his replacement, an American writer called Edward Hogan, exerted minimal influence.[44] As Salzburg was now an entirely Austrian affair, Puthon had full responsibility for keeping the peace between Furtwängler and von Karajan. The latter had wanted to direct, as well as conduct *Orfeo ed Euridice* at the Riding School (the first time an opera had been presented there), but finally allowed Schuh and Neher to work with him. The three also collaborated on *Figaro*. Furtwängler conducted *Fidelio*, and Fricsay returned for another modern opera, Frank Martin's *Der Zaubertrank*. Gradually post-war shabbiness gave way to elegance, and the growing international public seemed to enjoy the mixed classical and modern repertoire.[45]

In general the critics praised the von Karajan–Furtwängler tandem, though Martin's work was less well received. Some called it '*Trauertrank*'(a 'sad drink', rather than a 'magic drink'). Thanks to von Einem's influence, works by Alban Berg, Schoenberg and Stravinsky were also on the programme. Thimig's production of *Jedermann* was repeated in addition to the Austrian playwright Franz Grillparzer's *Des Meeres und der Liebe Wellen* which featured the triumphant return of Paula

Wessely; von Karajan received great critical acclaim, especially for his *Orfeo*.

Viktor Reimann, at the time Salzburg's most prestigious critic, thought *Orfeo ed Euridice* the most 'finished' Festival production, but felt that perhaps Neher and Schuh had overextended themselves by collaborating on three operas. And like his colleagues in the Twenties and Thirties, he raised the eternal question of the nature of the Salzburg audience. High ticket prices excluded most local people from their own festival; yet their taxes helped subsidize it. Reimann found *Jedermann* old-fashioned and desperately in need of a new production. He disliked the conductor's apparent power to choose his favourite operas, without regard to the old Salzburg 'idea'. In another article Reimann attempted to reformulate this 'idea'. In war-ravaged and divided Europe, Salzburg was in a unique position to become the 'new Weimar'. European culture was exhausted by the conflict, but the Austrians had, in the end, suffered less than the Germans, and less even than most of the victors. Salzburg could become the kernel of a revival of European culture in a deeper sense than in 1918, a true international centre designed to preserve 'musical and spiritual freedom' by opening its doors to music from both East and West, by serving as a meeting point for diverse cultural patrimonies and the classical and modern repertoire.[46]

Despite the success of the 1948 Festival, which saw Salzburg beginning to feel its old self, tensions simmered. Walter Legge invited von Karajan, Furtwängler and their wives to an intimate dinner in a Salzburg hotel, and there they 'vowed eternal friendship'. The next day, Legge writes, Furtwängler summoned Egon Hilbert and 'dictated a contract undertaking to conduct every year at Salzburg on condition that von Karajan should be excluded from Salzburg as long as Furtwängler lives.' Von Karajan would only be permitted to conduct the two orchestral concerts for 1949 that he had already been promised.[47]

Legge may have exaggerated Furtwängler's '*Diktat*', but he certainly caught the spirit of the rivalry. In October Tassilo Nekola (general secretary of the Directorium), von Einem, Puthon and Hilbert met to discuss the 1949 Festival. Von Karajan had demanded to conduct *Rosenkavalier* and *Zauberflöte*, and to act as his own stage director. He threatened to boycott the Festival if Carl Orff's *Antigone* were performed. Noting that Schuh had already been promised *Zauberflöte*, von Karajan's request was denied. The directors would not allow von Karajan to 'hold a pistol' to their heads. Furthermore, Furtwängler's presence was vital, and *he* wanted to conduct *Zauberflöte*.[48] This decision had a predictable effect on von Karajan: if he could not write the rules, he would not play the game. His manager made great difficulties for the 1949 concerts that had already been agreed to — Verdi's *Requiem* and Beethoven's Ninth Symphony — and it was only in March that the Festival directors agreed to authorize extra funds for the projects, after protracted negotiations with the Ministry of Education. Meanwhile the underlying tensions continued. Von Einem sent a nasty review of a von Karajan concert in Zurich to Puthon, and Messner was upset that the maestro was conducting the Verdi *Requiem*, which to him was a mere operatic fantasy masked in a religious framework.[49]

Despite the bitterness, the Festival of 1949 was a brilliant success, although it witnessed some sad departures. In September Richard Strauss, the last living founder, died. Hans Pfitzner, despite his refusal to conduct at Salzburg in 1933, had been invited back to give summer courses in the Mozarteum, but became ill and also died, as did Maria Cebotari. Von Karajan performed in Salzburg, but then began a seven-year 'exile'. Bruno Walter, now almost eighty, returned for the first time since 1937 and Lothar arranged a meeting between him and Furt-wängler. Two years earlier the two had exchanged hurtful letters when Furtwängler had been offered — and then denied because of public pressure — the directorship of the Chicago Philharmonic.[50] Now they sat in the Hotel Bristol and quietly discussed their differences. In Lothar's words, 'those who had been split apart by the world came closer together, and what had been bitter, lost its aftertaste.'[51]

Walter conducted Mahler's *Das Lied von der Erde* with Julius Patzak and the English contralto Kathleen Ferrier, as well as Mozart's G minor Symphony. The choice of programme was an act of genius: Mozart's second-to-last, and most moving symphony and Mahler's farewell to the world, both of which reflected the ageing conductor's twin loves, his teacher and his idol. On 21 August 1949, twenty-nine years less one day since the first *Jedermann*, Salzburg could really celebrate its past. New artists also graced the scene. The Hungarian American George Széll conducted *Rosenkavalier* with Wallerstein's staging and the old Roller sets. Wallerstein himself was to die later that year, in the United States. Kirsten Flagstad took over the role of Leonora in Furtwängler's *Fidelio*, and dazzled both the public and the critics. Fricsay, Schuh and Neher prepared the world première of Orff's *Antigone* and the dependable Krips conducted Mozart's little known opera, *Titus*, for the first time in

Salzburg. Here one could observe the hand of Paumgartner, that tireless advocate of the 'lesser' Mozart. In that year he also began a tradition which has lived on to the present day, the Mozart matinée — Sunday morning concerts which highlighted many of Mozart's buried treasures.

Two operas were performed at the Riding School, a reprise of *Orfeo ed Euridice* (with Krips in the pit) and *Zauberflöte*, with the collaboration of Furtwängler, Schuh and Neher. Furtwängler's symphonic reading lasted over three and a half hours, and the director and designer used the massive space in the theatre to overwhelm the audiences. When the Queen of the Night sang her arias, the awning above the stage was pulled back to reveal a starry night. For Strasser, this was the most moving *Zauberflöte* that he had ever experienced, standing in sharp contrast to Toscanini's version. The Italian's rapid tempi suggested an identification with the lighthearted Papageno; Furtwängler, in Strasser's view, opted for the sincerity and lyricism of Tamino.[52]

Reviewers all agreed that in 1949 Salzburg achieved a new freshness and vitality and that the standard was as high, if not higher, than before the war.[53] A new opera, the introduction of a strong element of twentieth-century music, the creation of the Mozart matinées, and the mounting of an almost unknown Mozart opera all combined to create a feeling that Salzburg had set itself upon a new dynamic course. Only the theatrical performances lacked impetus. As it was the two hundredth anniversary of Goethe's birth, Lothar and Leopold Lindtberg staged two of his plays, *Clavigo* and *Iphigenie auf Tauris*, but their efforts received little praise and few foreigners attended. Max Reinhardt, through sheer flamboyance, had staged plays which a foreign audience could enjoy as spectacles despite the language problem, but the arrival of the cinema, of modern mass communication and entertainment had already begun to undermine even Reinhardt's ideas in the Thirties. By the end of the Forties neither American, French nor British audiences were tempted to come to Salzburg for its theatre; the major focus from then onward was therefore to be on music and opera.

As has so often been explained in these pages, the local people had never cared greatly for the Festival. Indeed Tasilo Nekola, whose experience dated back to 1931, remarked that 'the Festival is the second most unpopular activity in Salzburg. No one has ever been able to discover the first'.[54] Franz Rehrl had tried to counteract this prevailing distrust by convincing the local people that tourism meant profits, but in truth the hotel owners, shopkeepers and bankers were in a distinct minority. Most people did not gain, or if they did, that gain was so tangential that it was hardly noticed. Now, however, with post-war transport so poor, Salzburg was forced to mount its own productions, and more and more local people were employed in building sets and making costumes. This new state of affairs coincided perfectly with the aspirations of Schuh, Neher and their colleagues, who wished to produce and rehearse operas specifically for Salzburg. No longer could the critics complain that Salzburg was simply the locale for the production of Viennese repertory productions. Salzburg was producing operas in Salzburg *for* Salzburg. This gave the Festival a new individuality, and the time was propitious. New festivals were emerging in Edinburgh, in Aix-en-Provence, in Holland and elsewhere. 'Festivalitis', as one critic called it, was becoming part of the post-war scene.[55] Salzburg could no longer rest on its laurels.

8

From Furtwängler to von Karajan

1950–9

By the 1950s, the population of Salzburg had grown considerably, to almost 100,000 people. Though the old city retained its beauty, characterless suburbs had begun to spread out in all directions, even engulfing Leopoldskron, now leased by an American institution which gave seminars there throughout the year. The Festival faced competition from Aix-en-Provence, from Glyndebourne (founded as a festival by John Christie and Fritz Busch in the Thirties) and from Edinburgh, which presented a wide variety of cultural offerings. Bayreuth too had started up again under Wicland Wagner's imaginative direction, and was making itself felt as the centre of new and adventurous operatic productions.

Thus Salzburg found it must rethink what it was trying to do. Should it modify or continue to expand? Should it bring in new opera and new music? And most fundamental of all, should one individual take primary responsibility for programme planning and performance? But if so, who should it be? The Fifties saw a long drawn-out power struggle for control which involved politicians, playwrights, composers, conductors, architects and journalists. It was a time of considerable conflict behind the scenes.

Gottfried von Einem and his close friend Wilhelm Furtwängler were the dominant figures on the Directorium at the beginning of the decade, though the conductor was only an 'informal' member. Furtwängler was still haunted by Herbert von Karajan; he had heard that von Karajan would refuse to return to Salzburg in 1950 unless he were given an opera to conduct and direct. He feared that the Directorium would give in to von Karajan and expressed his concerns to von Einem.[1] In March 1950 von Karajan let it be known that he would not perform in Salzburg. When Furtwängler heard this, he tried to justify his animosity: his views on von Karajan were 'purely professional', he said. He hated

139

cultural politics, for they served only to obstruct the performances of great art. When he fought against 'false Rasputins' (by which he meant von Karajan) it was for musical, not personal or political reasons.[2]

Thus Furtwängler's dominance in 1950 was complete. The number of operatic and orchestral conducting assignments given to him rivalled that of Toscanini in 1937 and even von Karajan's stillborn contract for 1946. Böhm was asked to conduct Strauss's *Capriccio*. Lisa Della Casa sang the role of the Countess in this long one-act opera, which is a delight for Strauss lovers, and an overblown bore for others.[3] Josef Krips conducted both Benjamin Britten's *The Rape of Lucretia*, sung in German, and Boris Blacher's *Romeo und Julia*. But Furtwängler reserved all the major operas for himself. He, Schuh, Neher and Holzmeister (who built the sets) collaborated on *Don Giovanni* with Tito Gobbi, Elisabeth Schwarzkopf, Anton Dermota, Erich Kunz, Irmgard Seefried, Josef Greindl and Ljuba Welitsch. *Die Zauberflöte* was repeated in the Riding School. Here too the cast was very strong, even down to the minor roles. The three ladies were sung by Della Casa, Elisabeth Höngen and Sieglinde Wagner, all renowned *prima donnas* in their own right. Finally, Furtwängler presented his classic reading of *Fidelio* with another matchless cast, which included Julius Patzak, Paul Schöffler, Schwarzkopf, Greindl, Dermota and Kirsten Flagstad.

The 1950 programme was one of the most extensive in the Festival's history. To celebrate the three hundredth anniversary of Bach's death, many of the master's orchestral, chamber and solo works were performed. Messner created a most ambitious church concert series which included Brahms's *Ein deutsches Requiem*, Handel's *Messiah*, Bruckner's F minor Mass and several Bach cantatas. Bruno Walter and Hans Knappertsbusch returned to conduct orchestral concerts, and Rafael Kubelik presented a programme of contemporary music which was lauded by the critics.[4] In a curious—and never repeated—departure from the normal Festival programme, the Trapp Family Singers (later made famous by *The Sound of Music*), who had migrated to the United States in 1938, returned to perform three concerts.

For the second time since the war, the Festival made a small surplus, thanks to state subsidies, now fixed by a new federal law, passed on 12 July 1950. Briefly, the law set up three bodies, the Directorium, the Kuratorium and the *Delegiertenversammlung* (Assembly of Delegates). The Directorium contained a maximum of five members, and was responsible for the planning of the Festival, while the Kuratorium, made up of local, provincial and federal officers, controlled the

Festival's budget, and had ultimate authority to name members of the Directorium. As such it had a certain veto control over the Directorium, although its membership was made up only of elected and appointed public officials. The Assembly of Delegates, which met on a yearly basis, and included fifteen federal, provincial and local senior bureaucrats, had only advisory status, and no real power. Financially, the Government promised to contribute forty per cent of the yearly subsidy requested by the Kuratorium; the city, province and Tourist Fund Commission would each contribute twenty per cent. The subsidy would roughly cover the difference between costs and the amount taken in through ticket sales.[5]

The Law of 1950 has worked well, because it created a tightly-knit structure that had always been lacking, and guaranteed a sizeable federal contribution. There was, however, a danger point: the overlapping of power between the Directorium and the Kuratorium. If and when there was artistic disagreement, or more fundamentally a dispute about personalities, the lines of responsibility became entangled, and the Kuratorium had the ultimate power to enforce its political will on the other organ. This state of affairs was to have particularly important consequences during the Fifties.

Shortly after the 1950 Festival ended, rumours circulated that the directors had asked von Karajan to return to Salzburg the following summer. When Furtwängler learned of this he was furious; the directors immediately dispatched Nekola to meet him in Munich. Furtwängler did not mince his words. He was prepared to resign. Nekola replied that the directors had indeed approached von Karajan, but only in order to humour malcontents in Salzburg and Vienna who claimed that Salzburg was 'ignoring' von Karajan; he was unlikely to accept the offer. Nekola was right. Von Karajan opted for Bayreuth in 1951, where he began a short—and unhappy—collaboration with Wieland Wagner. Once again Furtwängler had prevailed by using the most potent weapon in his arsenal: the threat to resign.[6]

The contretemps between von Karajan and Furtwängler was soon pushed into the background, however, when it was learnt that the directors had decided to have Alban Berg's *Wozzeck* performed in 1951. The decision was made in September of 1950 in the Directorium, which then sought to justify it to the Kuratorium. Paumgartner, with strong backing from von Einem, argued that the world (meaning the international press) had grown to expect Salzburg to perform contemporary operas; the Festival had received extremely favourable publicity thanks to such innovations. Although *Wozzeck* was uncompromisingly modern, it was over twenty years old, and should be performed, despite the financial risk involved. Provincial Governor Josef Klaus, for one, was not convinced. He admitted that he had never heard the opera, but the projected cost (150,000 Schillings) seemed prohibitive. Josef Kaut, a local Socialist functionary, the Cultural Counsellor for the provincial government and a close friend of von Einem, supported the Directorium. Finally the decision was made to go ahead.[7]

No purely artistic decision ever caused more of a stir in Salzburg. It was not only the *Sprechgesang* and the atonality of the work that angered the local citizens; the lurid nature of the libretto shocked them, and in December a bitter debate erupted in the *Landtag*. One Deputy accused the author of the original play, Georg Büchner, of being a 'cultural Bolshevik' while another claimed that *Wozzeck* was '*Schmutz und Schund*' (dirt and trash).[8] Despite incredible political pressure, and a vote by the *Landtag* to 'withdraw' the opera, the Directorium stood firm. It engaged Böhm to conduct, Neher and Schuh for the decor and stage direction. The performance had a decidedly mixed reception. The reviewer for the new English monthly *Opera* thought the production and the singing second-rate, but praised Böhm's reading of the score.[9] Austrian and German reviews were more positive, though some seemed to go out of their way to praise the concept of producing *Wozzeck* rather than concentrating on the strengths and weaknesses of the performance. One Viennese newspaper argued that it was important for a truly atonal opera to be heard, especially one reflecting the spirit of its time (the Twenties) which, like 'our own period' was a period of reconstruction; Salzburg deserved honours for having put on this compelling work, for in doing so it was differentiating itself from its many rivals. *Die Arbeiterzeitung* in Vienna simply described *Wozzeck* as a 'sensation' that went beyond the wildest imaginings.[10]

Despite such critical support, the prosaic fact remained that only forty per cent of the seats for *Wozzeck's* four performances had been sold. As Klaus had feared, it was a financial disaster.[11] Salzburg audiences were not prepared to subject themselves to such a demanding score nor to the supreme effort it took to understand and appreciate it. They had been coming to Salzburg for thirty years for escape, to amuse themselves, to be moved and uplifted by familiar sounds, not be be educated in the history of music, or in the fate of their century.

This conservatism was as old as the Festival itself. In the Twenties, Richard Strauss had not been able to fill the house when he conducted

Ariadne, nor had Salzburg audiences been impressed by the Leningrad Opera Studio when it made its guest appearance in 1928. Even the revered Bruno Walter, who conducted Mozart and Wagner to a full house, played before half-empty seats when he indulged in his love for the obscure operas of Carl Maria von Weber or Hugo Wolf. The post-war period had seen no change, despite the best efforts of the directors and the continual plaudits of the critics. Anything new or obscure had met with audience resistance; this created a tension which still exists between the avant garde and the conservatives. Was Salzburg to be a magnificent museum, or a vibrant evolving institution? Efforts to strike a compromise between the two extremes have been a central concern for the directors throughout the post-war era. The *Wozzeck* debate symbolized this tension.

Max Graf was angered by the whole *Wozzeck* affair, and published a stinging article in the Vienna *Kurier* in which he took the people of Salzburg to task for their 'hate campaign' against the opera. While many Festival-goers had come from England, France and America *because* of *Wozzeck*, Austrians, instead of being proud of one of their most far-sighted composers, condemned him. It seemed to be a national characteristic, not only to reject the new, but to treat national composers—from Mozart to Bruckner to Mahler—with disdain. In his own youth, Graf had seen Arnold Schoenberg and Oscar Kokoschka leave Vienna, which refused to accept them. The greatest musical talents of twentieth-century Austria, Berg, Schoenberg, and Webern, were performed everywhere but in their native land. The nation must appreciate its heritage, not treat it with scorn and hate.[12]

Neither Alban Berg nor Mozart, however, was the real 'star' of the 1951 Festival; this was *Otello*, conducted by Furtwängler with Ramón Vinay in the title role. Only the second Verdi opera to be presented in Salzburg, it was performed in honour of the fiftieth anniversary of the composer's death. Herbert Graf (Max Graf's son), one of the major stage directors of the Metropolitan Opera in New York, directed, and Stefan Hlawa, returning to Salzburg for the first time since 1943, designed the costumes and decor. Furtwängler also repeated his now familiar *Zauberflöte* which many thought should remain a permanent part of the Salzburg repertoire. The fourth opera, *Idomeneo* was conducted by the Hungarian Georg Solti in the Riding School. *Idomeneo* is probably the greatest *opera seria* ever written, but by definition it is a static work and a producer's nightmare. The impossibility of making scene changes in the Riding School served to emphasize the lack of movement.[13] Other highlights of the season were Leopold Stokowski's appearance in two all-Russian programmes and Furtwängler's rendering of Beethoven's Ninth Symphony for the first time in Salzburg since 1937.

Von Einem had a strong commitment to strengthening Salzburg's theatrical profile, and had engaged Gustaf Gründgens, Germany's most renowned stage director, to put on Shakespeare's *As You Like It*. The play received outstanding notices, as did Berthold Viertel's production of Heinrich von Kleist's *Der zerbrochene Krug* (*The Broken Jug*).[14] Schuh, who himself had considerable theatrical experience, believed that the only way to interest the Festival audience in theatre was to engage great directors, like Gründgens, but unfortunately the latter never staged a play in Salzburg again.[15]

1951 had begun with a blaze of political invective caused by the proposal to stage *Wozzeck*; it ended with a much publicized scandal. It must be remembered that 1951 was the height of the Cold War, McCarthyism was rampant in America and the Iron Curtain had become a fact. Austria was still an occupied country, negotiations for a state treaty dragged on, but the Russians seemed in no hurry to give Austria her independence. The von Einem affair can only be understood in the light of visceral anti-Communism which most Austrians shared.

The story began innocently enough. Bertolt Brecht had lost his German citizenship in 1935, and had spent the war years in the United States. He had never felt at ease there, and after having testified before the House of Representatives' Committee on Un-American Activities, he returned to Europe. As a 'stateless' citizen Brecht had few options, and took up temporary residence in Switzerland. In 1948 he got in touch with von Einem through his old friend, Caspar Neher. Von Einem was now a member of the Directorium, and committed to a full-scale renewal of the Festival; like many others, he was less than enchanted with *Jedermann*. When Brecht and von Einem met in January 1948, they discussed the possibility of Brecht writing a new play, a Salzburg *Totentanz* (Dance of Death) to replace *Jedermann*. Two months later von Einem enlisted the support of Hilbert, who was enthusiastic about the project.[16]

That autumn Brecht returned to Salzburg and had a long discussion with von Einem about the play. Brecht's initial plans were very ambitious: with his pre-war collaborator Viertel he wanted to establish a base in Vienna; from there he would take his own group of players to perform in Salzburg and Munich. Hermann Bahr and Max Reinhardt had had a similar idea at the beginning of the century, which had not come to fruition.[17] In the spring of 1949 Brecht, dissatisfied with his treatment by the Swiss authorities, made a formal request to the Austrian government to grant him citizenship; this would at least give him an opportunity to go forward with his plans for Vienna and Salzburg. Von Einem backed the proposal, as did the Salzburg local authorities, including the Provincial Governor Dr Karl Rehrl, brother of Franz. In August *Die Presse* noted with a certain surprise that Brecht had been asked to run the Deutsches Theater in East Berlin. When he heard about the article, Brecht immediately wrote to von Einem to deny the rumour. He was only going to produce a play in East Berlin; he had no official post at the theatre.[18]

Discussions concerning Brecht's request for citizenship continued for many months, both in Vienna and Salzburg. Finally, in April 1950, both state and province granted permission. Austria had acquired one of the most original—and most controversial—playwrights of the twentieth century. Brecht finally received his passport in November 1950; but there was little celebration. The whole process, though well known to local and national government officials, as well as those close the Festival, had received little publicity. In April 1951 a Viennese journal mentioned that Brecht was now an Austrian citizen, but no one took much notice. Meanwhile Brecht was in fact working full-time in East Berlin, and had little time to spend on the *Totentanz*.

In the autumn of 1951 several Viennese and Salzburg papers began a concerted press campaign against Brecht which, in the end, shook Austria to its foundations. The *Wiener Tageszeitung* claimed to have heard the rumour that Brecht would divide his time between Salzburg and East Berlin, and that he had already become engaged in discussions which would lead to his taking over the theatrical leadership of the Festival.[19] Within a few days the *Salzburger Nachrichten* chimed in to say how 'mysterious' it was that Brecht, the beacon of 'Communist avantgardism', could be considering coming to Salzburg. Salzburg's most popular daily (which supported the Conservative *Volkspartei*) now searched for those responsible for giving Brecht Austrian citizenship.[20] There must be 'hidden Communists' lurking in the provincial government or in the judiciary. Not to be outdone, the *Linzer Volksblatt* suggested that Brecht was probably a secret agent who worked for the 'Ostzone'. Viktor Reimann thought the real culprit was von Einem, who had been aided and abetted by the Socialists, those 'conscious or unconscious' agents of Communism, who had put the scheme over on the unsuspecting, uninformed and naïve politicians of the *Volkspartei*. Because of the stupidity of the Conservative cultural leaders, 'our country will be undermined by the Communists'. Austria would be 'spiritually bolshevized'.[21]

What made the affair more complicated—and more absurd—was that neither party could in good faith accuse the other of being 'guilty' of the heinous deed. There was a Socialist–Conservative coalition at the national level; Salzburg city was Socialist, the province Conservative, but, due to proportional representation, Socialists held many prominent positions. The Conservative Minister of the Interior had supported the request for citizenship, as had the Socialist Magistrate in Salzburg and the Socialist Minister of Education in Vienna. Still, mud-slinging there was. Socialist members of the *Landtag* accused Governor Klaus of planning to make Brecht the head of the Salzburg Festival.[22] On the same day three right-wing members of the National Parliament accused the government of being unaware of Communist infiltration. They charged that Brecht's work was built on the 'systematic destruction of Western cultural values'.[23]

Throughout all the arguments, von Einem maintained his support for Brecht. Since he had no political constituency, the composer was vulnerable, and thus became a convenient scapegoat. The meeting of the Kuratorium on 31 October 1951 was the stormiest ever. Klaus accused von Einem of being '*Eine Schande für Österreich*'[24] (a disgrace to Austria). If von Einem would not leave the meeting, Klaus would. Von Einem stormed out; the remaining members of the Kuratorium summarily dismissed him from the Directorium for 'disrespectful behaviour against the other members, including the Governor'.[25]

Within days the incident had grown into a full-scale affair. Von Einem felt that he had been treated unjustly. No one had allowed him to defend himself, the name of Brecht had never been mentioned, though this of course was the issue on everyone's mind.[26] Von Einem wrote public letters to the local press, and demanded a hearing. Reaction from his fellow artists was swift: Schuh, Böhm and Furtwängler came to his defence; Blacher, his former teacher, resigned from the Mozarteum; and Denis de Rougemont, the Swiss writer and head of the Congress of Cultural Freedom, a Geneva-based anti-Communist organization funded by the US government, organized a public protest in von Einem's favour.[27] Within Austria, there were calls for the resignation of the various ministers who had been involved. Klaus issued statements,[28] held press conferences and denied that the Brecht affair had anything to do with the dismissal of von Einem.

In the end, though von Einem never received the public apology and full reintegration into the Directorium which he demanded, a compromise solution was found. In late 1952 the directors, after having held an 'inquiry' into the incident, decided to reward von Einem by performing his opera Der Prozess (based on Kafka's The Trial) at the 1953 Festival. Klaus informed von Einem that there was no question of his returning to the Directorium, since it was impossible for a sitting director to pass judgement on matters affecting his own compositions, but he hoped that the Brecht incident was now forgotten, and that von Einem would continue to compose.[29] Klaus's disingenuous reasoning was lost on no one. Josef Kaut, now a member of the Directorium (thanks to von Einem) knew the real story: von Einem did not have the votes, Klaus did. Kaut wrote to a friend that the whole business made him 'want to vomit'. He held out hope that von Einem might be made a member of a restructured Artistic Council, though the moment was not yet ripe to advance such a suggestion.[30]

Der Prozess was duly presented in 1953. The first performance drew the curious, but then attendance dropped off dramatically, and the opera averaged only a forty per cent ticket sale; it took in 200,000 fewer Schillings than estimated.[31] Von Einem did not give up. He continued to lobby for the creation of an effective Artistic Council which would have a real influence on Festival programmes; he received strong support from Furtwängler, Kaut and Schuh, and at the end of 1953 the decision was made to allow von Einem to attend those Directorium meetings where the major topic would be programme planning.[32] The composer had been allowed back into the inner sanctum—at least on some occasions. He could not know that Furtwängler's days were numbered, and that von Karajan was waiting in the wings. He was now President of the Council which, among others, included his good friends Schuh and Neher. Even Klaus congratulated him on his new role. The Governor, in reality von Einem's most consistent enemy, pretended that it was thanks to his efforts that von Einem had received his new appointment.[33]

The question remains, why had the scandal occurred in the first place? It is difficult to explain, given the complexity of political, artistic and personal rancour which motivated the major characters in the drama. Von Einem has not forgotten, although the other principal figures are now dead. Certainly Brecht's citizenship and the ensuing press campaign played a part, but how important was this? Yet without the heightened publicity surrounding Brecht it is unlikely that emotions would have become so fraught. There were other factors: the historical Salzburg–Vienna rivalry weighed more heavily than the Socialist–Conservative schism. Then there was the figure of Josef Klaus, an ambitious and controversial man. As early as 1951 he was promoting the idea of building a new Festival Hall and putting himself forward as a suitable successor to Salzburg's favourite Governor, Franz Rehrl. As his own political fortunes were closely tied to the success of the Festival, he became deeply involved with Festival planning, much more so than Rehrl had ever been.

Herein lies the link between the *Wozzeck* controversy and the von Einem affair. Klaus had opposed *Wozzeck*, and though he had lost the battle, he had won the war, in the sense that *Wozzeck* proved to be the financial disaster that he had predicted. On the eve of the 1951 Festival he had called Hilbert and Puthon into his office and told them point-blank that he did not approve of the direction that the Festival was taking.[34] But neither Puthon nor Hilbert was the prime mover in that new direction; von Einem was. Von Einem's personality also played a role. He was (and is) a large, powerful, dynamic and opinionated man. In the past such figures had dominated Salzburg Festivals, but they had all been *performers* whose presence was perceived as the lifeblood of the Festival. If Kerber could literally throw someone out of his summer-house to spare Toscanini's feelings, if Nekola would scurry up to Munich to assure Furtwängler that the Festival directors did not really *want* Herbert von Karajan, it was because the Festival's very existence seemed to depend on the participation of these haughty and difficult artists. Von Einem had no such advantage; he had ideas, he had powerful friends, but as von Einem he could not fill up the seats. The Brecht affair was his Achilles heel, a ready-made issue for political demagogy. It brought him down; his friends saved him from extinction, but not from temporary humiliation. Meanwhile Brecht lived on in Berlin, never to return to Salzburg again; he later confided to von Einem before his death (in 1956) that he had written only a cursory outline for the *Totentanz*; he had then laid it aside because of the pressure of other obligations. Ironically his interest in his Salzburg project was fading just at the moment when his citizenship became a hot political issue.

The whole affair revealed a facet of Austrian life which had rarely been noticed by the outside world: its complex internal cultural politics and intense provincial intrigues. Neither the resignation of Clemens

Krauss in 1934 nor the Moissi scandal of 1931 had received much publicity outside the country. Now, in an age of instant communication, when Salzburg was more than ever the 'window to Austria', the affair was widely publicized and damaged Salzburg's image. A generation which had seen artistic freedom trampled into the ground was extremely sensitive to outright attacks on that freedom, so it was not surprising that Furtwängler and Böhm supported von Einem nor that, in their embarrassment, the beleagured politicians partially rehabilitated the composer. Yet the Festival emerged somewhat diminished from the experience.

As if by an act of retribution, the 1952 Festival was plagued by last-minute illnesses, which deprived it of much of its lustre. In the summer of 1951, the Directorium had decided to give *Danae* its long-postponedworld première. Before his death in 1949 Strauss had refused to allow the work to be performed unless Clemens Krauss (or, in an extreme case von Karajan) conducted. Paumgartner and von Einem disliked Krauss intensely, but they agreed to invite him on condition that he be given no assurance that his relationship with Salzburg would continue.[35]

Illness caused Böhm and Furtwängler to cancel at the last minute; their replacements, Rudolph Moralt and Mario Rossi, were greeted with poor reviews.[36] *Danae* did not fare much better. Inveterate Strauss lovers, like Willi Schuh, his biographer, and William Mann, gave *Danae* strong support. For Schuh, the work, despite its problematic libretto, was 'the magnificent centre of the festival'; a 'great epoch' of German operatic history had closed with the last Strauss première.[37] To Mann, who himself was to produce a monumental biography of the composer, the opera was an honourable addition to the Strauss *oeuvre*.

> Those who find room in their musical makeup for the hedonist approach [to opera] cannot help falling in love with the effortless lyrical style, and witty musical invention, with the rich . . . harmonic contrivance, and with the graceful vocal writing that Strauss lavished on *Danae*.[38]

Another English critic put his views more succinctly, in just four lines. He was 'distressed' by the experience of seeing *Danae*: 'musical senility dressed up as a *Welturaufführung* (world première) can be nothing but an aesthetic offence, however well put on.'[39] This rather unkind slap was closer to the truth. *Danae* was never repeated in Salzburg, nor is it often performed on the modern operatic stage.

A middling production of *Don Pasquale* rounded out the 1952 operatic repertoire. The strength of the Festival that year was in the quality of its orchestral concerts. Ferenc Fricsay, Krauss, Széll, Kubelik, Victor de Sabata and Igor Markevitch provided an impressive array; Benjamin Britten and Peter Pears collaborated in an evening of *Lieder*, including some of the composer's own works. Oddly, Pears, the outstanding English tenor of his time, was never invited back to Salzburg. But the absence of Furtwängler and Böhm cast a pall over the proceedings. Salzburg was used to the first-rate.

The real innovation in 1952 was in the realm of the theatre. Hilbert had asked Ernst Lothar to take over the production of *Jedermann* which had seemed to be getting less and less popular. There was no desire to offend Reinhardt's widow, Helene Thimig, and she was still encouraged to continue her acting responsibilities and to collaborate with Lothar. Thimig had a will of her own, however, and the situation, perhaps predictably, quickly deteriorated. She complained to the Minister of Education and persuaded the local press to print stories that accused Lothar of planning to 'falsify' *Jedermann*. Then, claiming illness, she refused to collaborate with him. When Lothar tried to engage a known Communist, Karl Paryla, to play the Devil in his new production, she called Lothar 'pro-Communist'. But when *Jedermann* was finally produced, both the audiences and critics realized that Lothar had tampered very little with the original Reinhardt conception, and the production was well received.[40]

Indeed, throughout the Fifties, Lothar wielded almost total power over Salzburg theatricals, and he continued to be a member of the Artistic Council. In 1954 the Directorium ordered a year's moratorium on theatre productions, in order to have time to reflect on the future of drama in Salzburg. The next year Lothar staged a highly successful performance of Schiller's *Kabale und Liebe* (an old Reinhardt favourite) and Jean Vilar of the *Théâtre National Populaire* presented Molière's *Don Juan* in French. Until the end of the decade Lothar, with 'varying success' (his words) staged a series of plays, including Goethe's *Egmont*, Lessing's *Emilia Galotti*, Werfel's *Juarez und Maximilian* and von Hofmannsthal's *Der Turm*. Oscar Fritz Schuh also contributed two productions, Eugene O'Neill's *Fast ein Poet* (*A Touch of the Poet*) and Archibald Macleish's *Spiel um Job*. Lothar believed that Salzburg plays must stay within the context of the Festival tradition, and that literary experiments were doomed to failure. Only first-rate works should be staged, and the productions must be matchless. Furthermore, Festival dramas should 'observe the political and individual idea of freedom'.[41]

Schuh was less happy about the direction that Lothar was taking. In late 1956 he wrote to von Karajan (who by then had been selected as Artistic Director of the Festival) that, though there had been distinguished theatrical presentations in Salzburg, there had been no consistent planning, that the theatre was running a very poor second place behind the opera. Schuh hoped that von Karajan's arrival, and the building of the new Festival Hall (the details of which he had not yet seen) would augur a new beginning, that the theatre would once again play the role that von Hofmannsthal and Reinhardt had forged in the early years of the Festival. Salzburg must engage great talents, like Gründgens and Viertel, and produce a structured long-term plan. Otherwise the theatre in Salzburg would remain on the Festival's periphery.[42]

Lothar was not to take part in Schuh's hoped-for renewal of the Salzburg theatre. A few days before the first production of the 1959 *Jedermann* the director received a review from a local newspaper which strongly attacked his production. The writer was not a regular critic, but an influential member of local broadcasting circles. Then Josef Kaut made a public speech in which he called the Lothar *Jedermann* production 'antiquated'. Lothar was not prepared to be attacked by one of his own directors, and immediately resigned. In his letter of resignation he asked Salzburg not to forget its debt to Reinhardt and von Hofmannsthal. He hoped that Salzburg would never again deviate from the path of justice and righteousness which it had forfeited during the Nazi era. According to Lothar, this statement was not well received, and some Salzburg citizens painted Nazi slogans all over the town. Lothar's thirteen-year association with the Festival ended most unhappily.[43]

In 1953 and 1954, Böhm and Furtwängler were back. Highlights included Herbert Graf's production of *Don Giovanni* in the Riding School; Paul Czinner made a film of this which documents Furtwängler's magisterial interpretation. Holzmeister created on the stage a sort of 'Don Giovanni City', reminiscent of the late lamented 'Faust City'. Some critics were not impressed. One suggested that he felt as if he were watching a tennis match, as the action moved from Elvira's window to the graveyard and then on to Don Giovanni's palace. If Otto Edelmann's Viennese Leporello did not please, Cesare Siepi's Don was universally admired, and considered the best since Pinza's.[44]

The Graf-Hlawa-Furtwängler collaboration on *Figaro* had a mixed reception. Critics thought the production 'fussy', and despite the glorious singing of Schöffler and Schwarzkopf, complained about Furtwängler's slow tempi.[45] In contrast the Böhm-Neher-Schuh *Così*, played in the Residenz, was a huge success. *Der Prozess*, as described earlier, did not find an audience. Its problems were many despite a properly frightening decor devised by Neher. The psychological profundities of the tale did not lend themselves to an operatic rendering, but, more seriously, von Einem was attacked for having failed to integrate the various musical sources of his score—from Puccini to Schoenberg—into a whole.[46]

In 1953 Clemens Krauss made his last appearance in Salzburg; it was fitting that he should do so conducting *Rosenkavalier*, a work he had introduced to the Festival in 1929. Krauss, unlike Furtwängler, Böhm or von Karajan, never held an important post after the war. He had made too many enemies along the way, and if his political sins were forgiven, his others were not. In 1953 he had hoped to be chosen to succeed Böhm at the Vienna State Opera. When he heard that the invitation was not forthcoming, he decided to honour a conducting engagement in Mexico, despite warnings from his doctor that such an undertaking might aggravate his heart condition. Krauss did not survive the trip.[47]

In 1954 Furtwängler conducted *Der Freischütz*, an opera which many felt was singularly inappropriate for Salzburg. Critics noted the slow tempi and were put off by the 'heaviness' of the score. However Böhm's reading of *Ariadne auf Naxos* met with considerable success, and George Széll conducted the world première of the Swiss Rolf Liebermann's *Penelope*, which introduced Anneliese Rothenberger's exquisite soprano to Salzburg for the first time. Though Liebermann's work was written in the twelve tone idiom, it was much less aggressive to the ear than, for example, *Wozzeck*. Critics praised it, but the audience stayed away, and ticket sales filled up only forty-five per cent of the seats.[48] The most talked-about event of the 1954 Festival was Dimitri Mitropoulos's two concerts of twentieth-century music (which included a piece by von Einem) with the Vienna Philharmonic. He made a profound impression on critics and public alike, and Philharmonic members themselves longed for a more permanent collaboration with him.[49]

1954 was a watershed year in the history of the post-war Festival. In August Furtwängler asked if he could take a leave of absence in 1955 in order to renew his artistic energies. Puthon would not have it. 'Dr Furtwängler is much more than a conductor in Salzburg; his personality puts a stamp on the Festival.' The old Baron persuaded

Furtwängler to relent.[50] A few months later, the man whom one English critic had characterized as being a 'demigod' in Salzburg was dead.[51] Certainly the great conductor had dominated the post-war festivals, though his powers had never been as absolute as Toscanini's. He was 68 when he died, and had been Germany's most prestigious conductor for a generation. That same year Hilbert stepped down from his positions in Vienna and Salzburg, and was sent to Rome to create an Austrian cultural centre, another victim of Viennese bureaucratic intrigue. Thus two strong, almost overpowering figures left the Salzburg scene at the same time, creating a void in the leadership. Into this empty space stepped Furtwängler's 'evil Rasputin', Herbert von Karajan.

Two events dominated the second half of the Fifties, the building of the new Festival Hall and the rise of Herbert von Karajan. They were to fix the direction of the Festival for the next quarter of a century.

The idea of a second Festival Hall had been in the air since the early Fifties. In 1951 a Viennese newspaper had suggested that the only way to make Festival performances available to the general Salzburg public was to increase seating capacity, and the only means to accomplish this was to build a new Festival Hall.[52] At the same time Governor Josef Klaus also became interested, and in 1953 formed a committee to explore the possibilities for such a building. Herbert Graf submitted the original plans; later the competition was thrown open to international architects. From the beginning there was opposition to the whole project. Both Kaut, within the Directorium, and von Einem from without, laboured to defeat the idea—partially, it appears, because of their intense dislike for Klaus.[53] But the Provincial Governor was single-minded and refused to be sidetracked. Various proposals were studied, then rejected, including several which would have placed the new Hall outside of the town, near Schloss Klessheim or Schloss Hellbrunn. These proposals were based on the very real fear that if the new Festival Hall were in the centre of town, traffic conditions, already difficult, would become impossible. Finally, Klaus and his committee decided that Graf's original proposal, which suggested that the Hall be built on the site of the old court stables, next to the existing Festival Hall, should be implemented. The Kuratorium approved the proposal and assigned Clemens Holzmeister, the only architect the Festival had ever known, and now in his eighties, to draw up plans. Holzmeister's job was made more difficult by the fact that, in order to build adequate backstage facilities, large segments of the Mönchsberg needed to be cut away. The new Festival Hall was not cheap: the original figure of 110,000,000 Schillings (over £200,000) was doubled in the end. Construction began in 1956, the year that von Karajan was appointed Artistic Director of the Festival. The maestro wanted the Festival Hall to be the most modern in the world, and presided over every detail of its construction. Meanwhile controversy raged.[54]

Some have suggested that the huge dimensions of the Hall, which encompasses the world's largest operatic stage, matched von Karajan's ambitions for Salzburg. Even today, it is considered 'von Karajan's Hall'. Others may conduct there, but only at his pleasure. The new hall had many obvious advantages over the old; in particular its acoustic qualities were second to none, a tribute to von Karajan's lifelong interest in acoustical techniques. There were no poorly sighted seats, and even those sitting in the back rows would not feel removed from events on the stage. This was an important improvement on older European and American opera houses. The massiveness of the stage was echoed by the huge orchestral pit. which could comfortably seat the entire Vienna Philharmonic as well as its members' families. The stage machinery was the most up-to-date imaginable. Yet the Hall despite its advantages, was not a feast to the eye, nor were the seats comfortable. Save for the chandeliers, baroque had been banished, and replaced by severity; the walls were composed of giant squares of wood, varying in colour from light to dark brown. There was no warmth, and the sheer breadth of the stage was distracting. But there was another problem, aesthetics aside, of a more pressing nature. Was the Hall appropriate for Salzburg?

An American once mentioned to this author that it reminded him of a basketball gymnasium. Its size precluded the playing of intimate operas; it demanded the huge, the extravagant, the grand. There were, of course, many works of this kind in the repertoire of the nineteenth century, but Salzburg was not in the business of celebrating Wagner, Verdi, Bellini or Meyerbeer. Oscar Schuh thought that the Hall was completely 'out of place' in Salzburg. Of the Mozart operas, only *Idomeneo* might lend itself to a stage of such a size, yet this was the one Mozart opera which the public had not embraced. Von Einem agreed.[55] Depending on one's point of view, Salzburg had either been 'liberated' or 'constrained'; liberated from the inadequacies of the old Festival Hall (and the Riding School, which could only be used for a few operas) or constrained by size to take untold liberties with the Salzburg programme. Mozart operas such as *Don Giovanni* and *Figaro* might be performed on the new stage, but they would be overpowered by its dimensions, their delicious subtleties lost. 'Grand' opera would indeed look well here; it would in fact be the only way to make the new Hall pay for itself. But in doing so, Salzburg would destroy its tradition.

The negotiations which had brought von Karajan to Salzburg were long and tortuous. Hilbert's removal had been fortuitous, for the Director of the *Bundesverwaltung* was not of the kind to be dictated to by von Karajan. As usual, various intrigues had brought him down. He wrote to von Einem about the 'baseness' and 'nastiness' of certain politicians, including Josef Klaus, which had engineered his dismissal, and then went off to Rome, in his words, a 'modern Tannhäuser, but I am convinced that I will return.'[56]

In the first Directorium meeting after Furtwängler's death, the members, including von Einem—who represented the Artistic Council—discussed ways and means of approaching von Karajan; it was agreed that it would not be politic to mention Furtwängler's name. They should offer von Karajan two concerts for 1955; there was no question of his putting on an opera; the soloists and stage directors had already been chosen. Furtwängler had made all preliminary arrangements for the new production of *Zauberflöte*, and Oskar Kokoschka, who was to design the costumes and scenery, had let it be known that he would resign if von Karajan were called on to conduct. In 1956, however, von Karajan could be offered *Don Giovanni*. All agreed that his presence would act as a great stimulus for the Festival. The Directorium also decided not to ask Krips to come in 1956. Von Einem asserted that his reputation was not high in America, where he now conducted. Salzburg should opt for the rising generation of young conductors, men like Solti and Fricsay.[57]

It turned out that von Karajan was not available for 1955, and discussions between the conductor and the Directorium for 1956, carried out in the spring of 1955, likewise fell through. Mitropoulos was asked to conduct the 1956 *Don Giovanni*. But these were not the only negotiations in progress. The Minister of Education, Drimmel, had had his own talks with von Karajan, and rumours began to circulate that von Karajan was demanding a three-year contract and the right to present two operas every year, which he would both stage and conduct. At a particularly stormy meeting of the Directorium in August 1955, Karl Böhm could not longer contain his rage. He threatened to resign all his responsibilities in Salzburg if von Karajan's conditions were met. Böhm pointed out that even Furtwängler, who in his view was a much greater conductor than von Karajan, had never asked for a three-year contract.

Such a contract would cause an 'imbalance' and ultimately hurt the Festival. Puthon retorted that the Festival directors had had no conversations with von Karajan, save for the matter of the 1956 *Don Giovanni*. Thereupon von Einem said that he had heard that Klaus had been engaged in private talks with the maestro. Von Einem fully agreed that von Karajan had exceptional talent, but if he were given great power, no other first-class conductor or stage director would be willing to play second fiddle to him in Salzburg. Puthon was torn. He needed von Karajan, but he did not want to lose Böhm. He promised that, whatever happened, there was no chance that von Karajan would receive a higher salary than Böhm. In any case, there were as yet no official negotiations. All of von Karajan's 'demands' were rumours. Böhm was satisfied.[58]

Two weeks later the Artistic Council issued a public statement, in which it proclaimed its 'warm desire' to bring von Karajan to Salzburg. In the last three paragraphs of the document, the Council had originally addressed itself to the 'fears which exist' that von Karajan might become too authoritarian and threaten artistic freedom. For, as the Council agreed, 'no responsible artist should exert a power that would give him a decisive preeminence of any kind over others.' At this point, Klaus intervened, and refused to allow the statement to be published, unless the last three paragraphs were suppressed. There was no desire, outside of the Artistic Council, to irritate the maestro.[59]

Formal negotiations between the Directorium and von Karajan initially began in the autumn of 1955. Puthon wrote a frank letter to von Einem in October. The Baron wanted 'this extraordinarily talented man' to come to Salzburg. He was sure that a way could be found both to preserve Salzburg's 'tradition' and bring von Karajan in. He knew that Schuh and Neher, neither of whom the conductor liked, feared for their jobs, but Puthon promised that as long as the Directorium existed, they would not be shunted aside.[60] The talks dragged on through the beginning of 1956. Puthon sent out a report on their progress in January 1956; it is worth looking at in some detail, for it gives a clear picture of the price that Salzburg would have to pay for von Karajan's participation. His opera programme plan from 1957 to 1960 was the following:

1957:
Rosenkavalier and *Falstaff* (von Karajan)
Figaro (Böhm)
Don Giovanni (Mitropoulos)
Orfeo ed Euridice (Szell)
The new Liebermann Opera

1958:   *Rosenkavalier*
          Jeanne d'Arc
          Figaro
          Orfeo ed Euridice
          La Traviata

1959:   *Salome*
          Lucia di Lammermoor
          Wozzeck
          Così
          Zauberflöte
          Jeanne d'Arc

1960:   *Fidelio*
          Don Giovanni
          Zauberflöte
          Elektra
          An Italian Opera, by either Rossini or Bellini.

Von Karajan also wished to see a new production of *Faust* in the new Festival Hall. After 1960, four of the five major Mozart operas would always remain in the repertoire, and a new production of each of the five would be mounted every five years. His last innovation was to propose that the Berlin Philharmonic give guest performances during the Festival.[61] In his discussions with the Directorium, von Karajan said that he wished to conduct and stage *Lucia di Lammermoor* and *La Traviata*, two operas which had never been seriously contemplated for Salzburg. In truth, save for these operas (which, in the event were never performed), the maestro's suggestions were not uninteresting, and fitted in well with the Salzburg tradition. The inclusion of the Berlin Philharmonic (he was now its conductor for life), though it might cause some consternation among the Viennese, could only improve the Festival. Both Mahler and Krauss had produced and conducted their own operas. Von Karajan's notion of a revolving cycle of new Mozart productions was forward-looking, if perhaps overambitious, but at least he fully realized that the new age called for ingenuity and creativity in opera, that a single production could no longer hold the stage for decades. Audiences looked for new stage effects, new interpretations; the age of the stage director was at hand: as indeed it is still with us.

However it was not von Karajan's proposals for a Salzburg programme which shocked; it was the role that he envisaged for himself, which went beyond anything ever experienced in Salzburg. As Artistic

157

Director he wanted the final say on all casts and all conductors for operas and orchestral concerts. If a singer or conductor fell ill, and a replacement was needed, von Karajan must be consulted, even if he were in Tokyo. He also proposed to stop the tradition of performing new (or at least contemporary) operas every year. He was not against modern opera as such, but he would only allow those operas into the repertoire which were of suitable merit. He refused to take risks with inferior works. Von Karajan maintained that he had no animus against Schuh and Neher, and would allow them to continue to work in Salzburg, but he would not cooperate with the Artistic Council as long as von Einem was a member. As to salary, he proposed that he be paid 50,000 Schillings for each performance ($2000 or £1400); major singers should earn 12,000 Schillings per night (£450).[62]

As might be imagined, von Einem was not pleased with Puthon's report. The reaction of the Artistic Council was also hostile for they thought that von Karajan's financial demands would ruin Salzburg. The highest wages that singers were receiving in 1956 were 6,000 Schillings a night, half of von Karajan's proposed figure. They also feared that von Karajan's power to select all the casts would have a devastating effect on the Festival. Singers or conductors with whom he was not on good terms would simply not come to Salzburg, whatever their worth. The Council noted that modern operas had given Salzburg a new and dynamic profile, and that it wished to see the tradition continued. Nor was the notion of a three-year contract favourably received, for it would set a dangerous precedent. Other artists would demand equal treatment and the Directorium would be hard put to to deny them. Finally, the Festival would be so 'frozen' that it would not always seek the best of new talent, as it had in the past, when it engaged artists on a yearly basis. Von Karajan's demand for von Einem's removal called forth predictable outrage, and smacked of dictatorship. Soon, it seemed, the Directorium as a decision-making body would be dead, and one man alone would exert unprecedented power. The only issue which the Council found at all worthy of discussion was von Karajan's programme for 1957–1960. Here there were points of convergence. Again, however, the conductor's attitude was the imperious, 'take it or leave it,' and this the Council could not accept.[63]

Reading von Einem's correspondence at the time, one senses his immense frustration, which came both from his old philosophical differences with von Karajan and his deep personal dislike for the man. Between January and March of 1956 the Directorium met several times to discuss the course of the negotiations, and neither von Einem nor any other member of the Artistic Council was invited. There was no doubt that the Directorium wanted von Karajan; von Einem's presence would only muddy the waters.[64] In March, negotiations were concluded.

Klaus then wrote a note to von Einem, informing him that he would remain on the Artistic Council, that modern works would be a continuing element of the programme, that Neher and Schuh would stay. Von Karajan had assured the Directorium that the artistic tradition of Salzburg would be preserved.[65]

The story does not end here. For six more years von Einem remained Director of the Council, but his powers waned, and his invitations to meetings of the Directorium became more and more infrequent. The first 'formal' meeting of the two antagonists occurred in August 1956. Von Karajan was in a conciliatory frame of mind, and told the Directorium that he had no plans to get rid of Böhm, Schuh, Neher or anyone else. He accepted his disagreements with von Einem, but said that these were philosophical in nature and could be worked out through quiet discussion. He had but one new proposal. He, like others, had noticed that the Festival public, while increasing in quantity, was decreasing in quality. He suggested that it was vital to develop a '*Stammpublikum*', a core public, which could be counted on to commit itself over the long term to Salzburg. This public would consist of true lovers of art, and not of occasional tourists. To encourage such people von Karajan wanted to create a subscription series for the Festival. This idea was not immediately accepted by the Directorium, but von Karajan later applied it to his Easter festival, and eventually to the summer one as well. The maestro also talked at length about the technical possibilities of the new Festival Hall, and promised to consider modern operas on their merits. Von Einem kept strangely silent throughout the meeting, as did everyone else.[66]

Later, von Einem was treated as an 'outsider' as von Karajan consolidated his power. Von Einem's 'spy' Kaut kept him informed, however, about important decisions. In 1959 Puthon, then almost 90, decided that he would retire the next year. Kaut wrote to von Einem that he would either support his friend or Egon Hilbert for the Festival presidency.[67] But the Kuratorium would support neither, and, with von Karajan's backing, Paumgartner was chosen. He was already over seventy, but still retained his life-long interest in presenting Mozart's lesser-known works. Von Karajan would grant Paumgartner freedom in this area, as long as the new President would allow von Karajan to dominate the other areas of the Festival.[68]

Meanwhile, Klaus had become a member of the federal government—he would later become Chancellor—and had written to von Einem to say that a 'new era' had now begun, one that would undoubtedly be compared with the age of Furtwängler.[69] Von Einem did not share Klaus's joy, and when von Karajan (who gave up his position as Artistic Director in 1960) returned to become a permanent member of the Directorium in 1962, he realized that there were now no checks on von Karajan's powers. Paumgartner was 'senile', Puthon was dead.[70] In the autumn of 1962 von Einem resigned from the Artistic Council which, like its predecessors, had essentially fallen into disuse. He had, for the umpteenth time, asked the President to include the Council's recommendations in the general programme discussions of the Directorium; Paumgartner had not even bothered to answer the letter. The game was over. Von Karajan had won; there had been no modern operas presented since 1961, and there were no plans to perform any.[71]

In the long run, von Einem's 'defeat' was only temporary, in the sense that von Karajan did not shut the door completely on contemporary opera, and was always prepared to include a large number of twentieth-century works on the general Festival programme. But it was a bitter personal defeat for von Einem, whose fifteen years with the Festival now came to an unhappy end. He had once asked von Karajan how the maestro could fulfill all his responsibilities, as head of the Berlin Philharmonic, Artistic Director of Salzburg and Vienna, head of the New Philharmonia and so on. Would it not be better to concentrate on one post, and focus all his resources on that? Von Einem recalls that von Karajan had smiled, and remarked that he loved 'Das Spiel der Mächtigen', the game of the powerful. By 1960 von Karajan had played that game in Salzburg, and his victory was complete.[72]

The late Fifties was a period of transition, controversy and expectation; despite the internal debate over von Karajan's powers and the nature of the new Festival Hall, which was often leaked to the press, the Festival itself continued to prosper—and to expand. Indeed the major development during this period was the expansion of the programme, and the participation of guest orchestras, an idea which until then had been anathema to the Directorium.

From 1955 to 1957, in the absence of a central figure, Karl Böhm's responsibilities increased. In 1956 he conducted a *Figaro* which featured the young baritone, Dietrich Fischer-Dieskau, in the role of the Count. Fischer-Dieskau had been discovered shortly after the war, and had made his first appearance in Salzburg during the 1951 Festival, where he enchanted audiences with a rendition of Mahler's *Lieder eines fahrenden Gesellen*. His return in 1956 marked the beginning of an extraordinary popular reign in Salzburg. Dimitri Mitropoulos's reading of *Don Giovanni*, again featuring Siepi, was a triumph, during this, the two hundredth anniversary of Mozart's birth. Ballet, which had always been of marginal importance in Salzburg, now played an expanded role. Margherita Wallmann, a veteran of the 'golden age', choreographed Stravinsky's *Persephone* and Honegger's *La Danse des Morts* in 1955, and the next year George Balanchine brought the New York City Ballet to perform a pot-pourri of dances set to orchestral pieces by a host of composers, including Mozart and Debussy. Spanish and American dance companies came in the following years, confirming Salzburg's new commitment to the dance, and to its international role. As usual, Salzburg had its pick of famous soloists: Arthur Grumiaux, Nathan Milstein, Claudio Arrau and Geza Anda all gave solo concerts in 1956. Bruno Walter, now nearing eighty, returned for the last time to conduct Mozart's *Requiem*. German *Lieder*, which had never had a great international following, now became an important and growing element of the Salzburg repertoire. Seefried, Schwarzkopf and Fischer-Dieskau gave this art form a new life.

The most important expansion of the programme, however, was directly related to von Karajan's arrival on the scene. The directors had acquiesced to his request to include guest performances of the Berlin Philharmonic at the Festival. Once the precedent was established, Salzburg did not turn back. In 1958 the Amsterdam Concertgebouw Orchestra under Wolfgang Sawallisch and George Széll gave five concerts, the next year the French Radio Orchestra (ORTF) appeared, as did the New York Philharmonic under Leonard Bernstein, America's most popular native conductor. Gone were the days when the Vienna Philharmonic had a total monopoly. In the end everyone prospered from the change. With an expanded programme, the Vienna orchestra could not possibly perform all the operas and orchestral concerts in six crowded weeks. It still retained the prestige of being the sole orchestra employed for opera. Guest orchestras which appeared with their regular conductors gave the audience an opportunity to compare and contrast the various strengths and weaknesses of the world's most prestigious ensembles.

Another trend during these years was the change in the attitude of the critics. They no longer felt any responsibility to 'save' Salzburg. The

Festival was on solid financial grounds — almost too solid, perhaps. And commercialism was rampant. An American critic wrote in 1956:

> . . . where Wagner is a cult in Bayreuth, Mozart is a business in Salzburg. In the Mozart industry everything is identified with the composer; even the famous marzipan balls are called Mozart Kügel. In their prosperous devotion to their composer, most Salzburgers are not even aware that Mozart, aged twenty-four, repudiated his home town in protest against the meanness of its archbishop, Hieronymus, and never returned.[73]

The directors had tried to keep prices below those of Bayreuth in the early Fifties; by the end of the decade Salzburg had become the most expensive Festival anywhere, and top seats cost the Austrian equivalent of seven pounds, ten times the price of a meal in an average restaurant. Again, as in the past, critics complained about Salzburg élitism.[74]

Yet what distinguished the new criticism, especially of the Anglo-American variety, was its relative objectivity. Reviewers rarely mentioned Salzburg's 'idea', her 'mission', or even her natural beauty, an overriding theme in pre-war criticism. Instead they noted how complicated life was becoming in the city because of the huge influx of summer tourists and Festival visitors. Salzburg's old city was becoming one huge traffic jam. Unlike in the past, critics now had the ability to make comparisons. By the late Fifties, air travel allowed the critic to sample performances all over the world, and that world was dotted with other music festivals. In the Thirties critics inevitably travelled less. Now they could spend the season in New York, rush off to Vienna, London or Hamburg, and then summer in Bayreuth, Salzburg, Munich, Aix-en-Provence or Edinburgh. They could contrast Siepi's Don Giovanni in New York with his performance in Salzburg, for singers, and conductors too, were continually on the move. The same was true of stage directors, like Herbert Graf, whose Metropolitan Opera productions could now be judged against his Salzburg efforts. Von Karajan himself took this new mobility to the extreme, for at one point he held six important posts at the same time. In the long run, this trend may have contributed to the lowering of standards. For the critic, however, it was a bonanza. He could write with knowledge and familiarity about performances, productions and interpretations. He knew when a singer was 'out of voice' because he might well have seen that same singer, two months previously and five thousand miles away, when he or she was in top form. This new world put extraordinary pressure on Salzburg, for if the Festival aspired to present the best

Mozart in the world, it had to prove itself every year and in every performance. Audience and critics would not tolerate the second-rate.

Von Karajan's *persona*, his image, was formed in the public mind before he came to Salzburg. He had become a 'star' of a peculiarly modern kind, for as the premier conductor of the jet age, who comported himself like an oriental deity, his 'showmanship' outstripped that of any musical celebrity before or since. This posed a great problem for the critics, who reacted as much to the man as to his work. It became difficult to think about von Karajan's interpretation of a score, with his closed eyes, his sweeping baton, his shock of grey hair, without remembering his Mercedes, the private plane, the skiing, the yacht, the old marriage, the new marriage, the whispered stories of his Nazi past. It is hard to be objective when reading criticism of von Karajan's performances, because one is aware that the critic had brought so much baggage with him into the concert hall. Once von Karajan took over Salzburg and gradually made it his own, many critics, especially those from England and America, seemed to lean over backwards to find fault with his performances. This contrasted with most Salzburg and Viennese papers, who positively gushed over Austria's favourite son. But whatever critics or gossip columnists wrote, von Karajan, like Reinhardt, Toscanini and Furtwängler before him, mesmerized his audiences and put Salzburg at the centre of the summer musical world.

Most critics agreed that his staging and conducting of *Fidelio* in the 1957 Festival was masterful. One reviewer thought that von Karajan had used the confines of the Riding School even more eloquently than had Reinhardt when he had staged *Faust*.[75] His other opera, *Falstaff*, brought back memories of Toscanini's famous 1935 production, though one critic noted that there was not a 'sparkle of laughter' in the orchestral playing.[76] The 1958 *Don Carlo*, also in the Riding School, was less appreciated, though Gründgens had made considerable efforts to render the Verdi opera plausible, despite being unable to make any scene changes. Some critics saw von Karajan's interpretation as approaching the vulgar.[77] In 1959, generally considered a bad year in Salzburg, von Karajan's *Orfeo ed Euridice* (another work closely associated with the Thirties) was considered by many to be hopelessly romanticized.[78]

If von Karajan was subject to telling criticism, perhaps because he *was* von Karajan, Karl Böhm, with less flamboyance and an almost non-existent podium personality, continued to receive positive reviews, both for his Mozart interpretations and his 1959 Salzburg première of Strauss's *Die schweigsame Frau*. If he disliked being Salzburg's 'second' conductor — and he did — he kept it to himself. His outward image of the quiet and modest *Kapellmeister* pleased critics and audiences alike.

Modern opera did not fare well in Salzburg in the late Fifties; this was not Karajan's doing, despite his well-known prejudices. Save for Liebermann's fairly successful *Die Schule der Frauen* in 1957, the operas presented — Samuel Barber's *Vanessa* (the New York Metropolitan Opera production, presented in 1958), Frank Martin's *Mysterium von der Geburt des Herrn* (1960) and Heimo Erbse's *Julietta* (1959) — were savaged by the critics and drew small audiences.[79] The monumental failure of *Vanessa* forced critics to rethink their attitude towards modern opera in Salzburg, and many eventually came to von Karajan's view, that Salzburg should only stage contemporary works when they were of sufficient quality to reward the effort. There was little sense in committing vast energy and expense to the performance of inferior works which would give a temporary ego satisfaction to their authors — and evenings of displeasure or boredom to everyone else.

The changes in the late Fifties caused many critics to engage in a serious debate about Salzburg's future. Some saw a new and expansive era at hand, others were horrified. Robert Jungk, of *Die Weltwoche* in Zurich, gave away his prejudices in the title of his article: 'Salzburg sells her soul.' He compared Salzburg to *Jedermann*, calling it *'Jederstadt'* or 'every city'. Salzburg, like *Jedermann*, was in need of redemption, he claimed, for it was selling its moral heritage on the altar of Mammon. The city had tripled in population since the Thirties. The elegant Festival public had made it rich. Three times as many people attended the Festival as in 1925. But, to the writer, the 'monster' Festival Hall and the 'ugly' new hotels that had sprouted everywhere were metaphorical symbols of 'every city's' decline. The projected new Festival Hall had begun with promise, there had even been talk of an international competition to choose its design, in which renowned architects such as Frank Lloyd Wright and Richard Neutra would take part, but soon Holzmeister, because of his political connections, had taken over. His idea, to carve the new Hall out of the Mönchsberg, appealed to few, but Klaus forced it through probably because he wanted to be remembered for a massive project, like Franz Rehrl's highway to the Grossglockner. At one point Klaus had justified his support for the new Hall in these words:

Salzburg finds itself in the role of a hotel keeper who does not have enough beds, and is faced with the choice of increasing the size of the hotel — or losing out to the competition.

To this, the critic replied that Salzburg's mission had nothing to do with hotel beds, or with gratifying the needs of the masses with outsize theatre stages or ugly, impersonal hotels. The founders, Reinhardt, Strauss and von Hofmannsthal, had wanted to bring the spirit of art into an unhappy world, which was disgusted with rampant materialism. That spirit had been meant to abide not only in the theatres and opera halls, but on every street corner, in the shade of every park, in the broad expanse of the town squares. Now, like *Jedermann*, that Salzburg spirit was declining in the pursuit of 'extravagance and greed'. Jungk ended his article with a fitting quotation, God the Father's advice to Jedermann:

Your strivings are only for earthly gain,
You scorn what is above.[80]

A Viennese journal attacked the new Hall in another light. Its sheer size would shatter Salzburg's pretensions to cater to an international music élite. Now the first ten rows of the Festival Hall might be filled with educated music-lovers; the rest of the seats would be occupied by 'high society types' from America and the rest of the world.[81]

R.H. Ruppel of Munich's distinguished *Süddeutsche Zeitung* questioned von Karajan's role. The failure of Barber's *Vanessa* had caused Ruppel to ponder the direction that the Festival was taking. *Vanessa* was a bad opera; worse, it should never have been staged in Salzburg, for it was totally alien to the Festival's tradition. Certainly von Hofmannsthal's original ideas concerning the equality of theatre and opera in Salzburg were outdated; monetary considerations necessitated the primacy of opera. Yet the programme conception, based on the South German – Italian tradition, had stood the test of time. *Vanessa* had 'betrayed' the idea of the Festival. If von Karajan had new ideas, if he wanted to lead Salzburg in a new direction, then he should articulate those ideas. At present Salzburg was performing operas, some old, some new, but there seemed to be no unifying concept behind the Festival. It was an Artistic Director's obligation to provide this. He must answer the question, *'Quo vadis illustrissime?'*[82]

Another article put Salzburg's past into perspective. Kurt Klinger's clear-headed analysis was closer to the truth than those of other critics, who decried the present and longed for the purity of the past. He argued that the founders, von Hofmannsthal, Strauss and Reinhardt were, above all, good publicists; to win converts to the Festival they had employed arguments that in many cases they did not believe themselves. Von Hofmannsthal's embrace of the 'absurd' views of the philosopher Nadler about the Bavarian – Austrian cultural tradition was a tactic to interest people in the Salzburg idea, nothing more. Both Reinhardt and Strauss had survived on their wits, and enriched themselves in their trade. Neither was a true idealist; there never had been such a thing as pure idealism in Salzburg. Ideas did not produce a Festival; money did. The directors of the Festival in the Twenties and Thirties acted at times honestly, at times dishonestly; they were inspired on occasion by idealistic motives, other decisions were taken out of sheer expediency. That was, and is, the way of the world of artistic representation.

> Today, von Karajan is acting in the same tradition, though times have changed. We must accept this for better or for worse, as well as the iron, sometimes brutal, laws of management. That von Karajan avoids making solemn pronouncements about the 'mission' of the festival is understandable; he realizes that the public who comes to Salzburg lives in a nihilistic world, and cannot be won over by pretty phrases.

Speeches about the Salzburg 'idea' were meaningless. To succeed the Festival must present works which pleased the public, no more no less. Von Karajan knew this; his critics did not. They were 'fantasists' who wrote about a Salzburg which never existed. There was no Festival 'artistic tradition' that could be separated from the necessity to satisfy the audience. The words of the founders must be reinterpreted for our own age. Von Hofmannsthal had said that 'common' and 'undignified' works had no place in the Salzburg programme; but what was 'undignified' and 'common' in 1920 might not be so today.

Klinger went on to point out that the Festival would only prosper if it related to the world as it was, not the the 'Bavarian–Austrian' heritage, a suspect concept which, in any case, meant nothing to the modern Festival-goer. The modern audience came from all over the world, and Salzburg too must invite artists from everywhere, from New York, from Tokyo, from Rio. In a world of a thousand festivals, Salzburg could still distinguish itself by the quality of its productions and its dedication to Mozart. It would be a mistake, however, for Salzburg to avoid competition and satisfy itself that it could put on the best Mozart performances in the world. The Festival must compete at all levels, and only use as its base its unrivalled mastery of Mozart's work. Mozart was the most universal of composers, and Salzburg's best means of honouring its native son was to become universal itself.[83]

Klinger may have exaggerated a bit — von Hofmannsthal during one period of his life *was* sincerely influenced by Nadler's ideas — but his major points are valid. In essence he criticized the superficial nostalgia which appealed to many of the critics. By implication he admitted that directors and audiences of an earlier age might have been motivated by idealism, at least some of the time. But putting on a Festival entailed a great deal more than grandiose pronouncements. Managerial skills were as important in 1935 as they were in 1958. In the Twenties and Thirties the world may have been a slightly simpler place, but the production of great art evolved from conflict, disagreement and intrigue. It would always be so. Von Karajan understood the complexity of the post-war world, and Salzburg's role within that world. He was not betraying the Salzburg 'idea'. He was adapting it to the rigours of the new age.

The Fifties occupied a special place in Austrian hearts, thanks to the Peace Treaty of 1955, which ended the occupation and politically defined Austria's role in the post-war world. In the long run the Treaty, signed after years of interminable negotiation and Russian obstructionism, did more to help form a national consciousness than all the speeches of politicians, and all the ruminations of intellectuals. But Austria paid a price for the Treaty. Her government had to accept permanent neutrality; it could join neither a military nor an economic multi-national bloc, neither NATO nor what was to become the Common Market (now the EEC). As a result, the country suffered in economic terms; its growth was much slower than that of its western neighbours. Politically, however, Austria was forced into a role which, as time went on, she began to exploit—and enjoy: she became a self-styled second Switzerland, an island of peace surrounded by Warsaw Pact and NATO nations involved in a full-scale armaments race. Geographically the country was hopelessly exposed, but at the same time she could use her neutrality to underline her role as a meeting point for East and West; and this has been a keynote of Austrian policy, whatever the party in power, ever since. There was also general agreement that the country's natural wonders, the Alpine west, should be publicized as never before, so as to augment the country's lifeblood, tourism. Austria began to define herself even more closely with her cultural heritage, her unique contribution to the Western world.

Salzburg was a key to that cultural heritage, and, as has been seen, as early as 1950 the federal government passed a statute guaranteeing considerable government financial support to the Festival and setting up a structure of official organs responsible for its artistic and financial administration. By the time the Peace Treaty had been signed, there was no doubt that the Salzburg Festival was on secure grounds; most performances were sold out, despite the high ticket prices, and most prominent conductors, singers and musicians in the world enraptured the growing audiences; the historic grumblings of the Salzburgers were silenced by the huge economic boon that the Festival brought.

The fundamental question posed at the beginning of this chapter—whether one individual should take primary responsibility for programme planning and performance—had finally been solved, for Salzburg always abhorred a vacuum. First it was Reinhardt, then Krauss, then Toscanini who took command. The 'interregnum' from 1946 to 1950, when no figure was dominant, brought forth an era of intense creativity as the Festival struck out in new directions. Then Furtwängler stepped in, and after his death von Karajan made his successful bid for power. He has wielded it ever since.

9

Von Karajan's Imperium

1960–87

The opening day of the 1960 Festival saw two gala concerts, each of which was suggestive of battles won and lost, of the confused priorities occasioned by Salzburg's massive new Festival Hall. At eleven in the morning, the Hall was officially opened. After the usual speeches, Herbert von Karajan conducted the 'Gloria' from Mozart's C minor Mass. That evening the maestro mounted the podium to conduct Salzburg's first *Rosenkavalier* since 1953, only the second production of the opera in the Festival's history, as Alfred Roller's old Vienna sets had endured a quarter of a century. Now scene designer Teo Otto, a veteran of Otto Klemperer's Kroll Theatre in Berlin during the late Twenties, collaborated with Rudolph Hartmann on a magisterial production which filled the huge stage to overflowing with Straussian charm, wit and melancholy. The two concerts, Mozart in the morning, Strauss in the evening, were the culmination of a spirited debate; Salzburg traditionalists thought it scandalous that Strauss, not Mozart, should be performed on the opening night. Von Karajan would not have it otherwise. In the end the official opening in the morning gave Mozart his due; in the evening Karajan got his way. So it would be for the next quarter of a century and beyond. Von Karajan would dominate Salzburg for a longer period than any of his predecessors, and the new Festival Hall in its massive grandeur, would be the vehicle for his artistry.

If *Rosenkavalier* was a tried and true Festival opera, which had been given many times in the previous thirty-five years, the same could not be said for Verdi's *Il Trovatore*, which von Karajan chose to stage and conduct for the 1962 Festival. The opera had a matchless cast in Leontyne Price, Giulietta Simionato, Ettore Bastianini and Franco Corelli, and again Otto created the scenic design. In a sense this event had already been prefigured in the conversations between von Einem

169

and von Karajan fifteen years before, when the maestro had argued that Salzburg audiences wanted to see popular operas performed by the world's greatest singers, and cared little about so-called Festival tradition. In the past, excuses had always been made when tradition had been flouted. When Toscanini vowed to conduct *Falstaff* in 1935, he had met immediate opposition from the Festival directors, but this had melted away when the maestro threatened not to come to Salzburg at all if his wishes were not met. Toscanini's motives had nothing to do with preserving a Salzburg tradition; he loved the opera—and wanted to spite Mussolini. The director had then lamely decreed that *Falstaff* would be performed because the opera was Salzburg's way of 'Europeanizing' the Festival. Some were quick to point out that, after all, the founders had worshipped the age of the Baroque, and that the Shakespeare play upon which the opera was based was a product of that age. The same argument was marshalled after the war, when Verdi's *Otello* graced the Salzburg stage. However, a rationale for *Trovatore* was not forthcoming, neither from the conductor-director, nor from the Festival's new president, Bernhard Paumgartner. There could be none, save for the obvious fact that Verdi's dense dramatic and extremely popular work lent itself perfectly to the vastness of the Festival Hall stage. Though a few reviewers mentioned this, most were carried away by the production and the singing, and audiences, some of whom paid over forty pounds for a ticket from a hotel porter, were ecstatic. That summer one heard little talk of Salzburg's other splendours; all was dominated by Giuseppi Verdi, *Il Trovatore* and Herbert von Karajan.

The extraordinary success of the opera proved von Karajan's theory to be correct, and over the next two decades the maestro conducted, generally at two-year intervals, his own productions of many of the world's greatest grand operas. Some of these, like *Elektra* (1964), *Falstaff* (1981) and *Salome* (1977), were squarely in the Salzburg tradition. Others like *Boris Godunov* (1965), *Carmen* (1966, 1985), and *Aida* (1979) were not. Most, save for *Aida* and *Carmen*, received critical acclaim. Few critics now questioned what relevance *Carmen* or *Aida* had to a Mozart festival. Oddly, von Karajan, whose mastery of Mozart operas, at least in the Fifties, was generally recognized, was unable to satisfy critics with his three major Mozart productions in the new Festival Hall: *Figaro* (1972), *Don Giovanni* (1968) and *Zauberflöte* (1974). Most reviewers noted that the delicacy and intimacy of Mozart was lost in the vastness of the new Hall, and all three operas tended to be overproduced. On occasion other conductors performed operas there, but only with von Karajan's permission. He quickly let it be known that, whatever the statutes read, it was indeed 'his' Hall.

If von Karajan could on occasion receive a roasting from the critics, his standing with the public was higher than ever before. Whether conducting an opera in the new Festival Hall, or an orchestral concert with 'his' Berlin Philharmonic, the maestro's mere presence generated excitement bordering on hysteria that no other conductor could command. The public clearly adored him; he could do no wrong. For many, no price was too high to attend a von Karajan performance, and Salzburg, despite increasing competition, remained securely in the centre of the world's music festivals.

It would be a mistake however, to think that, because of von Karajan's cavalier approach to the Festival's artistic tradition, Salzburg was only a showcase for his multifarious talents. Mozart was not forgotten, thanks to the efforts of Karl Böhm. Böhm became ensconced as the Festival's 'second' conductor. and continued to preserve the flame of Salzburg's first composer, Mozart, in the old Festival Hall. Böhm's Mozart performances of the period were matchless, and most are preserved on record. He was a small man, and never possessed the electrifying quality or the regal bearing of von Karajan. But Böhm had, like all great conductors, a strong will matched by a great belief in his own status, and, like them, he too threatened to resign when he did not get his way. This occurred in 1956, when the directors had given von Karajan a three-year contract. But then Böhm too had his contract extended, and the clouds parted. According to observers, Böhm was intelligent enough to know that the Festival lived and breathed on von Karajan's success, and von Karajan equally realized Böhm's qualities. As a result, though the men never became close friends, they worked out a *modus vivendi* which endured for two decades, Böhm accepting that von Karajan was always the *primus inter pares*. Böhm conducted his favourites, Mozart and Strauss, in the old Festival Hall and in the 1971 season was permitted to revive the once vilified *Wozzeck*—with outstanding success. His efforts were not unappreciated, by either audiences or critics. He commanded a strong following among the Salzburg faithful, and many saw in him, rather than in von Karajan, the authentic standard-bearer of the Salzburg idea.

Böhm died in August 1981, thus bringing to an end a Salzburg career of forty-three years, rich in diversity and accomplishment. On 26 August of that year the Vienna Philharmonic performed the Mozart *Requiem* in his honour. The conductor was a young American, James Levine, still in his mid-thirties, who had been coming to Salzburg since

171

1975. *Le roi est mort, vive le roi!* There was symbolism in the event, an almost tangible passing of hands. For by that time Levine, Musical Director of the Metropolitan Opera in New York, had established himself as an expert Mozartian, and much, much more. Salzburg needed to look no further for its 'second' conductor, and Levine, despite his youth, has fulfilled that role ever since.

Over the past quarter of a century the Festival has followed a pattern, a recipe for success which has survived mini-scandals, occasional broadsides from critics, attacks from government officials and a gradual decrease in the ageing von Karajan's activities. One of its major elements has been the Berlin Philharmonic, which had now become Salzburg's second orchestra in residence. Though the old rivalry with Vienna never really died out, the latter had the satisfaction of having exclusive rights to the opera house. The Berlin Philharmonic was employed only for orchestral concerts, usually under the baton of its lifetime conductor, von Karajan, but also from time to time under famous guest conductors. Serenades, solo concerts, *Lieder* recitals, chamber concerts and Mozart matinées were expanded, both to satisfy increased demand and to permit less well-heeled Festival-goers, unable to afford the high ticket prices for the operas and major orchestral concerts, to taste at least some of the pleasures of the Festival. Indeed, for the music-lover, these concerts were a feast in themselves. Nowhere else in the world could one hear the known and the less well-known works of Mozart played with such delight, or listen to such an extensive repertoire of *Lieder* in such a short period of time. These performances lacked the 'snob appeal' of those in the Festival Halls. There was rarely a dinner jacket or a designer creation in sight, but the settings, the Mozarteum, the exquisite rococo rooms in Schloss Mirabell or the Residenz, provided the elegance, the audiences the enthusiasm, the performers the dedication. Salzburg had something for everyone.

However, in the realm of theatre, always problematic since the days of Reinhardt, the pattern broke down. In the early Sixties, with von Karajan's backing, the Festival saw a rebirth of interest in the stage, as Leopold Lindtberg produced Parts I and II of *Faust*. A few of Reinhardt's players—Hermann Thimig, Ewald Balser, Paul Hartmann, Attila Hörbiger and Paula Wessely—were still active, to remind audiences of the theatre's glorious past in Salzburg. But after *Faust* the theatre slept until the early Seventies, when the Italian-born director of the Teatro Piccolo of Milan, Giorgio Strehler, made his triumphal—though short lived—entry into the Salzburg scene. His production of

Das Spiel der Mächtigen, a two-part drama, based on Shakespeare's Henry plays, caused a sensation in 1973–4. His departure under duress in early 1975 left the way open for Ernst Haeusserman, Lothar's son-in-law (and, like his father-in-law, as well as his early mentor, Max Reinhardt, Director of the Theater an der Josefstadt in Vienna) to take full responsibility for Salzburg's theatrical planning; this he accomplished with style until his death in 1984. He also directed *Jedermann* from 1973 onwards, keeping faith with the tradition started by Reinhardt. In other respects however Haeusserman did not believe in reliving the past; he had little taste for theatrical experimentation and realized that in the Seventies and Eighties there was no possibility of bringing in non-German-speaking audiences to the Salzburg theatre, as Reinhardt had done. It was better to have straightforward first-class performances of a German or Austrian classic, or even of Shakespeare, than to try to create a spectacle which would appeal to no one.

In 1960 the ninety-year-old Baron Puthon stepped down and was replaced by Bernhard Paumgartner, himself over seventy, a man full of honours in the musical world who had lived and breathed the Festival all his adult life, and represented a last living link with the heady days of 1920 and 1921. As a Mozart scholar and active purveyor of the composer's genius, Paumgartner had no peers. The new President was elected after the usual haggling, intrigue and infighting. He was no close friend to his former student, von Karajan, but was content to allow the maestro to make the major decisions concerning operatic and concert programmes and personnel, as long as he, Paumgartner, could exert his power over the other areas of musical performance. Paumgartner's life-long interest was to revive the lesser known early works of Mozart, such as *Lucio Silla*, *Bastien et Bastienne*, *Mitridate Re di Ponto*, *La Finta Giardiniera* and *Zaïde*. Most of these products of Mozart's youth, however, gained no enduring popularity, and after Paumgartner's death in 1981 were rarely revived. Part of the reason may have been economic. While vast sums were spent on superb productions in the Festival Halls, Mozart's early operas were performed in the Residenz, a hall with inferior accoustics, and with casts and conductors of less than star quality. It is a fact of operatic life that unknown or little-known works depend on inventive productions and top-rate performances in order to succeed with a sceptical public.[1] Paumgartner did not have the means to make these operas live again.

Ironically, his greatest triumph was his discovery of an oratorio composed by the Italian Emilio de' Cavalieri. *La rappresentazione di anima e di corpo* (*The Representation of the Soul and the Body*) was first performed in 1600 in Rome, almost a decade before Monteverdi's epoch-making *Orfeo*. In 1968 it was performed at Salzburg in the Riding School; the following year it was moved to the Kollegien Church and was then performed in the shadow of Fischer von Erlach's majestic altar for the next five seasons, enrapturing both critics and audiences.[2] In a sense *La rappresentazione* was Paumgartner's answer to those, now legion, who claimed that Salzburg could never return to the heady days of the Twenties, or to its original idea. Like Reinhardt and von Hofmannsthal, the President had plucked an unknown work out of the baroque past, and made it live through careful adaptation, Herbert Graf's simple but powerful production and the ambiance created by the church setting in which it was performed. Once again an inspired gesture had brought back Reinhardt's notion of half a century before, 'the city as stage'. Paumgartner had always seen the period of *Jedermann* and *The Great World Theatre* in the Twenties as Salzburg's most creative age.

Bowed down with the years, Paumgartner died in 1971, in his early eighties. He had strolled around the small town of Salzburg in 1920 with Reinhardt in search of the proper setting for *Jedermann*, had conducted the Festival's first Mozart offering in 1921, had educated two generations of music lovers about the glories of minor Mozart and had turned the serenade evenings and Sunday matinées into integral parts of the Salzburg scene. Indeed today the Mozart matinées are so popular that they are repeated twice weekly, on Saturday and Sunday mornings. The audiences pay relatively little for their morning's pleasure; they may look a bit scruffy, but they love Mozart and that, for Paumgartner, was what Salzburg was all about.

Josef Kaut succeeded to the presidency in 1971; he had been a member of the Directorium since the early Fifties, and had also held the post of Cultural Counsellor to the Provincial Government. Kaut was a Socialist of long standing, and in the Fifties had been an intimate friend of von Einem, as well as a visceral enemy of the then Provincial Governor, Josef Klaus. By 1971, however, Kaut, himself over seventy, had outlived most of his enemies as well as his friends. Like Paumgartner, Kaut had made his peace with von Karajan—otherwise he would have never been chosen. He was no musicologist, but twenty years on the Directorium had given him an incomparable knowledge of the workings of the Festival. In the Sixties he published a major history of the Festival which is amazingly candid, given his closeness to power.

At the end of his life he produced a second volume which was no more and no less than a settling of old scores with various individuals, in particular with von Einem, Strehler, and the playwright Thomas Bernhard, all of whom had caused him grief.[3] Kaut saw his role as that of a publicist and a defender of Salzburg, and played it well. He argued articulately against those who attacked the Salzburg star system, the lack of new music, the incoherence of the Festival programme. Kaut knew his audience's taste, and shared von Karajan's aversion to presenting contemporary opera for the mere sake of being able to brag that Salzburg was in the avant garde. He presided over a decade of artistic and financial prosperity such as Salzburg had never known before. He had, therefore, no inclination for change.

Kaut died in 1983. Over the objections of many who were close to the Festival, von Karajan engineered the choice of Albert Moser, President of the *Musikverein* in Vienna, a native of Graz and a life-long musical administrator, as the new President. Moser had been a friend of von Karajan's for thirty years, had no artistic pretensions and saw his office primarily as a forum for improving Salzburg's public relations.[4] His selection did not sit well with the local potentates. They did not like von Karajan's *Diktat*, nor the fact that Moser continued to live in Vienna, ran the *Musikverein* and only came to Salzburg once or twice in the winter and during the Festival, whereas previous presidents had either been from Salzburg or had made it their home. But von Karajan's threat of resignation turned the tide. Shades of Toscanini—and Furtwängler!

Throughout the von Karajan era there has been no lack of criticism of the Festival, particularly from local, Viennese or German critics who are perforce in closer contact with Salzburg than those from other countries. Some of their themes are well known: lack of direction and of a coherent artistic policy, failure to encourage interest in new music, the high price of tickets, the shabby state of the theatre, the musical ignorance of the wealthy Salzburg audiences. In past decades many critics decried Salzburg snobbishness; now they moan about the city's carnival atmosphere brought about by the advent of mass tourism. Indeed traffic jams in central Salzburg can rival those anywhere, buses of brash tourists of all nationalities line the Salzach, restaurants and cafés are jammed. Most of these tourists will never set foot in a concert—anywhere—but they make life uncomfortable for those who will, and destroy the intimacy and charm which are Salzburg's trump card. Needless to say, though Salzburg merchants may growl about the unpleasantness caused by the crowds, they are very happy to sell them their wares. Culture equals business as Franz Rehrl said long ago.

There was, however, one criticism which led to a certain amount of soul-searching among the Festival directors. Siegfried Melchinger, writing in *Theater Heute* in 1964, remarked that Salzburg seemed to be running out of creative energy. The great post-war epoch of Neher, Schuh and von Einem was over, programmes were put together haphazardly and there was no individual on the Directorium (and this included von Karajan) with sufficient breadth of experience in all of the arts—theatre, opera, music (including contemporary music) and dance—who could take charge and mould the Festival into a vital living force. The pre-war Reinhardt–von Hofmannsthal–Strauss era was over, as was the age of Böhm, Furtwängler and the unequalled Viennese Mozart ensemble. The Austrian–Bavarian festival of the Twenties had become a European festival under Toscanini; now it was of international importance, but it could never achieve its potential under parochial and fragmented leadership.[5]

Seven years later, in the most thorough study of Salzburg critics ever made, a pair of researchers pursued in-depth interviews with almost a hundred reviewers who had attended the 1971 Festival. Many had had a long association with Salzburg. Interestingly enough, most echoed some of Melchinger's complaints. They were dissatisfied with the programmes, felt that contemporary music was being shunted aside for reasons of financial expediency, decried the conservatism of the Festival directors and Festival audiences, and even suggested that the quality of several of the productions for that year was not of Festival standard. Over sixty per cent suggested that a strong programme director might make all the difference. And most believed that the theatre could be, and should be, given a new lease on life.[6]

1971 also saw the Festival subject to a different kind of criticism, this time from the people of Salzburg itself. Though Austria had no Vietnam generation *per se*, the country was no stranger to the frustrations of the young in the Sixties. In Salzburg this protest against the older generation took the form of the creation of an anti-Festival, *Die Szene der Jugend*, which, as its title implies, was aimed at the youth of Salzburg who both loved art and despised the bourgeoisie who paid a fortune for their tickets. The anti-Festival took to the streets, put on outdoor plays, operas, dances and poetic recitations. Ticket prices (when tickets there were) were minimal. Avant garde productions were encouraged, and even Oscar Fritz Schuh helped to produce.[7] As time went on, the anger of the locals subsided, the *Szene* became more organized—and inevitably less shocking—and the city began to grant it small subsidies. Ironically, it is now advertised in the brochure of the Festival which it was created to mock.

Salzburg's most recent brush with scandal occurred in the winter of 1983, when the State Auditor's report on Festival finances was leaked to the press. The reverberations are still continuing. Once before, in 1935, a State Auditor's report had criticized the Festival's profligate spending, but in that simpler age, there were no press leaks; Puthon and Kerber bargained with the Auditor, and that had ended the matter. 1983 was different because the Viennese and Salzburg press took great pleasure in pointing out how rich everyone with any connection to the Festival was becoming, and this at the taxpayer's expense. Festival functionaries, it appears, were receiving eighteen months' salary for twelve months' work (the usual rate in Austria is fourteen months' salary). Artists who performed in Salzburg were receiving salaries far above the international wage scale. Furthermore, no expense was spared for operatic productions. The Auditor noted that, even for rehearsals, Don Giovanni's glass (which he dutifully breaks at the end of his champagne aria) was invariably crystal, and that the silver rose presented by Octavian to Sophie in Act Two of *Der Rosenkavalier* was made of silver, whereas the Berlin Opera production made do with plastic.[8] The Festival directors replied that great art was beyond price.

Then all those with a complaint against the Festival joined the fray, including the then Socialist Cultural Counsellor for the province, Dr Herbert Möritz. He was concerned that the Festival, while wasting such huge sums of money, made so little effort to accommodate the local population, most of whom who could never dream of attending these expensive productions. And his words were echoed by the Socialist Minister of Education, Helmut Zilk, who refused to accept free tickets to Festival performances. By an odd stroke of fortune, Zilk left the Ministry in late 1984 and was replaced by Möritz, who now claims to be satisfied with the direction Salzburg is taking to open up its performances, usually by offering seats at general rehearsals to the local populace.[9] Möritz's new responsibilities have radically changed his perspective; he does not wish to discuss his earlier views, and now supports the idea, which he earlier fought vigorously, of a third reconstruction of the old Festival Hall. The purpose of the reconstruction is symbolic of Salzburg's continuing success with its public. At the moment it is impossible to put on performances simultaneously at the old Festival Hall and the Riding School. Artists use common dressing rooms, and the noise of one performance would

177

usually disturb the other. The changes will be costly, but when completed will allow the Festival to increase the number of performances to satisfy its ravenous public.

And it is just the presence of that public, always enthusiastic, always reliable, that has enabled the Festival directors to ignore, albeit politely, much of the inevitable, and usually repetitive, criticism it has received. Only in one area has there been a certain change of perspective in recent years, that of twentieth-century and contemporary music; and even here the directors have gone to great lengths not to alienate a public which has little taste for the new. Much of the credit for this new direction can be given to Gerhard Wimberger a conductor, composer and professor at the Mozarteum, who became a member of the Directorium in 1972, and to Otto Sertl, the General Secretary of the Festival from 1980 to 1985. Wimberger brags that almost fifty per cent of the orchestral programmes now feature music written after 1900. Of course much that was new and shocking in the Twenties and Thirties, including the works of Stravinsky, Bartók, Prokofiev and Berg, for example, is now familiar to modern audiences. However Wimberger wants to see even more contemporary works on the programme, and the Festival on occasion has commissioned such works, though Salzburg will never be a centre for musical experimentation.[10] Three modern operas were presented between 1972 and 1986, two of these world premières: Carl Orff's *De temporum fine comoedia* (1973), Friedrich Cerha's *Baal* (1981) and Luciano Berio's *Un re in Ascolto* (1984). All of these works were expensive to mount and the Festival directors realized that, whatever the publicity, money would be lost. As a result the administration worked out a scheme which only functions, it must be said, when too many people are chasing too few tickets for the more popular operas. Potential ticket buyers who wish to see, say, *Don Giovanni* or *Carmen*, must also buy tickets for new operas (when they are being performed) or other concerts and recitals whose programmes are somewhat more adventurous, and thus risk being poorly attended. In this way Salzburg manages to sell out practically every concert in any given year.[11] Thus world premières of modern operas and new music are still an occasional part of the Festival, a compromise between audiences, who could probably do without them, critics who could not do without them, and directors trying to forge a *juste milieu*.

Critics have always complained about the snob appeal of Salzburg, though none has ever presented a scheme by which the Festival could both pay for itself and have a sufficiency of lower-priced seats. Today

Salzburg no longer pretends to cater for everyone, for the city is too small to cope with a mass influx of tourists. Certain areas are now banned to tourist traffic, which has helped considerably, but the newly-created open spaces are often filled to overflowing. As a result few artists are seen in the old cafés which were once a major centre of social life; instead they tend to gather in Parsch, an elegant suburb which tourists rarely visit, or in hotels on the Mönchsberg or the Gaisberg.

Another recent change is the extreme mobility of performers. Since there are dozens of major festivals occurring all over the world, to many artists Salzburg is but one stop on their own festival tour. They do not stay on after their performance. Except for a few critics who have been attending Salzburg for years—like H. H. Stuckenschmidt, dean of German critics, who holds court most days in various restaurants in the city—there is little of the camaraderie and close-knit social fabric associated with the Reinhardt–Zweig era, when performers, critics, audiences and directors met frequently at parties and in cafés. This may displease ageing veterans, but most modern visitors have never experienced anything else, and are used to the relative anonymity of daily life in Salzburg. 'If this is Tuesday it must be Salzburg' is a comment that now could come not only from tourists on package trips, but also from many Festival performers.

Critics have frequently written about the progressive lowering of standards. Of course their criteria are entirely subjective, and the nostalgia quotient is high; each generation of critics has looked back to a more glorious Salzburg. This began in the late Twenties, and will presumably always be with us. Certainly the charged atmosphere of the Thirties was unique, as was the flavour of innovation and excitement which permeated Salzburg after the war. Whether the actual performances of the Thirties, Forties and Fifties were superior to a later age is a question which is much harder to answer.

One artist who has thought deeply about the subject is Anton Dermota, now in his seventies, who as a young tenor first sang in Salzburg under Toscanini in the mid-Thirties; his career at the Vienna State Opera spanned four decades. In his memoirs he comments on the changes he has seen. Standards for singers have dropped, he believes, thanks in part to the multiple opportunities that an artist with a potentially great voice now has. There is less likelihood of a singer of potential star quality serving a long apprenticeship, learning many roles, nurturing his or her talent. Instead, the singer is quickly pushed (and often needs little prodding) into the peripatetic world of continual travel and performance on every continent. Artists' agents encourage singers early in their careers to specialize in certain carefully chosen roles, even if, in the end, these may turn out to be unsuited for their voices. Inevitably, this trend both dooms ensemble opera, for superior singers refuse to remain in one place long enough to create that ensemble, and often shortens careers. The number of singers who have become 'burned out' at a relatively early age, thanks to the frenetic pace of their professional lives, is legion.[12] Dietrich Fischer-Dieskau concurs with Dermota's judgement. Fischer-Dieskau has combined an extraordinary international career with deep interest in musicology, which has permitted him to avoid the dangers of over-exposure. He also chose his operatic roles with scrupulous care, and some of his best work was singing Mozart roles in the Salzburg of the late Fifties and early Sixties.[13] The unforgettable Mozart ensemble opera, born of the collaboration of Neher, Böhm and Schuh, graced Salzburg for two decades after the war; it is no more. Certainly Mozart is today sung well in Salzburg, but one can often hear it better done in Aix or at Glyndebourne. There Mozart may be performed by lesser singers, but adequate rehearsal time and the quest for ensemble perfection dominate all else.

Franz Endler has been following Salzburg closely for thirty of his fifty years, and his is the most influential voice in Austrian music criticism; he, and others, see a new danger: the predominance of the stage director.[14] In this century we have passed through the age of the singer to that of the conductor and now to that of the scene designer and stage director. Jean Pierre Ponnelle has been responsible for most Mozart productions in Salzburg for the past decade. He loves to work in Salzburg, and is lionized by the public. He is satisfied with his position and desires no greater responsibilities.[15] Ponnelle's talents are appreciated world-wide. His renown is such that Festival-goers often refer to 'Ponnelle's *Flute*' when commenting on his highly successful production which has graced the Salzburg stage for a record eight years in a row. Twenty years ago, these same people might have referred to 'Levine's *Flute*'. Mozart's name is no longer mentioned.

Another dominating director of the Sixties and early Seventies was Giorgio Strehler. Unlike Ponnelle, his ambitions were unlimited, and he had the solid backing of Reinhardt's widow, Helene Thimig, who saw Strehler as the sole living director whose flair and genius reminded her of her late husband.[16] This Italian began his collaboration with Salzburg in 1965, with an original and evocative production of *Die*

Entführung, certainly the greatest production of the opera that the Festival had ever known. For the next few years the Directorium tried to engage Strehler to make a long-term commitment to Salzburg. His irascible personality and indecision slowed down negotiations. Finally, in 1971, Strehler signed a contract as a 'consultant' to the Directorium. He planned with von Karajan to mount new productions of all the major Mozart operas, and to direct a series of plays. Like Reinhardt, Strehler never bothered about cost; unlike the master, he was temperamentally unsuited to deal with the various official bodies, the Directorium and Kuratorium, who sought his involvement but would not finance his artistic whims, which went far beyond the Festival's spending capability. In the end, only two of Strehler's major projects came to fruition: the first, *Das Spiel der Mächtigen*, was an immensely complex play in two parts. It was staged in 1973 and 1974. The work demanded a huge cast, extensive rehearsal time and astronomical initial expenses. In the first year, Strehler's eccentricities, his moodiness, occasional hysteria and organizational weakness produced at best a semi-rehearsed product; the following year, the play was vastly improved, and received good notices, but the directors decided that it was impossible to continue with such a production due to the huge costs it entailed.

The second major Strehler project was his collaboration in 1974 with von Karajan on *Die Zauberflöte*. Again inadequate rehearsal time plagued the production which made full use, some said overuse, of the new Festival Hall's considerable technological capabilities. What the audiences finally saw was a poorly rehearsed and overly produced opera, which pleased no one. Von Karajan let it be known that he would not conduct the work the next year; he did not wish to be associated with a disaster.[17] By the beginning of 1975 Strehler was gone. He had wanted to become a member of the Directorium, had desired to become Salzburg's major operatic and stage director (even Reinhardt had stayed away from opera in Salzburg) but had achieved neither. His resignation eased the task of the overwrought Directorium, though it was realized that Salzburg had lost a creative genius, a man who at least could have brought new life to Salzburg theatre, whose mere presence had created excitement unknown since Reinhardt's day. But the Festival needed at least a minimum of cooperation among its artists; Strehler wanted to make it into a one-man show. And worse, with *Zauberflöte* he failed to produce the expected masterpiece. That, probably more than his rampant egoism, destroyed him.[18]

The Strehler interlude, with all its passion and name-calling, did not completely undermine the position of director in Salzburg, for Ponnelle, with fewer pretensions, still prospers, but it did underline the dangers that a powerful stage director could create. One was financial. New productions, especially when performed a limited number of times for only two or three years, were extremely expensive. Secondly, modern stage technology had made it possible to work magic, but therein lay a problem; stage directors were tempted to use these technological means simply because they existed. They could dazzle audiences with their expertise and illusions. But what of the opera itself? Here Franz Endler thinks that the quest for novelty has worked to the detriment of Salzburg opera. Solid productions are changed for the sake of change, to allow the conductor and stage director to receive the publicity and fulfilment that surrounds a new production. And the stage director, in his constant search for a new angle, a new approach, often finds himself experimenting for experiment's sake. This is not a practice confined to Salzburg; it exists in opera houses throughout the world. Do audiences demand such new productions? Is their level of boredom such that they will not tolerate the same staging and scenery for more than a couple of years? Endler thinks not. It is publicity-seeking artists, not satiated opera-goers, who demand the new productions.

Karl Löbl, a veteran critic, is now an administrator with the Austrian Radio and Television Company (ORF) and has been writing and reading Festival criticism for thirty-five years. He admits to being a bit jaded. When he picks up a newspaper and begins to read a review which mentions the Salzburg snobs, the inflated ticket prices, the poorly-thought-out-programmes, he does not bother to read the by-line. He knows that it is another young critic cutting his teeth. Indeed, he admits, his own criticisms twenty-five years ago contained the same points. Now Löbl finds the familiar catalogue of complaint tiresome. Each generation of critics must have its say, and the litany of Salzburg's alleged faults remains more or less the same.[19]

Since Löbl has been criticizing for so long, his scepticism is both understandable and forgiveable. But what he does not say is that, in the Salzburg scheme of things, critics count for little. They are treated with consummate politeness by the Festival press bureau and by municipal and provincial officials. Indeed Festival public relations are outstanding. Critics who have come for several years are often granted a medal from the province by the Governor. They are certainly not punished if they write poor reviews, for their presence is what is important, not what they write. Festival tickets for the major productions are sold out months in advance, so there is no danger that a poor review might lead to a drop in attendance. The Salzburg directors would be uncomfortable only if critics chose to ignore their Festival. Very few do. One notable self-proclaimed exile is Andrew Porter, the distinguished music critic of the *New Yorker*, who has not been in Salzburg for over two decades because of his distaste for the Festival's conservative approach. Another exile, also an Englishman, is Harold Rosenthal, Editor of *Opera*, although he does arrange for other critics to be sent to the Festival and publishes their reports in the annual Festival issue of the magazine.[20] Rosenthal finds the hero-worship of von Karajan which permeates Salzburg distasteful, and does not wish to be a part of it.

But these critics are in the minority; to most, assignment to Salzburg is looked upon as a bonus. Edward Greenfield of the *Guardian* has been attending the Festival for fifteen years; during the day he sports *Lederhosen* and hobnobs with artists; in the evening he listens attentively but admits that it is harder for him to write a bad review in Salzburg than in London, such is his love for every aspect of the city and its Festival. H. H. Stuckenschmidt of the *Frankfurter Allgemeine Zeitung* echoes Greenfield's words, candidly admitting to having a love affair with Salzburg.[21] André Tubeuf, the distinguished French musicologist and critic, has been coming to Salzburg for twenty-five years. He knows everybody connected with the Festival, has seen practically every performance, has the largest collection of Salzburg memorabilia in private hands. Those summer weeks are for him the high point of his year.[22] Occasionally critics are treated with less than tender loving care. Endler remembers being attacked by a mob of von Karajan lovers some years ago when he dared to criticize the maestro. It is generally true that Viennese critics are less beloved in Salzburg than others. The old provincial hostility is still alive; when any mishap occurs in Salzburg, it is immediately reported—and sometimes embellished—by the Vienna press. It has always been so, and such rivalry will probably never change.[23]

In recent years the Festival directors have gone to great lengths both to demonstrate that the Festival was bringing much-needed foreign currency to Salzburg's (and Austria's) coffers and to point out how satisfied and loyal audiences were. Indeed Salzburg's financial drawing power is a persistent (some say too persistent) theme of Festival propaganda. It is no accident that, from the early seventies until 1985, one of the members of the Directorium was a banker.[24] In response to the continual criticism that Salzburg citizens feel estranged from the Festival, the directors have produced figures which show just the opposite. Representatives of the ticket bureau suggest that it is a myth that the people of Salzburg cannot procure tickets for their own Festival. Fifty per cent of the tickets are now sold in Salzburg itself, though one official remarked with a wry smile that he had no idea what percentage of these went to local travel agencies or to the ever-accommodating hotel porters, many of whom proceed to sell them to (primarily foreign) Festival-goers at mark-ups of from twenty to five hundred per cent.

But the final word on the Festival cannot come from critics, from directors or from cold financial figures. The Festival exists only because of its audience, and that audience has shown an extraordinary fidelity to the venture. A report released in 1981 showed that fully fifty-five per cent of those Festival-goers who responded to the questionnaire had been attending for the past six years; thirty-nine per cent of the total had come more than ten times.[25] Thus there exists an extremely loyal core public, many of whom belong to the Festival-sponsored organization *Salzburger Förderer*, who as paying members get an early opportunity to choose tickets for the following year's performances. Thus for every wealthy Texan who arrives breathless at the Hotel Goldener Hirsch and pays two hundred pounds for a ticket for 'whatever is being performed tonight', there are hundreds of loyal Salzburg lovers who know very well what is being played, and have paid months in advance so that they can see it.

A special edition of the *Salzburger Alpenjournal* in the early Sixties produced three numbers devoted entirely to the Festival. One asked German critics how Salzburg could be improved, a second requested the opinions of Austrian critics on the same question, the third asked the public to respond. Not surprisingly, critics hauled out the old nostrums; but every member of the public who was interviewed was satisfied with Salzburg as it was. Thus the perennial moans, repeated by one critic after another, about what is wrong with Salzburg do not worry the Festival directors unduly; they know that the public is content.[26]

However, Salzburg should not allow itself to rest on its laurels, letting material success create smug conservatism. President Moser is well aware of this. One bad year would not hurt ticket sales for the next, he suggests; but if a series of Festivals was badly received by the public, then Salzburg might fall upon difficult times. Moser now looks forward to the great celebration of 1991, the two hundredth anniversary of

Mozart's death, when all of the composer's major operas will be performed. But in looking ahead too far, it is easy to stumble.[27] The 1985 Festival was not vintage Salzburg; it was reminiscent of 1958 and 1959, when the directors concentrated too closely on the opening of the new Festival Hall to the detriment of the whole.

As long as von Karajan has breath, he will pick the productions, the conductors and the singers for 1991. Indeed his contribution to Salzburg has been immense. First and foremost, he is the only active artist who participated before the war; he is the link between Reinhardt and our own day. Moreover von Karajan's contribution goes far beyond the relative strengths and weaknesses of the operas and concerts he has conducted; his magnetic personality draws people from all over the world. Although he is sometimes accused of distorting the 'spirit' of Salzburg for his own ends, any objective perusal of the programmes over the past quarter of a century suggests just the opposite. Mozart has been extremely well served. Von Karajan's grand operas have not supplanted Mozart; they have broadened the scope and appeal of the Festival. In his own way he has also preserved what is left of ensemble opera. Like Reinhardt, he is beloved by the performers with whom he chooses to work. He is a man of detail, and his preparations for operatic productions are long and painstaking; he literally moulds his singers into their parts, and their loyalty to him is unquestioned.

Von Karajan now stands alone. Two conductors who made a great impression in Salzburg, and might have been his rivals, Ferenc Fricsay and Dimitri Mitropoulos, died young, at the beginning of von Karajan's unofficial imperium. Leonard Bernstein, who is a near contemporary, and Carlo Maria Giulini have made infrequent visits to Salzburg. The newer generation of conductors—Claudio Abbado, Riccardo Muti, Lorin Maazel and James Levine—have risen quickly in a world starved for first-rate conductors, and are increasingly more active in Salzburg, but do not yet possess the necessary charisma. Although they may not have all the attributes of Toscanini, Walter or Furtwängler, they have continued to carry on the tradition of their great predecessors, maintaining the highest standards, honouring Mozart and making the Salzburg Festival a unique event.

The streets that Max Reinhardt sauntered through in 1920 are hardly changed. The fortress which looked down upon so much beauty is still intact, the cafés are still full, Leopoldskron and Zweig's house still remain, living testaments to that vanished age. The majestic D minor chords which open *Don Giovanni* do not sound any differently today

185

than when Richard Strauss hit the downbeat in 1922 for the same opera. There is an eternity in the great musical and operatic compositions of the past few centuries, as there is in the prose of the great playwrights, just as there is an eternity in the hills, valleys, churches and castles of that extraordinary stage setting, the city of Salzburg itself. This is what Reinhardt's eyes feasted upon, this is the world that Toscanini, Hofmannsthal, Walter and all the others brought to life through the evocation of great art. Thus in the deepest sense, the Salzburg idea, the idea of the transcendence of the individual through the medium of art, will never die.

Notes

CHAPTER 1

1 W. A. Bauer and O. E. Deutsch (eds), *Wolfgang Amadeus Mozart, Briefe und Aufzeichnungen* (7 vols; Kassel, 1962–75); letter, 7 August 1779, cited in Alfred Einstein, *Mozart* (New York, 1945), pp. 54–5; letter, 26 May 1781.

2 Josef Kaut, *Festspiele in Salzburg* (Salzburg, 1969), p. 16.

3 Hans Conrad Fischer, 'Die Idee der Salzburger Festspiele und ihre Verwirklichung', dissertation, Munich, 1954, p. 45. Fischer's history is comprehensive, though he lacked archival material, and carried the story only to the immediate post-war period. Kaut's work is useful — he was at the time one of the Directors of the Festival and later became its President. Other books on Festival history are: Otto Beer, *Kleines Salzburger Festspielbuch* (Vienna, 1947); Wolfgang Schneditz, *Salzburger Festspielbuch* (Salzburg, 1958); Roland Tenschert, *Salzburg und seine Festspiele* (Vienna, 1977). On Festival criticism, see Max Kaindl Hönig, *Resonanz, 50 Jahre Kritik der Salzburger Festspiele* (Salzburg, 1971).

4 Oskar Holl, 'Dokumente zur Entstehung der Salzburger Festspiele', in *Maske und Kothurn*, Vienna, 1967, Heft 2/3, pp. 149–51.

5 Fischer, op. cit., pp. 48–9.

6 Ibid., p. 51.

7 *Maske und Kothurn*, loc. cit., pp. 151–2.

8 Ibid., see pp. 155–68 *passim* for the correspondence of Gehmacher and Damisch.

9 Kaut, op. cit., p. 20.

10 Franz Hadamowsky, *Reinhardt und Salzburg* (Salzburg, 1963), pp. 16 ff.

11 Letter, Max Reinhardt to Salzburger Festspielhaus Gemeinde (hereafter referred to as SFG), 18 July 1918; Archives, Salzburg Festival.

12 See Diana Burgwyn, *Salzburg* (Salzburg, 1982), p. 92.

13 Fischer, op. cit., pp. 96, 189.

14 Oliver Sayler, *Max Reinhardt and his Theatre* (New York, 1923), p. 200.

15 Hugo von Hofmannsthal, *Festspiele in Salzburg* (Vienna, 1952), pp. 12–14.

16 SFG, *Kundgebungen zur Errichtung des deutschösterreichischen Festspiel-hauses*, Vienna, 21 April 1918.
17 Stefan Zweig, *The World of Yesterday* (New York, 1943), p. 295.
18 SFG, *Mitteilungen*, November 1919, p. 15.
19 Bernhard Paumgartner, *Erinnerungen* (Salzburg, 1969), p. 118.
20 Fischer, op. cit., p. 162.
21 Hugo von Hofmannsthal, *Jedermann*, ed. Edda Leisler, Gisela Prossnitz (Frankfurt, 1973), pp. 193, 194. This edition includes essays on the play. Also, letters, SFG to Franz Rehrl, 15 and 22 July 1920; Landesarchiv, Salzburg, Franz Rehrl Archiv (hereafter referred to as RA).
22 Hofmannsthal, *Jedermann* op. cit., pp. 254–9.
23 Sayler, op. cit., p. 191.

CHAPTER 2

1 Ernst Hanisch *et al.*, *Österreich, 1918–1939: Geschichte der Ersten Republik*, Vol. II, p. 930 (Vienna, 1983).
2 Ibid., p. 905.
3 Ibid., pp. 903, 921–3.
4 Strauss-Hofmannsthal, *Briefwechsel* (Zurich, 1952), 5 October 1920, p. 394.
5 Letter, SFG to Finance Minister, 4 June 1921; Allgemeines Verwaltungs-archiv, Vienna (hereafter cited as VWA).
6 Letter, Minister of Finance to Minister of Education, 18 June 1921; VWA.
7 *Neue Freie Presse*, Vienna, 16 August 1921; *Theatre Arts Magazine*, New York, July 1921, p. 217.
8 Strauss-Schalk, *Briefwechsel* (Tutzing, 1983), 20 July 1921, p. 219.
9 Strauss-Hofmannsthal, op. cit., 19 August 1921, p. 219.
10 Memo, Minister of Education, 1922 (no date); VWA.
11 Otto Strasser, *Und dafür bin ich bezahlt* (Vienna, 1974), pp. 45–6.
12 *Die Fackel*, No. 601–607, 24 November 1922, pp. 3–5.
13 *Salzburger Chronik*, 22, 25 July 1922; *Neue Zürcher Zeitung*, 18 August 1922.
14 *Kleine Volkszeitung*, Vienna, 31 August 1922; *Gazette de Lausanne*, 29 August 1922.
15 *Wiener Allgemeine Zeitung*, 26 August 1922.
16 *Neue Freie Presse*, 17 August 1920.
17 *L'Eclair*, Paris, 18 July 1922; *Literary Digest*, London, 23 September 1922.
18 *Musikblätter des Anbruchs*, Vienna, 1 July 1922, pp. 2–3.
19 Kaut, op. cit., p. 293.
20 Strauss-Hofmannsthal, op. cit., 29 August 1922, p. 411.
21 Ibid., 4 September 1922, pp. 411–12.
22 Strauss-Schalk, op. cit., 31 October 1922.
23 *Neue Wiener Journal*, Vienna, 30 March 1923.

24 Letter, SFG to Vienna Philharmonic, 11 May 1923; Archives, Vienna Philharmonic.
25 Gottfried Reinhardt, *The Genius* (New York, 1979), p. 26.
26 Strauss-Schalk, op. cit., 29 September 1923, p. 358.
27 *Die Wacht*, 26 February 1924.
28 *Der Eiserne Besen*, 15 August 1924.
29 Letter, SFG to Vienna Philharmonic, 29 April 1924; Archives, Vienna Philharmonic.
30 Erika Sabrsa, 'Die Opern von Richard Strauss bei den Salzburger Festspielen', dissertation, Vienna, 1963, p. 29.
31 *Salzburger Chronik*, 5 October 1924.
32 W. Huber, ed., *Franz Rehrl: Landeshauptmann von Salzburg 1922–1938* (Salzburg, 1975), p. 169.
33 Letters: Rehrl to Minister of Education, 2 January 1925; RA.
34 Letter, SFG to Max Reinhardt, 12 January 1925; Archives, Vienna Philharmonic.
35 Letters: Vienna Philharmonic to SFG, 19 February 1925; Erwin Kerber for the SFG to Ministry of Education, 21 February 1925; SFG to Vienna Philharmonic, 3 March 1925; Archives, Vienna Philharmonic.
36 Letter, SFG to Bundespräsident, 25 May 1925; VWA.
37 *Neue Mannheimer Zeitung*, 2 September 1925; *Reichspost*, Vienna, 6 June 1926.
38 *Neue Zürcher Zeitung*, 24 August 1925.
39 *New York Times*, 13 August 1925.
40 *Salzburger Volksblatt*, 2, 11 September 1925.
41 Gusti Adler, *Vergessen Sie nicht die Chinesische Nachtigall* (Munich, 1980), p. 94.
42 *Neue Freie Presse*, 14 August 1925.

CHAPTER 3

1 *Wiener Zeitung*, 22 November 1925.
2 *Music Courier*, New York, 15 April 1926, p. 46.
3 Letter, Rehrl to Baron Franckenstein, 22 May 1926; RA.
4 Letter, Franckenstein to Rehrl, 19 June 1926; RA.
5 Letter, General Consul, Trieste, to Auswärtige Amt, 8 May 1926; Archives, Auswärtige Amt, Haus und Hof Archives (hereafter cited as Haus und Hof).
6 Dr Erich Gobert, *Wirtschaftspolitik und Fremdenverkehr* (Salzburg, 1926), pp. 11, 24; RA.
7 Huber, op. cit., pp. 172–3. *Landesprotokoll*, Salzburger Landtag, 7 April 1926. It was Easter week, and the implication is that Salzburg was giving its festival a rather too generous gift.

8 Kaut, op. cit., p. 351. Every individual whom the author has interviewed who knew Puthon, has corroborated this statement.
9 SFG, *Sanierungsplan*, Salzburg, 1926; RA.
10 *New York Times*, 16 August 1926; *Theatre Arts Monthly*, New York, November 1926, p. 753.
11 *London Morning Post*, 6 September 1926.
12 Adler, op. cit., p. 191.
13 *Der Eiserne Besen*, 28 August 1926.
14 *Neue Zürcher Zeitung*, 20 August 1926.
15 Strauss-Hofmannsthal, op. cit., 9 June 1926, p. 471 (letter, Hofmannsthal to Strauss).
16 *Reichspost*, Vienna, 5 September 1926; Huber, op. cit., p. 181.
17 *Musikbote*, Vienna, October 1926, Vol. 7, pp. 206–7.
18 Huber, op. cit., p. 183.
19 Letter, Auswärtige Amt (hereafter cited as AA) to Austrian Embassies, 29 January 1927; Haus und Hof.
20 Letters: Director of Bundestheaterverwaltung to Rehrl, 21 December 1926; Rehrl to Director, 27 December 1926; RA.
21 *Deutschösterreichische Tageszeitung*, Vienna, 2 February 1927.
22 Letter, Max Reinhardt to Franz Rehrl, 4 April 1927; RA.
23 Letter, Director of Bundeskanzlerei to Franz Rehrl, 2 December 1926; RA.
24 Letters: Bundeskanzleramt/AA to Austrian Embassies, 4 April 1927; Austrian Consul, Matto Grosso, to AA, 29 May 1927; Austrian General Consul, New York, to AA, 24 June 1927; Haus und Hof.
25 *Salzburger Chronik*, 20 July 1927.
26 Adler, op. cit., p. 211.
27 *New York Herald*, 23 July 1927.
28 *Christian Science Monitor*, 17 September 1927. Kerby, during his visit, put forth the idea that Salzburg should mount its own productions; see *Salzburger Chronik*, 23 January 1927.
29 *Theatre Arts Monthly*, New York, November 1927, pp. 850–2.
30 *Die Stunde*, Vienna, 10 August 1927; *Commoedia*, Paris, 19 August 1927.
31 *Christian Science Monitor*, 17 September 1927.
32 Letter, Franz Rehrl to Minister of Education, 29 October 1927; VWA.
33 Letter, Minister of Education to Franz Rehrl, 13 December 1927; VWA.
34 Letters: Ministry of Education to Ministry of Finance, 20 November 1927; Minister for Trade and Tourism to Minister of Education, 28 February 1928 (he suggested 50,000 Schillings for the Festival); Franz Rehrl to Minister of Education, 4 May 1928; Final Report, Minister of Education, 17 June 1928; VWA.
35 *Neue Freie Presse*, 20 March 1928.
36 *Ostdeutsche Morgenpost*, Beuthen, 23 August 1928; *Eiserne Besen*, 14 September 1928.

37 *Candide*, Paris, 6 September 1928; *La Volonté*, Paris, 5 September 1928.
38 *Münchner Zeitung*, 22 January 1928.
39 *Neue Zürcher Zeitung*, 15 August 1928.
40 *Salzburger Volksblatt*, 10 November 1928.
41 *Neue Freie Presse*, 2 February 1929.
42 Gottfried Reinhardt, op. cit., p. 373.
43 Letters: Puthon to Rehrl, 22 August 1928; von Hofmannsthal to Rehr, 17 December 1928; Gedächtnisprotokoll, 7 December 1928; letter, Franz Rehrl to von Hofmannsthal, 15 December 1928; RA.
44 *Salzburger Volksblatt*, 16 January 1929.
45 Report, Paumgartner *et al*, 1928, pp. 2, 3, 18, 25; RA.
46 Report, 'Der Programgestaltung der Salzburger Festspiele', 1929, pp. 2–11; RA.
47 'Salzburger Randglossen; Der Fall Reinhardt', pp. 1–5; RA.
48 Letter, AA to Austrian General Consuls, 9 March 1929; Haus und Hof.
49 Letter, Pressbüro, SFG to AA, 10 May 1929; Haus und Hof; *Wiener Zeitung*, 27 January 1929.
50 Note, Education Ministry, 22 June 1929; VWA.
51 *Neue Zürcher Zeitung*, 4 September 1929; *Neue Freie Presse*, 23 August 1929.
52 *Neue Freie Presse*, 30 August 1929.
53 Adler, op. cit., pp. 228–30.
54 *Salzburger Chronik*, 31 August 1929.
55 *Journal des Débats*, Paris, 11 September 1930. Letter Bundeskanzleramt to AA, 9 March 1930; Haus und Hof.
56 Strasser, op. cit., p. 81.
57 *Commoedia*, 21 August 1930; *Berliner Tageblatt*, 13 August 1930.
58 *Neue Freie Presse*, 28 August 1930.
59 Speech, 10 August 1930, at the reception of the Grosse Goldene Ehrenzeichen, Salzburg; Max Reinhardt Archives, Binghamton, New York.
60 Letter, Max Reinhardt to Franz Rehrl, 11 October 1930; RA.
61 *New York Times*, 27 August 1930.
62 *Le Temps*, Paris, 29 August 1930.
63 *Wiener Volkszeitung*, 2 August 1930.
64 *Salzburger Volksblatt*, 18 November 1930.

CHAPTER 4

1 The most comprehensive survey of Nazi cultural policy in the music sphere is Fred K. Prieberg, *Musik in NS Staat* (Frankfurt, 1982).
2 Hanisch, op. cit., pp. 908, 915, 921.
3 Bruno Walter, *Theme and Variations* (New York, 1947), p. 312; *Dépêche de Toulouse*, 16 August 1933.

4 Hanisch, op. cit., p. 922.
5 Gunter Fellner, *Antisemitismus in Salzburg, 1918–1938* (Vienna, 1979), p. 100.
6 Letter quoted in *Salzburger Volksblatt*, 8 July 1929.
7 K/23m, 1929 (no date); RA.
8 Fellner, op. cit., pp. 107–8.
9 Minutes, *Aufsichtsrat*, 20 October 1930; VWA; Strasser, op. cit., pp. 86–8.
10 *Neue Freie Presse*, 14 August 1931.
11 Adler, op. cit., pp. 292–306; Alfred G. Brooks (ed.) *Max Reinhardt: A Centennial Festschrift* (Binghamton, NY, 1973), pp. 14–16 (hereafter referred to as Brooke, *Festschrift*).
12 Margherita Wallmann, *Les Balcons du Ciel* (Paris, 1976), p. 30.
13 *Excelsior*, Paris, 3 September 1931.
14 *Neue Zürcher Zeitung*, 30 August 1931.
15 Report, 14 September 1931, pp. 1, 2, 11, 12; VWA.
16 *Salzburger Volksblatt*, 7, 17 September 1931.
17 *Der Eiserne Besen*, 1 September 1931.
18 *Allgemeine Zeitung*, Vienna, 8 October 1931.
19 *Salzburger Chronik*, 3 February 1932.
20 *Salzburger Chronik*, 29 April 1932.
21 *Neue Freie Presse*, 27 July 1932.
22 *Christian Science Monitor*, 17 September 1932; *La Rampe*, Paris, 15 October 1932.
23 *Vossische Zeitung*, Berlin, 13 October 1932.
24 Prieberg, op. cit., pp. 43–4; Goebbels's Diaries, 7 August 1932; Bundesarchiv, Koblenz (hereafter cited as BA).
25 Letter, German Consul, Salzburg, to Foreign Ministry, Berlin, 19 July 1933; BA.
26 Letters: Foreign Ministry to Propaganda Ministry, 28 July 1933; Propaganda Ministry to Foreign Ministry, 23 August 1933; BA.
27 Letter, 17 October 1935; BA.
28 Prieberg, op. cit., p. 128; *Paris Soir*, 31 May 1933.
29 Walter, op. cit., p. 312.
30 Erwin Kerber, *Ewiges Theater*, (Munich, 1935), p. 52ff; Hugo von Hofmannsthal, *Festspiele in Salzburg* (Vienna, 1952), p. 29ff; Fischer, op. cit., pp. 192–3.
31 *Theatre Arts Monthly*, New York, October 1933, p. 771.
32 Wallmann, op. cit., p. 60.
33 Adler, op. cit., p. 307.
34 Gisela Prossnitz & Edda Leisler, 'Max Reinhardt's Faust Inszenierung in Salzburg', in *Maske und Kothurn*, 1970, Heft 2, pp. 135–8.
35 *La Tribuna*, Rome, 1 August 1933; *Neues Wiener Journal*, 22 August 1933; *Reichspost*, Vienna, 29 August 1933.

36 *Candide*, Paris, 24 August 1933; *Journal de Genève*, 11 August 1933.

37 *Prager Presse*, 24 August 1933. In general, German music journals were allowed to cover the Festival in 1933, and contained uncensored reviews. For example: *Deutsche Musik Zeitung*, September 1933; *Kölnische Zeitung*, 2 September 1933, *Vossische Zeitung*, 17 August, 9 September 1933.

38 *Neue Zürcher Zeitung*, 3 August 1933; *Europe Centrale*, Paris, 15 July 1933; *Pester Lloyd*, Budapest, 5 August 1933; *Candide*, 24 August 1933.

39 *Prager Presse*, 23 August 1933; *Europe Centrale*, 9 September 1933.

40 *Salzburger Chronik*, 21 October 1933; Stefan Zweig, op. cit., pp. 346–8.

41 *Salzburger Volksblatt*, 27 November 1933; Letter, Minister of Education to SFG, 26 August 1933; SFG to Minister of Education, 23 August 1933; VWA.

42 Minutes, *Aufsichtsrat*, 30 January 1934; VWA.

43 *Auszuge aus dem Memorandum Hilde Sperrs*, 1933 (no date); Haus und Hof.

44 Report, undated, 1933 Austrian Press Attaché, Rome, to AA; Haus und Hof.

45 Letter, Les Amis de Salzbourg, Brussels, to London Salzburg Society, 7 March 1934, Haus und Hof.

46 Letter, Austrian Ambassador, London, to AA, 19 July 1934; Report, Foreign Ministry, 1934 (no date); Letter, British Empire Salzburg Society, 17 March 1934; Franz Rehrl to Foreign Ministry, 25 June 1935; Haus und Hof. This was in response to a note that Rehrl received from the British Ambassador in Vienna, who said that he had been approached by Frau von Wünscheim, who promised to use her 'influence' to get him tickets for the forthcoming Festival.

47 Letter, Austrian General Consul, New York, to AA, 6 February 1936; Haus und Hof.

48 Letter, Austrian Ambassador, Budapest, to Foreign Ministry, 5 June 1934; Haus und Hof; Letter, Ministry of Trade to Ministry of Education, 21 February 1935; SFG to Ministry of Education, 13 March 1935; VWA.

49 Letter, Foreign Ministry to Ministry of Education, 3 April 1936; Director, Austrian Tourist Agency/Trade Ministry, Vienna, to Landesverkehrsamt, Salzburg, 18 November 1935; Report, Austrian General Consul, Prague, to Foreign Ministry, 25 November 1935; Haus und Hof.

50 Bundeskanzleramt, Letter, Suvich to Dollfuss, 1 May 1934; Bundeskanzleramt to Ministry of Education, 7 May 1934; Dollfuss to Suvich, 17 April 1934; VWA.

51 Gabriel Puaux, *Mort et transfiguration de l'Autriche, 1933–1955* (Paris, 1966), p. 126; See also *Bulletin de la Société des Etudes Mozartiennes*, Paris, 1932, pp. 146–53.

52 Puaux, op. cit., p. 122.

53 Letter, Ministry of Education/Beaux Arts to Foreign Ministry, 12 April 1933; Archives, French Foreign Ministry.

54 Letters: Peyrebere to Brussel, 17 June 1936; Brussel to Foreign Ministry, 22 June 1936; French Ambassador, Vienna, to Foreign Ministry, Paris, 9 January 1935; Archives, French Foreign Ministry.
55 Interview, Erich Leinsdorf, July 1983.
56 Harvey Sachs, *Toscanini* (New York, 1975), p. 220.
57 Prieberg, op. cit., p. 75.
58 Prieberg, op. cit., p. 75; Sachs, op. cit., p. 226; *Time*, 19 June 1933.
59 Telegram, Bundestheaterverwaltung, June 1933; Haus und Hof.
60 Prieberg, op. cit., p. 75.
61 Letter, B. Huberman to A. Toscanini, June 1933; Private archives.
62 Letter, AA to Huberman, 25 August 1933; Haus und Hof.
63 Strasser, op. cit., pp. 100–14; Hugo Burghauser, *Philharmonische Begegnungen* (Zürich, 1980), pp. 50–7.
64 Burghauser, op. cit., p. 47; Sachs, op. cit., p. 228.
65 Letter, Burghauser to Bundestheaterverwaltung, 10 May 1933; Burghauser to Ministry of Education, 28 June 1933; Report, Ministry of Education, 10 July 1933; Haus und Hof.
66 Burghauser, op. cit., p. 111.

CHAPTER 5

1 Burghauser, op. cit., p. 58.
2 *Salzburger Chronik*, 23 May 1934.
3 Letter, UK General Consul, Munich, to UK Ambassador, Berlin, 28 July 1934; Public Record Office, Great Britain, Foreign Office archives.
4 Letter, Habricht to Goebbels, 7 May 1934; BA.
5 Letter, Reichsendleitung to Reichsmusikkammer, 28 April 1934; BA.
6 Letter, W. Funk to Furtwängler and Strauss, 25 May 1934; BA.
7 *Salzburger Volksblatt*, 11, 28 June 1934.
8 Report, 16 June 1934; Letter, SFG to Minister of Education, 20 June 1934; VWA.
9 *Salzburger Volksblatt*, 26 June 1934; *Salzburger Chronik*, 26 June 1934.
10 Letter, SFG to Ministry of Education, 28 July 1934; VWA.
11 SFG bi-weekly reports, July, August 1934; VWA.
12 Sachs, op. cit., p. 231.
13 As quoted in *Salzburger Chronik*, 14 September 1934.
14 Adler, op. cit., p. 305.
15 Thimig, op. cit., p. 177.
16 Adler, op. cit., pp. 323–5.
17 Brooks, *Festschrift*, op. cit., pp. 131–2.
18 Carl Zuckmayer, *A Part of Myself* (London, 1970), pp. 41, 44.
19 *Theatre Arts Monthly*, New York, September 1934, pp. 653–4; *Literary Digest*, 18 August 1934; *Excelsior*, Paris, 18 August 1934.

Notes

20 *Time*, 3 September 1934.
21 *Salzburger Chronik*, 11 September 1934.
22 *Le Temps*, Paris, 28 August 1934.
23 Statistical Data, Salzburg Festival, 1936; VWA.
24 Minutes, *Aufsichtsrat*, 22 October 1934; VWA.
25 Sachs, op. cit., p. 238.
26 Letter, Austrian General Consul, Milan, to Austrian Ambassador, Rome, 2 November 1934; Haus und Hof.
27 Note, Direction of International Concert Directory to AA, 16 September 1935; VWA; Letter, AA to Education Minister, 18 September 1935; SFG to Education Minister, 29 October 1935; Haus und Hof.
28 Strasser, op. cit., p. 84; Sachs, op. cit., p. 232; Detail can be found in B. H. Haggin, *Conversations with Musicians* (New York, 1959), pp. 227–31.
29 Strasser, op. cit., pp. 86–90; Prieberg, op. cit., pp. 66–8.
30 Letter, French Ambassador, Vienna, to French Foreign Minister, 14 December 1934; Archives, French Foreign Office.
31 Infobrief, 17 August 1934; BA. The German press is ordered to report on all Austrian cultural manifestations, so as to rebuild relations between the two countries.
32 *Völkische Beobachter*, Munich, 7 September 1934.
33 *Stuttgarter N.S. Kurier*, 12 August 1935.
34 *Volkische Beobachter*, 30 July 1935.
35 Goebbels's Diaries, 13 July 1937; BA.
36 Press conferences, 11 March 1937, 1 July 1937; BA.
37 Report, 3 December 1937; BA.
38 Letter, Reichsmusikkammer to Ministry of Propaganda, 9 August 1934; BA.
39 Letter, Reichsmusikkammer to Ministry of Propaganda, 16 October 1934; BA.
40 Report by Walter Funk, Reichskulturkammer, 21 July 1935; Berlin Document Center; Report, Minister for Internal Affairs, 19 January 1935; BA.
41 Report, section IX, Propaganda Ministry, 13 November 1934; BA.
42 Werner Krauss, *Das Schauspiel meines Lebens* (Stuttgart, 1958), pp. 137–8.
43 Letter, Karl Böhm to R. Schlösser, President, Reichsmusikkammer, 27 August 1935; Report, Propaganda Ministry, 6 November 1935; Letter, German Embassy, Vienna, to Foreign Ministry, Berlin, 10 October 1935; BA.
44 Thimig, op. cit., p. 194.
45 Von Papen Reports, October, 1935; BA; Walter, op. cit., p. 311.
46 Letter, Austrian Consul, Cologne, to Foreign Ministry, Vienna, 16 October 1935; Haus und Hof.

47 Police report, Salzburg, 20 November 1935; Haus und Hof.
48 *Le Journal*, Paris, 2 August 1936.
49 Statistical data, 1937, Salzburg Festival; VWA.
50 Report, Salzburg Press Bureau, 28 February 1938; RA; letter, Franz Rehrl to King of Italy, 14 June 1935; Haus und Hof.
51 *Paris Soir*, 18 July 1937.
52 Interview, Tasillo Nekola, July 1984; Fischer, op. cit., p. 129; Benno Fleischmann, *Max Reinhardt* (Vienna, 1948), p. 200.
53 Minutes, *Aufsichtsrat*, 13 July 1936; VWA; Sachs, op. cit., p. 264. Throughout 1936 and 1937, the State Auditor was the *bête noire* of the Festival directors; his 50-page report (Report, Rechnungshof, 14 December 1935; VWA) accused the Festival authorities of wasting money on salaries, productions, perquisites, and the dispensation of an exaggerated number of free tickets. The Education Minister, Pertner, tended to take the side of the people of Salzburg; the issue, though never publicized, caused great consternation and led to some (symbolic) cutbacks and much correspondence between the Festival, the State Auditor and the Minister of Finance, who likewise was suspicious of Salzburg's free-spending ways.
54 Anton Dermota, *Tausendundein Abend* (Vienna, 1978), p. 83.
55 Report, Education Ministry, 11 March 1937; VWA.
56 *Die Fackel*, February 1936, pp. 1–22.
57 Brooks, *Festschrift*, op. cit., pp. 53–75; Gottfried Reinhardt, op. cit., pp. 259–60.
58 Thimig, *Wie Max Reinhardt Lebte* (Frankfurt, 1975), p. 107.
59 Strasser, op. cit., p. 110.
60 Erich Leinsdorf, *Cadenza* (Boston, 1976), pp. 40–1.
61 *Le Temps*, 1935 (no date); *Le Monde Musical*, 30 September 1935, pp. 264–5.
62 Letter, Austrian Ambassador, Paris to AA, Vienna, 15 February 1936; Haus und Hof.
63 Goebbels's Diaries, 12 October 1937; BA; Sachs, op. cit., p. 261. George Marek, *Toscanini* (New York, 1975), p. 182; Burghauser, op. cit., pp. 90–1; Berta Geissmar, *The Baton and the Jackboot* (London, 1944), p. 31.
64 Leinsdorf, op. cit., p. 50.
65 Interview, Erich Leinsdorf, July 1983.
66 Haggin, op. cit., p. 171; *Salzburger Chronik*, 31 July 1937, is a good example of a 'praising with faint damnation' approach to opera criticism.
67 *Letters of Thomas Mann* (New York, 1971), pp. 238–40, 31 October 1935.
68 *Le Journal*, Paris, 22 August 1936; *The Morning Post*, London, 8 August 1935; Jacques Foschotte, *Les Hauts Lieux de la musique* (Paris, 1950), p. 46.
69 *Candide*, Paris, 20 August 1936.

70 Report, Bundeskanzleramt, 24 August 1937; VWA.

71 Foschotte, op. cit., p. 48.

72 *Salzburger Chronik*, 17 August 1937.

73 Report, 24 August 1937; RA.

74 Letters, Reinhardt to Gusti Adler, 13, 14 October 1937; Reinhardt Archives, New York.

75 Letter, Reinhardt to Adler, Autumn 1937 (no date); Reinhardt Archives, New York.

76 Letters, Reinhardt to Adler, 2 November, 6 December 1937; Reinhardt Archives, New York.

77 Letter, Max Reinhardt to Sara D. Roosevelt, 26 November 1937; Theatersammlung, Vienna, Archives.

78 Salzburg Festival Press Report, 15 April 1938; RA.

79 Telegram, Toscanini to Rehrl, 16 February 1938; RA.

80 Telegram, Toscanini to Walter, 21 February 1938; RA.

81 *La Bourse Egyptienne*, Cairo, 24 April 1938.

82 Report, Franz Rehrl to Minister of Education, 25 February 1938; RA.

83 Letter, Austrian Ambassador, The Hague, to Guido Schmidt, Foreign Minister, 25 February 1938; Haus und Hof.

84 Letter, Rehrl to Minister of Interior (Seyss-Inquart), 28 February 1938; Haus und Hof.

85 Puaux, op. cit., p. 120.

86 *Berliner Tageblatt*, 6 March 1938; Letter, Wiedemann (Reichkanzlerei) to von Wusow (Foreign Ministry), 28 February 1938; Berlin Document Center.

87 Walter, op. cit. p. 307.

88 Markel, op. cit., p. 184.

89 Annette Kolb, *Abschied von Österreich* (Amsterdam, 1950), pp. 216–17.

CHAPTER 6

1 Ernst Hanisch, *Nationalsozialistische Herrschaft in der Provinz Salzburg im Dritten Reich* (Salzburg, 1983), pp. 25–7 (hereafter cited as *NS Salzburg*).

2 Ibid., p. 340.

3 Ibid., p. 68.

4 *Salzburger Zeitung*, 7 April 1938.

5 Reichsstaatthalter VI, letter, Reittner to Mühlmann, 18 May 1938; VWA. Hanisch, *NS Salzburg*, pp. 104–8.

6 Strasser, op. cit., p. 131.

7 Letter, Mozarteum Chorus, Salzburg, to Field Marshall, Salzburg, 10 April 1938; BA.

8 Letter, State Secret Police to Ministry of Propaganda, 27 May 1938; BA.

9 Letter, Frau Bernhard Paumgartner to Goebbels, 29 June 1938, BA.

10 Strasser, op. cit., pp. 131, 144–5.
11 Reinhardt, op. cit., pp. 241–3.
12 Reichsstaatthalter VI, letter, Reittner to Mühlmann, 18 May 1938; VWA.
13 Letter, UK Ambassador, Vienna, to Foreign Minister, 7 April 1938; Public Record Office, Great Britain, Foreign Office.
14 Press conferences, 12 May 1938, 23 June 1938; BA.
15 Press conference, 7 July 1938; BA.
16 *Vendemaire*, Paris, 3 August 1938; *Time*, 1 August 1938.
17 Letters: Glaise-Horstenau to Goebbels, 2 July 1938; Goebbels to Glaise-Horstenau, 9 July 1938; BA.
18 *Neue Zürcher Zeitung*, 8 August 1938.
19 *Marianne*, Paris, 17 August 1938.
20 *Saturday Review of Literature*, 22 August 1942, pp. 3, 4, 17.
21 *Journal des Débats*, Paris, 11 August 1938.
22 *Tribune des Nations*, Geneva, 3, 25 August 1938.
23 Reichsstaatthalter III, report, 29 September 1938; VWA.
24 Press conference, 29 September 1938; BA.
25 Fischer, op. cit., p. 244.
26 Reichsstaatthalter, report, SFG, 10 December 1938; VWA.
27 Reichsstaatthalter, prospectus, 1939 Salzburg Festival; VWA.
28 Press conferences, 27 April, 22 June, 27 July 1939; BA.
29 Dermota, op. cit., p. 132; *Salzburger Volksblatt*, 10, 15 August 1939.
30 Strasser, op. cit., p. 156.
31 Foschotte, op. cit., p. 105.
32 Strasser, op. cit., pp. 168–9.
33 Goebbels's Diaries, 3 August 1941; BA.
34 *Frankfurter Zeitung*, 7 August 1941.
35 Goebbels's Diaries, 10 November 1941; BA.
36 Press conferences, 20 June 1941, 23 May 1942; BA.
37 Fonds Montpensier, Paris, brochure, 1939 Salzburg Summer Course; Press conference, 13 July 1942; BA.
38 Letter, Krauss to Hitler, 25 April 1938; Berlin Document Center, file, Krauss.
39 Letter, Chief Representative of the Reich, Vienna, to Deputy to the Führer, Munich, 7 October 1940; BA.
40 Dermota, op. cit., p. 140; *Salzburger Festspiele Almanach*, 1942.
41 Letter, Gaukamer, Salzburg, to Russinger, Caretaker, Schloss Leopoldskron, 22 June 1942, Max Reinhardt Archives, New York; for the further history of the Schloss see Hanisch, *NS Salzburg*, pp. 96, 97.
42 *Kölnische Zeitung*, 2 September 1942.
43 Report, Martin Bormann, 14 January 1944; Berlin Document Center, file, Richard Strauss.
44 *Salzburger Zeitung*, 16 August 1944.

45 Norman Del Mar, *Richard Strauss* (3 Vols, London, 1962–72), Vol. I, pp. 171-5.
46 Interview, Albert Moser, February 1985.
47 Strasser, op. cit., pp. 185–8; Karl Böhm, *Ich erinnere mich ganz genau* (Vienna, 1974), pp. 85–7; Dermota, op. cit., p. 146.

CHAPTER 7

1 Report, Otto von Pasetti, 16 June 1945; National Archives (hereafter cited as NA); SHAEF Report, 29 April 1945; NA. On Allied denazification policy in post-war Austria, an invaluable work is Oliver Rathkolb, *Politische Propaganda der Amerikanischen Besatzungsmacht in Österreich, 1945 bis 1950*, dissertation, University of Vienna, 1981.
2 Letter, J. Minifie to R. Barnes, 9 June 1945; NA.
3 Cable, Minifie to ISB (Information Services Branch, which dealt with cultural questions), 16 July 1945; NA.
4 Report, Pasetti, 4 June 1945; NA.
5 Report, Pasetti, 16 June 1945; NA.
6 Interview, Renate Buchmann, August 1984.
7 *Stars and Stripes*, 16 August 1945.
8 *Stars and Stripes*, 22 August 1945.
9 Strasser, op. cit., pp. 182–3; Goebbels's Diaries, 19 November 1938, 20 June 1940; BA.
10 Report on Karl Böhm, Pasetti, 15 May 1946; NA; On Werner Krauss, see Ernst Lothar, *Das Wunder des Überlebens* (Vienna, 1962), p. 317.
11 Report, ISB, Henry Alter, 29 November 1945; NA.
12 Ibid.
13 Report, Pasetti, 27 May 1946; report, US element, Allied Denazification Bureau, 24 July 1946; NA. The Americans were very upset with Hilbert at the time, for he stated that 'it is of greater importance to re-establish Austrian cultural institutions than it is to denazify'.
14 ISB Report, March 1945; NA.
15 Report, Alter, 15 March 1946; NA.
16 Report, Pasetti, 3 June 1946; NA.
17 Letter, Puthon to ISB, 31 May 1946; Pasetti, report, 15 May 1946; Info slip, ISB, 20 June 1946; NA.
18 Memo, Lothar to Chief, ISB, 8 August 1946; NA.
19 Minutes, Allied Denazification Bureau, 19 December 1946; NA. Strasser, op. cit., p. 213.
20 Denazification Report, Counter Intelligence Corps, 7 August 1948; Report, denazification, 11 February 1948, Salzburg; NA.
21 Survey, ISB; Reports, 13 May, 12 June 1948; NA.
22 Letter, Theatre and Music Office, ISB, Vienna, to Head, ISB, 26 December 1945; NA.

23 Lothar, op. cit., p. 288.
24 Pasetti, report, 2 August 1946 (in private hands).
25 Lothar, op. cit., pp. 313, 314.
26 Pasetti, reports, 1, 2 August 1945 (in private hands).
27 Interview, Jacques Bornoff, Paris, March 1980; Interview, Buchmann.
28 Lothar, op. cit., p. 325.
29 Report, Lothar, 31 August 1946; NA.
30 Oscar Fritz Schuh, *Salzburger Dramaturgie* (Vienna, 1951), p. 11.
31 Interview, Viktor Reimann, August 1985.
32 Schuh, op. cit., pp. 5, 30–2.
33 Radio interview, Gottfried von Einem, series 'Neighbours Abroad', 25 August 1947; Gesellschaft der Musikfreunde, Vienna, Von Einem Archives (hereafter cited as VE Archives).
34 *Österreichische Musikzeitschrift*, Vol. 7/8, July, August 1947, pp. 169–70.
35 *Salzburger Festspiele Almanach*, 1965, p. 42.
36 See Bernhard Paumgartner, op. cit., pp. 151–65, for his general view of the post-war cultural scene.
37 Report, 31 August 1947; NA.
38 Letter, Lothar to Bruno Walter, 21 September 1946; NA.
39 Letter, Richard Strauss to Landeshauptmann, 1947; Landesarchiv, Salzburg. Report, Lothar, 30 November 1946; NA.
40 Report, Lothar to ISB, 31 August 1947; NA.
41 Interview, Gottfried von Einem, February 1985; 'Salzburg und die moderne Oper' (1950); VE Archives; Interview, 1947, 'Gottfried von Einem und das musikalische Theater: die Zukunft'; VE Archives.
42 Friederich Saathan, *Eine Chronik* (Vienna, 1982), pp. 145–6.
43 Letter, von Karajan to Puthon, 1947; Landesarchiv, Salzburg.
44 Report, Hogan, 26 July 1948; NA.
45 *Die Welt*, 4 September 1948.
46 *Salzburger Nachrichten*, 28 August 1948; See also, for Reimann's views on *Jedermann*, *Salzburger Nachrichten*, 28 July 1947, 21 July, 28 August 1948.
47 Elisabeth Schwarzkopf, *On and Off the Record* (Zurich, 1981), p. 228.
48 Minutes, Directorium, 25 October 1948; VE Archives.
49 Letter, Puthon to von Einem, 15 August 1949; VE Archives.
50 Bruno Walter, *Briefe* (Frankfurt, 1969), pp. 308–12.
51 Lothar, op. cit., p. 338; Report, Music and Theatre Office, Salzburg, 22 August 1949; NA.
52 Strasser, op. cit., pp. 225–6; *Time*, 8 August 1949.
53 *Contrepoints*, Paris, no. 6, 1949; *Münchner Merkur*, 22 August 1949.
54 Interview, Tasillo Nekola, August 1984.
55 *De Linie*, Amsterdam, 9 September 1949.

Notes

CHAPTER 8
1 Letter, Furtwängler to von Einem, 26 November 1949; VE Archives.
2 Letter, Furtwängler to von Einem, 27 March 1950; VE Archives.
3 *Opera*, Vol. 6, 1950, pp. 10–13.
4 *Wiener Kurier*, 8 August 1950.
5 Report, T. Nekola, to Directorium, 19 October 1950; VE Archives.
6 Minutes, Kuratorium, 9 September 1950; VE Archives.
7 See *Der Standpunkt*, Meran, 10 August 1951.
8 *Die Furche*, Vienna, 1 September 1951.
9 *Opera*, 1951, pp. 624–6.
10 *Die Arbeiterzeitung*, Vienna, 19 August 1951.
11 Attendance Report, 1951; Archives, Salzburg Festival.
12 *Wiener Kurier*, 1 September 1951.
13 *Opera*, 1951, p. 627.
14 *Il Tempo*, Rome, 24 August 1951.
15 Oscar Fritz Schuh, *So war es, war es so* (Vienna, 1984), p. 114 (hereafter cited as Schuh, Autobiography).
16 Kurt Palm, *Von Boykott zur Anerkennung: Brecht und Österreich* (Vienna, 1983), p. 65.
17 Ibid., p. 69.
18 *Die Presse*, Vienna, 6 August 1949; Palm, op. cit., p. 74.
19 *Wiener Tageszeitung*, 28 September 1951.
20 *Salzburger Nachrichten*, 20 October 1951.
21 *Salzburger Nachrichten*, 13 October 1951.
22 Minutes, Salzburger Landtag, Session of 24 October 1951, p. 34.
23 Minutes, Nationalparlament, Session of 24 October 1951, p. 346.
24 Palm, op. cit., p. 90; Interview, Gottfried von Einem, February 1985.
25 Palm, op. cit., p. 90; Saathen, op. cit., p. 178.
26 Letter, von Einem to J. Klaus, 13 December 1951; VE Archives.
27 Letter, Denis de Rougement to von Einem, 12 December 1951; VE Archives.
28 Saathen, op. cit., pp. 178–80.
29 Letter, J. Klaus to von Einem, 11 November 1952; VE Archives.
30 Letter, Kaut to von Einem, 21 November 1952; VE Archives.
31 Statistics, 1953; Archives, Salzburg Festival.
32 Letter, Kaut to von Einem, 29 December 1953; VE Archives.
33 Letter, J. Klaus to von Einem, 2 January 1954; VE Archives.
34 Saathen, op. cit., p. 181.
35 Minutes, Directorium, 9 August 1951; VE Archives.
36 *Opera*, 1952, pp. 595, 633.
37 *Neue Zürcher Zeitung*, 21 August 1952.
38 *Opera*, 1952, p. 592.
39 *Opera*, 1952, p. 634.

40 Lothar, op. cit., pp. 393–5.
41 Ibid., p. 397.
42 Letter, O.F. Schuh to H. von Karajan, 28 October 1956; VE Archives.
43 Lothar, op. cit., pp. 398–9.
44 *Opera*, 1954, p. 611.
45 *Opera*, 1953, p. 600.
46 *Opera*, 1953, pp. 595–8; *Berichte und Informationen*, Salzburg, 21 August 1953.
47 Strasser, op. cit., pp. 236–7.
48 Statistics, 1954; Archives, Salzburg Festival.
49 Strasser, op. cit., pp. 246–7.
50 Minutes, Directorium, 15 August 1954; VE Archives.
51 *Opera*, 1954, p. 605.
52 *Demokratisches Volksblatt*, Vienna, 28 July 1951.
53 Letter, Kaut to von Einem, 29 November 1953; VE Archives.
54 Kaut, op. cit., pp. 290–2.
55 Letter, Schuh to Kaut, 12 December 1959; VE Archives.
56 Letter, E. Hilbert to von Einem, 22 November 1954; VE Archives.
57 Discussion Points, Directorium meeting, 14 December 1955; VE Archives.
58 Protokoll, Directorium, 19 August 1955; VE Archives.
59 Protokoll, Kuratorium, 27 August 1955; VE Archives.
60 Letter, Puthon to von Einem, 22 October 1955; VE Archives.
61 Herbert von Karajan, 'Proposals for Salzburg Festival, 1957–1960'; VE Archives.
62 Report, Salzburg Festival, 'Negotiations with von Karajan', by Baron Puthon, 28 January 1956; VE Archives.
63 Comments on negotiations, Artistic Council, 28 January 1956; VE Archives.
64 Letter, von Einem to Puthon, 15 February 1956; VE Archives.
65 Letter, J. Klaus to von Einem, 14 March 1956; VE Archives.
66 Minutes, Directorium, 1 August 1966; VE Archives.
67 Letter, Kaut to von Einem, 9 February 1959; VE Archives.
68 Interview, Gottfried von Einem.
69 Letter, Klaus to von Einem, 9 February 1961; VE Archives.
70 Letter, von Einem to E. Preussner, Head of Mozarteum, 18 July 1962; VE Archives.
71 Letter, von Einem to Kuratorium, 3 October 1962; VE Archives.
72 Interview, von Einem.
73 *Atlantic Monthly*, May 1956, p. 70.
74 *New Yorker*, 2 December 1956, pp. 58–9.
75 *Opera*, 1957, pp. 624–5; *Stuttgarter Zeitung*, 12 August 1957.
76 *Opera*, 1957, p. 628.

77 *Opera*, 1958, pp. 619–20.
78 *Opera*, 1959, pp. 645–55.
79 *Opera*, 1958, pp. 621–2, 1959, p. 652; *Verders Ganz*, Oslo, 8 September 1958.
80 *Die Weltwoche*, Zürich, 26 July 1957.
81 *Forum des Akademikers*, Vienna, 1958.
82 *Süddeutsche Zeitung*, 30 August 1958.
83 *Forum des Akademikers*, Vienna, 1958.

CHAPTER 9

Archival material in Salzburg and Vienna is not available for this period.
1 Interview, Viktor Reimann, Salzburg, summer 1984.
2 *Figaro Littéraire*, 26 August 1968.
3 Kaut, *Die Salzburger Festspiele* (Salzburg 1982).
4 Interview, Moser, February 1985.
5 *Theater Heute*, Hanover, June 1964. *Carrefour*, Paris, 24 August 1966, notes the breakdown of ensemble opera in Salzburg.
6 Imma Higgs, Hans-Heinz Fabris, *Kritikanalyses* (Salzburg, 1971), pp. 13–21.
7 Schuh, Autobiography, op. cit., p. 183.
8 *Salzburger Nachrichten*, 17 February 1984.
9 Letter, Herbert Möritz to the author, 1984.
10 Interview, Gerhard Wimberger, August 1984.
11 Interview, Hans Temnitischka, Ministry of Education, January 1985.
12 Anton Dermota, op. cit., pp. 322–4.
13 Letter, Dietrich Fischer-Dieskau to the author, 1984.
14 Interview, Franz Endler, August 1985.
15 Interview, J.P. Ponnelle, August 1984.
16 Helene Thimig, op. cit., p. 193.
17 Interview, Endler.
18 See Kaut, *Die Salzburger Festspiele* (Salzburg, 1982), pp. 98–101.
19 Interview, Karl Löbl, Salzburg, 1984.
20 Letters: Andrew Porter to the author, 1983; Harold Rosenthal to the author, 1983.
21 Interview, Edward Greenfield, Salzburg, August 1984; Interview, H.H. Stuckenschmidt, Salzburg, 1984.
22 Interview, André Tubeuf, July 1984.
23 Interview, Endler.
24 See Salzburger Dokumentationen, *Die Auswirkung der Salzburger Festspiele auf Wirtschaft und Arbeitsmarkt* (Salzburg, 1981), pp. 19–20, 36–67.
25 Salzburger Dokumentationen, op. cit., p. 30.
26 *Alpenjournal*, special Festival editions, 1962, 1963, 1964.
27 Interview, Moser.

Index

Index

Index

Index

Krauss, Clemens, 34, 36, 37, 49, 53, 54, 56, 60, 61, 67, 76, 78, 80, 82, 83, 85, 86–7, 88–9, 114–16, 119, 121–2, 123, 125, 132, 148–9, 150, 152, 157, 168

Krauss, Werner, 16, 82, 90, 91, 99, 111, 122, 124, 125

Krips, Josef, 88, 89, 126, 128, 133, 136, 137, 140, 155

Kubelik, Rafael 140, 150

Kunz, Erich, 99, 115, 117, 140

Künzelmann, Ferdinand, 9

Kurz, Selma, 22, 36

Legge, Walter, 126, 133, 135

Lehar, Franz, 113

Lehmann, Lilli, 5, 6, 7, 45

Lehmann, Lotte, 36, 40, 61, 64, 76, 82, 94, 95, 96, 98, 99, 101

Leinsdorf, Erich, 77, 97

Leningrad Opera Studio, 44, 131, 143

Leopoldskron, Schloss, 8–9, 15, 17, 26, 60–1, 65, 68, 70, 92, 94, 96, 100, 115

Levine, James, 171–2, 180, 185

Lewis, Sinclair, 79

Ley, Robert, 58

Liebe der Danae, Die (R. Strauss), 116, 132–3, 149

Lindtberg, Leopold, 137, 172

Lipp, Wilma, 117

List, Emmanuel, 61

Löbl, Karl, 182

London Salzburg Society, 71, 72–3

Lothar, Ernst, 125, 132, 134, 150–1, 173

Lubin, Germaine, 61

Lucerne (Festival), 113

Lucia di Lammermoor (Donizetti), 157

Lucio Silla (Mozart), 173

Ludwig, Emil, 70

Lux, Josef-August, 104

Maazel, Lorin, 185

MacDonald, Ramsay, 54

Mahler, Gustav, 5, 12

Malade Imaginaire, Le (Molière) 26–7, 68

Mann, Thomas, 13, 98

Mann, William, 149

Manners, Lady Diana, 28

Markevitch, Igor, 150

Mauriac, François, 85–6

Mayr, Richard, 22, 43, 52, 61

Des Meeres und der Liebe Wellen (Grillparzer), 134

Meistersinger, Die (Wagner), 94, 95, 96, 99, 108, 109, 110, 112

Melchinger, Siegfried, 176

Mell, Max, 14

Mengelberg, Willim, 49, 85, 115

Menuhin, Yehudi, 119, 129, 133

Messner, Joseph, 37, 40, 47, 56, 87, 119, 120, 136, 140

Midsummer Night's Dream, A (Shakespeare), 40–1, 42, 84, 95

Miklas, Wilhelm, 103

Milstein, Nathan, 161

Mirakel, Das (Vollmoller), 26, 28, 29, 31, 41

Mitridate Re di Ponto (Mozart), 173

Mitropoulos, Dimitri, 152, 155, 156, 161, 185

Moissi, Alexander, 15–16, 23, 51, 54, 60, 62–3, 149

Molinari, Bernardino, 87

Monteux, Pierre, 96

Moore, Grace, 129

Moralt, Rudolph, 149

Möritz, Dr Herbert, 177

Moser, Albert, 116, 175, 184–5

Mozart, Wolfgang Amadeus, 2–3

Mozarteum, 3, 5, 6, 7, 14, 20, 21, 65, 105–6, 115, 120, 136, 146, 172, 178

Much Ado about Nothing (Shakespeare), 112

Much, Karl, 30

Mühlmann, Kajetan, 105, 106, 107

Munch, Charles, 129, 132

Mussolini, Benito, 74–5, 77, 110

Muti, Riccardo, 185

Mysterium von der Geburt des Herrn (Martin), 164

National Socialists (Nazis) 19, 27, 28, 57, 58, 59, 62–3, 66, 69, 70, 77–8, 79, 81, 82–3, 88, 89, 90–2, 102, 103–8, 113, 118

Nationalist Party (Austria) 18, 19, 22, 50, 58, 65

Neher, Caspar, 116, 117, 129, 130, 134, 135, 136, 137, 138, 140, 142, 144, 147, 152, 156, 158–9, 176, 180

Neidlinger, Gustav, 115

Nekola, Tassilo, 94, 135, 137, 141, 148

Neutra, Richard, 164

207

Index

New York Metropolitan Opera, 44
Ney, Elly, 114
Nilson, Einar, 1
nozze di Figaro, Le (Mozart), 5, 22, 29, 40, 99, 100, 109, 113, 115, 125, 128, 129, 133, 134, 151–2, 154–5, 156, 157, 160, 170

Oberon (Weber) 64, 67
Onegin, Sigrid, 66
Orfeo ed Euridice (Gluck), 61, 64, 96, 100, 109, 134–5, 137, 157, 163
Otello (Verdi), 143, 170
Otto, Teo, 169

Pallenberg, Max, 26, 35, 68, 69, 83
Papen, Franz von, 91, 92, 99
Paryla, Karl, 150
Pasetti, Otto von, 119, 120, 123, 124, 125, 127, 128, 132
Pataky, Koloman von, 61
Patzak, Julius, 120, 136, 140
Pauly, Rose, 22
Paumgartner, Bernhard, 1, 14, 20, 21, 37, 40, 44, 47, 56, 61, 65, 69, 87, 105–6, 111, 124, 128, 129, 130, 131–2, 134, 136–7, 149, 159, 160, 170, 173–4
Pears, Peter, 150
Penelope (Liebermann), 152
Peyrebere, Mme de, 75–6
Pfizner, Hans, 36, 66, 136
Pinza, Ezio, 82, 87, 99, 109, 151
Poell, Alfred, 114
Poelzig, Hans, 14, 25
Ponnelle, Jean Pierre, 180, 182
Porter, Andrew, 183
Preis, Josef, 29
Preussler, Robert, 19
Price, Leontyne, 169
Prihoda, Vasa, 114
Prohoska, Felix, 120, 128
Prozess, Der (Von Einem), 147, 152
Puaux, Gabriel, 75, 76, 102
Puthon, Baron Heinrich, 34, 39, 46, 48, 53, 63, 83, 84, 87, 105, 115, 119–20, 125, 128, 129, 130, 134, 135, 136, 148, 152–3, 156, 158, 159, 160, 173, 177

Rainer, Friederich, 104, 111, 112, 115
Ramek, Rudolf, 29

Rape of Lucretia, The (Britten), 140
rappresentatione di anima e di corpo, La (Cavalieri), 173–4
Räuber, Der (Schiller), 44
Ravel, Maurice, 70
re in Ascolto, Un (Berio), 178
Rehrl, Franz, 19, 28–9, 30, 33, 35, 37–40, 42–3, 46, 51, 52, 54, 58, 71, 72, 73, 75, 84, 98, 101–2, 103–4, 106, 107, 137, 148, 164
Rehrl, Karl, 145
Reichwein, Leopold, 91–2
Reimann, Viktor, 135, 145
Reiner, Fritz, 77
Reinhardt, Edmund, 52
Reinhardt, Gottfried, 26
Reinhardt, Max, 1, 5–6, 7, 8–10, 12, 17, 24–5, 27, 28, 29, 30, 31, 35–6, 38–9, 43, 44, 46, 47, 48, 49, 50, 51, 52, 53, 54–5, 56, 62, 70, 76, 84–5, 92, 93, 94, 95–6, 99, 100–1, 107, 109, 110, 121, 127, 128, 129, 130, 131, 145, 150, 151, 163, 165, 166, 168, 172, 173, 174, 181, 185, 186; *Jedermann* (1920), 14–16; *The Great World Theatre* (1922), 21–4; *Le Malade imaginaire* (1923), 25–7; *A Midsummer Night's Dream*, 40–2; *Twelfth Night*, 60–1; *Faust* (1933), 67–9; and Hollywood, 84–5, 95–6, 100–1, 102; and anti-Semitism, 63, 65, 89, 91
Reining, Maria, 99, 109, 114
Reitter, Albert, 105, 107
Rennert, Gunther, 133
Rethberg, Elisabeth, 22, 109, 110
Rethy, Esther, 99, 109, 120
Richter, Hans, 3, 4
Riding School, Outdoor *(Felsenreitschule)*, 14, 67, 84, 107, 130, 134, 137, 140, 143
Rieder, Archbishop Ignatius, 14, 16, 21–2, 24, 28, 29
Rode, Wilhelm, 66
Rodzinski, Artur, 96, 132
Roller, Alfred, 5, 12, 29, 35, 48, 99, 136, 169
Romeo und Julia (Blacher), 140
Roosevelt, John, 93
Roosevelt, Mrs Sara Delano, 93, 100
Rosé, Arnold, 30, 106–7
Rosegger, Peter, 106

208

Index